Freedom as Social Cooperation

Ezequiel Spector

Freedom as Social Cooperation

A Theory of Liberal Democracy

palgrave
macmillan

Ezequiel Spector
Faculty of Liberal Arts
Adolfo Ibáñez University
Peñalolén, RM - Santiago, Chile

ISBN 978-3-032-12216-2 ISBN 978-3-032-12217-9 (eBook)
https://doi.org/10.1007/978-3-032-12217-9

Spanish edition published by Marcial Pons, 2025

This Palgrave Macmillan imprint is published by the registered company Springer Nature Switzerland AG
The registered company address is: Gewerbestrasse 11, 6330 Cham, Switzerland

Acknowledgements As the months of the government-mandated quarantine in Argentina went by in 2020, I found myself confined to my small apartment in the Palermo neighborhood of Buenos Aires, rethinking many aspects of how I was approaching my philosophical work. I had been working in political philosophy for several years, yet I felt there was something fundamentally off in what I was doing—though I couldn't quite put my finger on it. At the time, I was serving as an assistant professor at the Law School of Torcuato Di Tella University, teaching legal philosophy and constitutional law.

Toward the end of 2020, I received the news that I had been awarded a visiting assistant professorship at the University of Arizona's Center for the Philosophy of Freedom. During those two years—and thanks to what I learned while working with David Schmidtz at the Freedom Center—I finally discovered what had been troubling me about my own approach. I had long worked under the assumption that moral philosophy is more fundamental than political philosophy: I would begin with *a priori* reasoning about what is ethically desirable and only then draw political conclusions about what institutions are just. As it turned out, the solution was simply to reverse the order. I began working from the idea that political philosophy should discipline our reasoning in moral philosophy: it is the political question of how we can best live together that determines what moral duties we have. I owe thanks to David Schmidtz, who—perhaps without even realizing it—rescued me from the intellectual stagnation in which I had been mired.

In 2022, I received a generous offer from Adolfo Ibáñez University in Chile to join the Department of Liberal Arts as a research professor and to found and direct a new Master's program in Philosophy, Politics, and Economics. At the time, Francisco Covarrubias, then Dean of the department, was looking for someone who shared the very vision of philosophy that I had developed in Arizona. My visiting appointment in Arizona was coming to an end, and I gladly accepted the challenge of moving to Chile to embark on this new chapter.

As I prepared for the move, an idea kept circling in my mind: what if this philosophical approach, new to me, could be taken one step further? What would happen if I used the political-philosophical question of how we can best live together not only to determine moral duties but, even more ambitiously, to define core political concepts such as freedom? Is it possible to create a plausible *a posteriori* notion of freedom? By the time I had settled in Chile, I was already entertaining the possibility of elevating political philosophy to a new level—one in which it not only shapes our moral philosophy but also serves as a kind of conceptual engineering, guiding us toward fresh and more illuminating understandings of political ideas like freedom.

Adolfo Ibáñez University provided me with an exceptionally vibrant and stimulating academic environment in which to develop this new approach. I am grateful to Francisco Covarrubias—now the university's president—for welcoming me into the remarkable team that makes this institution what it is.

The development of this idea took two years, during which I balanced undergraduate and graduate teaching with the administration of the newly established Master's program in Philosophy, Politics, and Economics. Throughout this period, I benefited greatly from the comments and insights of Manuel Atienza, Julio Montero, Alejandra Salinas, Cristina Crichton, Marcelo Alegre, Joaquín Millón Quintana, Eduardo Stordeur, Horacio Spector, Ezequiel Monti, and Paola Bergallo. I am deeply grateful for their generosity.

The Spanish version of this book was published by the prestigious Spanish publisher Marcial Pons in March 2025, following excellent feedback from an anonymous reviewer, to whom I am also sincerely thankful.

The present work is a revised and translated version of that publication. Being able to publish my work with such an important press as Palgrave Macmillan is a true honor. I would like to express my gratitude to the two anonymous reviewers and to Bronwyn Geyer, the editor, for her interest in my project.

I hope that the work that follows does justice to the people and institutions that have supported its development. Although this book is the product of my own intellectual journey, it is also the result of conversations and generosity from others. If the central ideas presented here succeed in illuminating even a small part of the political and philosophical questions that inspired them, it will be because I had the good fortune of working within communities that encouraged rigor, honesty, and imagination. For that, I remain profoundly grateful.

Competing Interests The author has no competing interests to declare that are relevant to the content of this manuscript.

CONTENTS

CHAPTER 1

Introduction

"No man is an island," wrote the English poet John Donne in the seventeenth century. This phrase makes sense if we interpret it to suggest that no one is self-sufficient. Without some form of cooperation, no one can achieve their life goals.

In popular survival series on platforms like Netflix, the harsh reality of isolation is vividly portrayed. These shows often strand individuals on remote islands or in isolated wilderness, forcing them to survive. Time and again, the narrative reveals a stark truth: those who choose to separate themselves from the collective struggle frequently face dire consequences—whether it be dwindling resources, vulnerability to danger, or ultimately, death. Such stories underscore the essential human need for cooperation and connection, illustrating that survival is rarely a solitary endeavor but a shared journey where mutual reliance becomes the key to overcoming adversity.

In its ideal form, modern society can be seen as a vast network of cooperation where individuals collaborate to reach their full potential. We travel safely on public roads because the state ensures our security. We earn a living because others value our work and are willing to pay for it. We have access to food thanks to producers, supermarkets, and several businesses. We learn at schools, thanks to the guidance of teachers. We recover from illnesses due to the care provided by doctors and other healthcare professionals in hospitals. We dress ourselves because

E. Spector, *Freedom as Social Cooperation*,
https://doi.org/10.1007/978-3-032-12217-9_1

of manufacturers and retailers, ranging from small shops to large malls. We explore new destinations via boats, trains, and planes—and the people who operate them. We enjoy art thanks to painters, musicians, actors, and other artists. We lead healthy lives by engaging in physical activities through sports clubs. We build friendships and fall in love because we spend our free time attending social events. Even when we seek solitude, the walls that shield us are built by many hands, and the laws that protect our peace—against noise, disruption, and disorder—are crafted and enforced by others, reminding us that every refuge depends on the collaboration of others.

Homo sapiens became the wisest of primates 40,000 years ago when they learned to make agreements with one another (Horan, Bulte, and Shogren 2005: 2).[1] Many steps in our evolution involved expanding our capacity for cooperation. Developing ways to support each other so that everyone can create and pursue their plans is a distinctly human trait.[2] If humans had lived as hermits, none of our skills would have been enough to realize our projects. Our abilities gain value through cooperation. As Aristotle noted, humans are fundamentally political (social) beings (Aristotle 1999 [350 BC]: 5).

This work explores the cooperative fabric of modern society, where forming and realizing life plans is unimaginable without a collaborative backdrop; where designing and implementing life projects cannot be separated from a context of cooperation. The central thesis of this work is straightforward: since humans have expanded their horizons by working together, a full understanding of freedom in the social world must include the dimension of cooperation. After all, if *natural* freedom—the freedom of an animal in the jungle—is acting on wild instincts without restrictions or agreements with other animals, then, conversely, social freedom must be understood as the formation of collaborative bonds with fellow human beings. It is through these ties and shared commitments that freedom in society truly unfolds, transforming isolated existence into a collective potential that enriches and sustains us all.

[1] As Adam Smith states, "Nobody ever saw a dog make a fair and deliberate exchange of one bone for another with another dog" (1981 [1776]: bk. I, ch. ii).

[2] Certain forms of cooperation can be observed in some non-human animals, ranging from bees to apes (Bowles and Gintis 2011: 2). Nevertheless, what is distinctively human are *complex* cooperative agreements (for example, commercial practices) that serve as a context for designing and carrying out life *projects* over time.

The concept of freedom (or liberty)[3] has been widely discussed in political philosophy. Some authors argue that freedom is the absence of interference by others: for example, we would not be free to run if someone were holding us by the arm. This is known as "negative freedom."[4] Others claim that being free means having self-control, self-realization, or some other kind of capacity: for instance, we would not be free to run if we suffered from a form of depression that prevented us from getting out of bed. This is referred to as "positive freedom."[5] Finally, there are those who argue that being free means not depending on anyone's will: for example, we would not be free to run if there were no laws guaranteeing protection against those who might wish to interfere with our plan to run. This is called "republican freedom" (or "freedom as non-domination").[6]

This book has two aims. The first is to challenge the prevailing views on freedom by presenting a new perspective grounded in our cooperative nature: "freedom as social cooperation" (FSC). From the FSC perspective, freedom is not merely the absence of interference (negative freedom), nor a specific mental or material condition (positive freedom), nor a form of independence (republican freedom). Instead, *freedom is a cooperative practice for shaping and realizing life plans*[7]—an environment where people collaborate over time so that everyone can design and pursue their projects. Thus, FSC views social cooperation not just as a means to achieve freedom but as *constitutive* of freedom itself. While critically addressing the limitations of negative, positive, and republican conceptions, this work also recognizes that FSC incorporates valuable

[3] Although some authors have drawn a distinction between "freedom" and "liberty" (Williams 2001, Dworkin 2011), in this book these terms are used interchangeably.

[4] The distinction between negative liberty and positive liberty is attributed to Isaiah Berlin (2002 [1958]). It is a distinction similar to the one drawn earlier by Benjamin Constant (1819).

[5] The notion of positive liberty is extremely broad and will be discussed in detail in Chapter 2. For a preliminary overview, see Nussbaum (1988) and Sen (1999).

[6] This conception will also be discussed in detail later. For now, see Pettit (1997) and Skinner (2008).

[7] To be sure, the expression departs from the standard use of the term "freedom." This deviation is intentional: the formulation aims to underscore that freedom is understood here not as an individual attribute or possession, but as a collaborative and socially sustained practice.

elements from these traditions, enriching and expanding the understanding of freedom. By developing this new conception, the book provides a framework for understanding freedom as a dynamic, cooperative process—one that is essential for the development of individuals living together.

FSC does not seek to capture the *true essence* of freedom but to articulate a notion of freedom that depends on and responds to social and institutional contexts. It does not intend to embody an abstract ideal but rather to reflect the best practices of humans living in society—specifically how people have managed to create environments of cooperation where they can develop and realize their projects. These social practices have evolved in various forms, ranging from simple models used by primitive tribes to the complex institutions of modern liberal democracies.

Thus, FSC represents a conception of freedom that grasps how individuals shape and pursue life plans *within society*. It should not be surprising, then, that FSC includes the idea of social cooperation; after all, social cooperation lies at the heart of societies where individuals have successfully developed and realized their goals—especially within liberal democracy, which represents humanity's highest achievement in this regard.

The second aim, closely aligned with the first, is to employ FSC as a theoretical foundation for understanding the political and economic institutions that define liberal democracy, thereby developing a theory of liberal democracy grounded in FSC. As will be shown, while FSC offers a philosophical conception of freedom, its application to concrete political and economic institutions yields results that are familiar and consistent with established principles—such as the dispersion and decentralization of power and influence, as well as the mutual support between the public realm and private enterprise. At a philosophical level, FSC presents a general conception of freedom grounded in social cooperation, but in practice, it is embodied in political and economic institutions that decentralize and disperse power while maintaining complementary roles.

This convergence underscores how FSC not only enriches our theoretical understanding but also reaffirms the core institutional arrangements that have long been recognized as essential to liberal democracy. By showing that FSC can explain the rationale behind these institutions, I seek to distill the highly complex political system of liberal democracy into a single, simple formula: FSC.

If I succeed in achieving this second objective, then FSC will also serve as a guide for improving the institutions of liberal democracy. In other words, if FSC can function as the underlying reason for this political system, it is reasonable to argue that changes to its institutional design should aim to address shortcomings that might move it away from this ideal.

Why should freedom and cooperation be understood as a single, unified concept rather than as distinct and separate ideas? This is a legitimate question. One might argue that freedom can be defined in a simpler or more "rustic" way—such as mere non-interference or basic autonomy—and that while cooperation is undeniably important, it remains a separate phenomenon. From this viewpoint, freedom and cooperation may have different meanings and functions, even if both are important components of a liberal democratic society.

The response rests on the principle that an integrated and unified theory provides a more coherent and compelling account than one that divides concepts into isolated entities. Liberals endorse liberty as a central political value, while also deeply valuing social cooperation and liberal democracy. Rescuing this basic intuition, FSC offers an elegant and unifying framework by grounding freedom within the fabric of cooperative relationships, thereby integrating these concepts into a coherent whole. Rather than treating freedom and cooperation as separate pillars that merely coexist, FSC conceives freedom as essentially social—rooted in cooperative interactions that also sustain liberal democratic institutions. This integrated perspective preserves the normative significance of freedom esteemed by liberals while offering a more comprehensive and explanatorily powerful account of how freedom, social bonds, and democracy depend on one another. In doing so, FSC transcends fragmented conceptions, presenting a parsimonious yet rich understanding of freedom that aligns closely with liberal commitments.

This book should interest a wide audience. First, it appeals to those working in political theory and political philosophy, and particularly to those dedicated to studying and understanding the idea of freedom. Indeed, the first part of the book develops a new conception (FSC) that seeks to go beyond traditional notions: a conception that, while incorporating valuable elements from those earlier ideas, also positions social cooperation as the central component of freedom.

Second, this work should be useful for legal scholars interested in exploring the foundations of liberal democracy, especially legal philosophers and constitutionalists (as well as students in these fields) who are eager to find a better justification for the political system they teach in law schools. Accordingly, the second part of this book is devoted to using FSC to develop a theory of liberal democracy that can explain the rationale for its political and economic institutions.

Third, this material may inspire those who hold public office and influence institutional design (legislators, secretaries, public policy advisors, etc.). After all, if liberal democracy can be interpreted as a system aimed at guaranteeing FSC, then FSC can serve as a beacon to guide their proposals and decisions, as well as a way to justify and support them.

The book aims to achieve a balance between making a theoretical contribution to philosophical literature and fulfilling a pedagogical purpose by serving as a way to explain the institutions of liberal democracy and how they may vary from country to country. While scholars may be more interested in the theoretical contribution and find the explanation of how liberal democracies function somewhat familiar, this explanatory portion is specifically designed to help students in the social sciences field understand how this institutional arrangement works in modern societies.

Broadly speaking, the system of liberal democracy is under attack from various fronts. On one side, left-wing populism seeks to convince us that the institutions of liberal democracy are bourgeois creations that, sooner or later, must be dismantled for serving the interests of the dominant classes. On the other side, right-wing populism tries to persuade us that individual rights must give way to considerations of national security or even to the need to restore the moral fabric of society.

The COVID-19 pandemic and the wars in Ukraine and the Middle East have further complicated the situation. Pandemics, wars, and natural disasters, among other events, allow governments to declare states of emergency that—even if necessary—often erode institutions such as the separation of powers, checks and balances, and individual rights.

In this context, the task of continuing to enrich the ideal of liberal democracy is a way to help it maintain its appeal and prominence on the political map. Particularly in these times of political confrontation, FSC is a timely way to strengthen liberal democracy, as it reminds us that the only way to be free is by working together.

Let me now explain the structure of the book. Chapter 2 reviews the conceptions of freedom that have been proposed so far: various forms of negative freedom, positive freedom, and republican freedom. This overview will be useful for distinguishing FSC from those previous conceptions.

Chapter 3 is the core of the work: the theoretical development of FSC and an explanation of its main features. According to FSC, freedom is a cooperative practice for creating and realizing life plans. It is a specific form of cooperation that, as I will explain, "depends on all participants, but on none in particular." Furthermore, as I will elaborate, this notion of freedom is robust, in the sense that it encompasses a notion of equality and human dignity.

To explain the concept of FSC, I use various hypothetical examples, the main one of which I term "primitive cooperation." This is a situation similar to what contractualist philosophers have called "state of nature," though with its own characteristics, making it a clear example of how social cooperation can provide the context for creating and realizing life plans. The aim of this model, then, is not to offer a historical thesis, but rather to illustrate the conception of freedom developed in this work. After explaining FSC, I show that it brings together the most attractive aspects of previous conceptions of freedom, while remaining an autonomous conception grounded in the idea of social cooperation.

In Chapter 4, I use FSC to develop a theory of liberal democracy. The line of reasoning I follow is that the structure of liberal democracy is a more evolved, but not fundamentally different, version of the organizational form found in "primitive cooperation." The greater sophistication of liberal democratic institutions can be understood as solutions to certain problems that would arise in such a more precarious scenario. But, again, this model is a heuristic tool to illustrate FSC and show its potential to ground a theory of liberal democracy. It is not a historical account of how liberal democracies emerged.

In particular, this chapter focuses on political institutions. I argue that FSC can explain institutions such as the state, suffrage, federalism, and features of the political system like the separation of powers and checks and balances.

Chapter 5 continues the development of this theory of liberal democracy. Here, I analyze how FSC can account for the functioning of the economic system, with institutions such as private property, markets, and money, as well as institutions that aim to correct market failures, like antitrust legislation, labor law, and unions. I also examine, in light of

FSC, the typical forms of state financing: taxation, public debt, and, in some cases, monetary issuance.

Chapter 6 discusses the role of the state as a provider of goods and services. As I will explain, the state is dedicated not only to preserving the environment in which people interact, but also to complementing it by offering basic goods and services. I provide a detailed analysis of some of the main goods and services offered by modern states. I start with circulation infrastructure, which I divide into "static" (such as side-walks, streets, and roads) and "mobile" (such as subways, trains, and airplanes). I then continue with health services, the education system, the media, support for vulnerable groups (which I call "integration tools"), and pension systems.

Finally, Chapter 7 offers some conclusions and an overview of two topics that remain open. The first is the application of FSC to the institution of the family. I argue that FSC provides tools to explain much of family law in liberal democracies. The second is the application of FSC to the international community. I suggest that FSC can also account for how international law and international organizations operate. However, I clarify that a more detailed analysis of these topics lies beyond the scope of this work and will likely be the subject of a future study.

CHAPTER 2

What Is Freedom? A Review of the Prevailing Perspectives

2.1 The Realm of Non-Interference

Freedom is often understood as the absence of interference by others: you are free to do X if and only if no one prevents you from doing X. Thus, according to this conception, freedom is threatened by certain external factors—namely, the actions of other human beings. Consequently, to enjoy freedom is to enjoy a sphere in which others do not interfere.[1]

One of the characteristics of this conception, then, is that only obstacles created by other human beings count as restrictions on freedom (Berlin 2002 [1958]: 172–173; Kramer, M. 2003: 3). You may be unable to see because you were born blind, but this inability does not limit your freedom to see—although your freedom would be limited if, for example, someone was covering your eyes. You may be unable to jump more than 20 centimeters, but this inability does not restrict your freedom to do so—although your freedom would be restricted if, for example, someone

[1] The idea of negative freedom underlies the works of various authors in the liberal tradition: Hobbes 1998 [1651], Locke 2003 [1689], Constant 1819, Bentham 1843, von Humboldt 1993 [1852], Berlin 2002 [1958], Mill 2009 [1859], Hayek 1960, Spencer 1960, Nozick 1974, and Steiner 1994. Mill's case requires further clarification: while he defends negative freedom by arguing that the state should not interfere in the individual sphere, his concept of political liberty is grounded in the importance of individuals achieving self-realization through the development of their individuality—a notion that aligns with a form of positive freedom.

E. Spector, *Freedom as Social Cooperation*,
https://doi.org/10.1007/978-3-032-12217-9_2

was holding you back. You may lack the money to buy a luxury car, but this inability does not restrict your freedom to do so—although your freedom would be restricted if, for example, someone prevented you from accessing your money.[2]

In the political realm, the notion of negative liberty is especially appealing to those who wish to limit the expansion of the state into people's lives (Hayek 1960: ch. 1, Nozick 1974). For example, in the classical liberal tradition, the central concern is not what the state can do for citizens, but what it should not do: basically, the state must refrain from interfering with courses of action that do not harm others (Mill 2009 [1859]:18–19). Thus, according to this line of thought, people should be free in the sense of enjoying a sphere where, given their circumstances, they can live as they wish without interference from the state or any other party.

2.2 The Power within: Motivation, Self-Control, Self-Realization, and Beyond

Many philosophers contend that the negative conception falls short of capturing the full human experience of freedom and therefore advocate for a more robust notion. The positive conception of freedom encompasses a wide variety of views and theories, some of which differ significantly from others. Therefore, a definition of positive freedom should be broad enough to capture all these variations. In this sense, we could say that *positive freedom is the fact of having control over oneself and of achieving (or at least being able to achieve) one's fundamental goals or acting according to certain motivations.*

Immanuel Kant, for example, holds that people are autonomous only to the extent that they act according to the moral demands of practical reason (Kant 1991 [1797]: 26–27). In particular, Kant argues that practical reason is expressed through two types of demands: non-moral and

[2] The idea that economic limitations do not threaten negative freedom has been criticized. Gerald Cohen (2001), for example, argues that if we do not have money to buy a train ticket, we are not free to travel on that train because, if we tried to board without a ticket, the conductor or the police would be able to interfere. Cohen concludes that those who defend capitalism do not embrace a notion of negative freedom simpliciter, but rather a *moralized* negative freedom, which holds that only some interferences are morally wrong—specifically, those that violate property rights (Cohen 1988: 252, 256, 295).

moral. Non-moral demands are hypothetical imperatives—they change depending on the goal we set for ourselves; for example, if our goal is to graduate as lawyers, the non-moral demand arising from practical reason is that we complete a law degree. Moral demands, on the other hand, are categorical imperatives—they do not depend on our particular goals (feeding our children, for instance, is a categorical imperative, as we must do it regardless of our desires). To Kant, autonomy, or freedom, is the capacity to act in accordance with categorical imperatives, which are based on reason and operate independently of our inclinations and desires.

Unlike Kant, G. W. F. Hegel maintains that inclinations and desires do play an important role in the exercise of freedom (Hegel 1969 [1812]: 37). This does not mean, however, that in Hegel's view any inclination or desire constitutes an exercise of freedom. Like Kant, he accepts the distinction between reason and freedom on the one hand, and merely contingent inclinations and desires on the other. Therefore, as with Kant, Hegel believes that freedom does not require us to adopt any course of action we want, but rather those we have *reasons* to adopt—reasons that are independent of contingent inclinations and desires. Nevertheless, Hegel argues that being free also involves being inclined and desiring to adopt these courses of action, and, equally importantly, *understanding* the reasons for adopting them. Thus, we can say that, for Hegel, freedom requires (1) adopting courses of action we have reasons to adopt, (2) doing so in accordance with the corresponding inclinations and desires, and (3) understanding the reasons for acting in that way. For example, a mother who, out of love, fulfills her duty to protect her children and also understands the rationality of acting in that way would meet all three conditions (Patten 1999: 61–63).

Finally, according to Hegel, acting freely also includes a fourth element: to be free, a person needs others to voluntarily recognize them as a free being.[3] In this way, due to this relational component, we can say

[3] Similarly, Joel Anderson and Axel Honneth (2005: 129–131) argue that any plausible theory of freedom should take the relational element seriously. The authors contend that individualistic conceptions of freedom, such as the notion of freedom as non-interference, mistakenly assume that people are self-sufficient. Consequently, their conception of freedom seeks to account for how individual autonomy depends on (and is preserved by) certain forms of social relationships. Their thesis is that the exercise of autonomy depends on certain attitudes toward ourselves—namely, self-respect, self-confidence, and self-esteem—and that these attitudes are made possible by the way others perceive us. In

that, according to Hegel, one's freedom is tied to the freedom of others (Garnett 2021: 17).

Karl Marx, for his part, understands freedom as the realization of our human nature, which entails working for the common good and perceiving ourselves as beings who contribute to that shared purpose. This requires, for example, exercising collective control over productive resources and producing to meet our common needs—something that demands the abandonment of the capitalist system. When we act in accordance with our nature, we achieve self-realization. Conversely, when we are alienated from our own nature—as Marx argues happens in capitalist societies—we are reduced to a pseudo-human existence and lack true freedom (Marx 2005 [1844]: 151). Thus, to Marx, freedom also has a relational dimension, since it is attained by acting as a member of a community rather than as an isolated individual (Marx 1975 [1844]: 234).

Thomas Green also understands freedom as self-realization. More precisely, he argues that true freedom is found only when a lasting sense of fulfillment is achieved, which is possible only through the perfection attained by exercising capacities that are distinctively human (Green, T. H. 1986 [1879]: 228–229). Green maintains that, in the political realm, this entails the promotion of the common good (Green, T. H. 1986 [1881]: 199; Green, T. H. 1986 [1895]: 90). The work for the common good by members of a community, Green asserts, creates a civic bond among them, making each individual's self-realization a collective achievement.[4] No one can achieve self-realization in isolation; rather, the self-realization of all is accomplished together—it is reciprocal (Green, T. H. 2003 [1883]: 217–220).

Furthermore, Green holds that certain institutions are necessary to attain this freedom: people complement one another within shared institutions that express human nature and its fundamental purposes. However, these institutions do not function by *compelling* or *encouraging* people to be free; rather, they *enable* individuals to develop independently and reach the perfection that *true* freedom entails (Green, T. H., 1986

the next chapter, I explore this approach, known as relational autonomy, in greater detail to distinguish it from my own conception, as the two can easily be confused.

[4] John Dewey also offers a theory in which freedom inherently involves communal bonds. I will explore this theory in greater detail in the next chapter, particularly to contrast it with FSC.

[1881]: 202). According to Green, this notion of freedom is compatible with diverse life plans, which is why he considers his theory a form of ethical pluralism (Simhony 2021: 73).

Jean-Jacques Rousseau, on the other hand, understands freedom as inseparable from collective self-government. According to him, freedom is achieved through participation in the decision-making process by which the community exercises control over itself (Rousseau 2002 [1762]: 163–164).[5] For Rousseau, the central question is what form of association can, by its own strength, defend the lives and property of its members while simultaneously guaranteeing the freedom of each individual, understood as the condition in which each person obeys only themselves.

According to Rousseau, the answer to this question is the social contract, in which each person, along with their rights, yields themselves to the community as a whole, thereby creating a union that, being stronger than any individual, can protect each of its members. Since the conditions are equal for all, no one has an interest in demanding special benefits from others. Likewise, because everyone yields to everyone else, in terms of each person's freedom, it is as if no one yields to anyone. Indeed, all the rights one has over others are also rights that others have over oneself. In this sense, each person loses as much as they gain, but the balance is positive when considering that the community, empowered by collective strength, protects each individual. As Rousseau expresses it: "Each of us puts his person and all his power in common under the supreme direction of the general will, and, in our corporate capacity, we receive each member as an indivisible part of the whole" (Rousseau 2002 [1762]: 164).

The positive conception of freedom has been criticized for carrying the risk of authoritarianism (Spector, H. 2015: 2647). The concern is that if being free is not about doing whatever one desires, but about pursuing certain goals formulated with a degree of vagueness, then governments might oppress the population in the name of freedom, under the pretext of helping them achieve those goals and thus liberate them from their own deviations. For example, regarding Green, Berlin remarks that he "was a genuine liberal: but many a tyrant could use this formula to justify his worst acts of oppression" (Berlin 2002 [1958]: 180).

[5] Similarly, Hanna Arendt (1961: 148–149) argues that freedom entails political engagement within an established republic.

Similarly, the danger is also present in the idea of positive freedom as collective self-government: the government might adopt an organic conception of society, according to which society is a living organism that acts rationally—that is, with self-control—only when its parts act harmoniously according to the plan of its rulers, who form the brain of this great body. But the danger persists even if one interprets the notion of collective self-government more democratically—for instance, as the idea that freedom is participation in collective decision-making. It could happen that this requirement is met, yet oppression still exists (for example, a society governed by majority rule where everyone votes, but the majority systematically abuses the minority).

Some defenders of positive freedom have reformulated this conception in ways that remove its potential to become an authoritarian ideal, without losing the substance that makes positive freedom a more robust conception than negative freedom. Generally, these approaches define freedom in terms of certain capacities or resources rather than in terms of *ends* that must *necessarily* be achieved. To be sure, a subtle judgment about what is good can be discerned in some of these approaches, yet they clarify that having the *opportunity* to live a valuable life is already sufficient for freedom, even if the individual later chooses not to take advantage of this opportunity or only partially does so. Other approaches, on the other hand, categorically state that they do not intend to assume any conception of the good life and limit themselves to defining "freedom" as the acquisition of the necessary means for individuals to live the life they choose.

In the first group, we find, for example, Amartya Sen's theory. He defines freedom as the essential capabilities needed to live a life we have "reason to value" (Sen 2006: 4–5). These capabilities are described in terms of sets of attributes (such as enjoying good health) and practices (such as having affectionate relationships with others) to which we have *genuine access* (Sen 1979: 218; Sen 1985: 9). But what additional capabilities exist beyond the two examples mentioned? Sen does not provide an exhaustive list (Sen 2005: 158). Instead, he argues that communities should decide, through deliberative processes, what is necessary to lead a valuable life (Sen 2004).

Sen acknowledges that, given the diversity of worldviews, it is difficult for people to reach unanimous agreement. However, he believes there can be consensus on fundamental elements related to basic needs, such as health, education, and nutrition. Interestingly, although Sen's approach seems to imply a particular view of what forms of life are valuable, he is careful to clarify that any plausible notion of freedom must be sensitive to personal preferences. For example, adequate nutrition may be essential to living a valuable life, but this does not mean that someone who chooses to fast for religious reasons, despite potential health risks, lacks freedom. As long as they have had the real opportunity to eat properly, the person is free. According to Sen, any analysis of whether people are free must take their *choices* into account (Sen 2006: 52).

A similar perspective has been defended by Martha Nussbaum. Her aim is to offer a variation of this approach that, following Aristotle, fully captures the range of human powers. Like Sen, Nussbaum defines capabilities as genuine opportunities to achieve certain ends; however, she adds that in specifying these ends, we must consider the essential activities of human beings as well as their intrinsic dignity (Nussbaum 1997: 286–289, Nussbaum 2000: 72). She maintains that certain basic capabilities are unquestionably essential for performing these activities and living a life with dignity. Therefore, unlike Sen, she provides a specific list of these capabilities: life, bodily health, bodily integrity, the senses (including imagination and thought), emotions, practical reason, the ability to relate to other human beings, the ability to relate to non-human beings, the ability to enjoy recreational activities, and control over one's environment (for example, the capacity to exercise property rights as well as political participation) (Nussbaum 2011: 19, 33–34).

It is important to emphasize that this list does not prescribe how people must live: individuals are free to choose whether and how to use these capabilities. This means the list is compatible with a variety of life plans that can lead, through different paths, to human flourishing. In fact, like Sen, Nussbaum believes any evaluation must be sensitive to people's choices. To Nussbaum, respecting someone who, for religious reasons, does not eat adequately and thereby risks their health is also part of respecting their intrinsic dignity. It is the possession of these capabilities that holds value and contributes to human flourishing, regardless of whether—and how—the individual chooses to use them (Nussbaum 1997: 286, 288–289).

In the second group, we find, for example, Charles Taylor's thesis. Taylor argues against what he calls the "crude" view of negative freedom attributed to Thomas Hobbes, according to which freedom consists merely in the absence of external obstacles (Taylor, C. 1979: 192–193).

Taylor contends that any plausible notion of freedom must distinguish between different kinds of external obstacles, depending on which purposes these obstacles frustrate. For instance, a law prohibiting us from crossing a red light is qualitatively different from a law forbidding us to practice our religion. This qualitative difference holds even if both forms of interference are of the same intensity—that is, the same type of prohibition subject to the same sanction and enforced with equal effectiveness by the government. Yet, these two rules are qualitatively distinct because, in one case, the law frustrates purposes we do not consider fundamental (perhaps arriving early at a restaurant to reserve a table), while in the other, it frustrates purposes we ourselves have deemed fundamental (Taylor, C. 1979: 183). In the first case, we do not regard our freedom as meaningfully affected; in the second, we do.

Taylor argues that if we start from this (highly plausible) premise, then it is the fulfillment of our fundamental purposes that takes precedence, relegating to a secondary role the nature of the obstacles threatening their fulfillment. It follows, then, that freedom can also be threatened by internal obstacles, since these can also divert us from our fundamental purposes (here, "fundamental purposes" does not refer to an objective standard of perfection but rather to the goals individuals themselves have set as fundamental) (Taylor, C. 1979: 192 and 180).[6] Ultimately, the Hobbesian conception of freedom overlooks the very reason why freedom is a valuable ideal: it enables us to fulfill our fundamental purposes (Taylor, C. 1979: 183).

In a similar vein, Lawrence Crocker argues that a plausible theory of freedom leads to what he calls "left libertarianism" (Crocker 1980: 9). As he puts it, his aim is to convince "negative libertarians" (defenders of negative freedom) to embrace the positive notion of liberty (Crocker

[6] Taylor (1979: 180) argues that people sometimes have desires that conflict with their basic purposes—for instance, when someone succumbs to the temptation to keep sleeping and misses a religious ceremony that was very important to them. Yet, this does not imply that Taylor endorses a specific view of the good life, as he refrains from judging which basic purposes are valuable, at least in his work critiquing the negative conception of freedom and proposing a positive notion that avoids authoritarian implications. Taylor's position becomes more nuanced in his work on identity (1989), where he argues that morality has an objective existence and grounds human *identity*. This reasoning, combined with the idea that freedom involves following *our basic* purposes, seems to lead to the conclusion that being free entails acting in accordance with an objective moral standard.

1980: 2). To do so, he contends that there is no morally relevant difference between external interference by other human beings (the focus of negative liberty) and other forms of interference, such as incapacity or poverty (Crocker 1980: 7 and 119). Ultimately, in his view, freedom consists in having a variety of options, ***none of which is objectively better than another***. In his words, "the positive liberty I will be defending is a matter of the presence of options and opportunities, not a matter of self mastery.... While the Hegelian account of liberty might count as paradigmatically positive for Berlin, Hegel is not a positive libertarian as I understand that phrase, and as I understand Hegel" (Crocker 1980: 4).

Along similar lines, John Christman (2009, 2013a, 2013b) argues that positive liberty should be understood as an ideal concerning *how* people form their desires (whether through rational reflection on various alternatives), rather than the *content* of those desires. His goal is to provide a notion of liberty that is neutral regarding its content: a procedural theory of freedom that does not judge which choices are better but focuses exclusively on whether the decision was made freely. According to Christman, this requires that the person have had the necessary material resources to pursue different paths and have undergone a rational reflection process that led them to choose one of them. (Recall that, although Sen and Nussbaum also emphasize the importance of certain means, some of which can be understood as material resources, their conception of freedom may be seen as reflecting judgments about more or less valuable ways of life).[7]

[7] Not everyone accepts the distinction between negative and positive liberty. Gerald MacCallum (1967), for example, argued that there are not different notions of liberty, but rather different ways of interpreting a single notion. More precisely, liberty consists of a single "triadic relation"; what the negative and positive views (and other possible views) disagree on is not this general formula, but how the variables that constitute it should be interpreted. According to this general formula, when we speak of "liberty," we refer to (a) an agent (b) who is not constrained from (c) doing, not doing, becoming, or not becoming something. Different views may differ in what counts as the "agent," what counts as a "constraint," or how to define the goal that the agent is free to achieve. For example, those who support a negative conception consider constraints on liberty to be only external interferences, while those who defend a positive conception consider internal states of the agent, such as psychological impediments, to also limit liberty.

2.3 Freedom from Arbitrary Power

An increasingly influential group of philosophers, led by figures such as Philip Pettit and Quentin Skinner, reject both the negative and positive conceptions of liberty and instead favor what is known as "republican freedom." This kind of freedom is not new: it was implicit in the doctrines of the ancient Romans, as well as in the writings of several medieval authors,[8] shaping what is today called the "neo-Roman" view of the republican tradition (Skinner 2002: 247–248).[9] Republican freedom defines liberty in terms of the "absence of domination." This type of freedom has distinctive features that set it apart from both negative and positive liberty.

On one hand, republican freedom differs from negative liberty because, according to the republican conception, freedom is not simply the absence of interference, but rather the presence of certain institutions that *prevent* arbitrary interference (Pettit 1997, Skinner 1998, Pettit 2001). Examples of such institutions include a democratic constitution, the separation of powers, and democratic elections. The republican view understands freedom as the absence of domination, meaning the absence of others' *capacity* to *arbitrarily* interfere with our choices (Pettit 1997: 52).

As Berlin acknowledges, from the negative perspective, a person can be free even if living under a dictatorship, so long as the dictator *chooses* not to interfere with their life. There is no necessary connection between negative liberty and any particular form of government (Berlin 2002 [1958]: 176–178). But is it not counterintuitive to claim that one can be free under a dictatorship, or that a slave can experience significant freedom as long as the master is compassionate and generous? Is not mere subjection to the arbitrary power of a dictator or master enough to nullify our freedom? (Pettit 1997: 22). According to the republican conception, we are free only if we live in a society with political institutions that *guarantee*

[8] In particular, Skinner refers to a number of Medieval common-law texts, most notably those of Henry de Bracton and Thomas Littleton.

[9] This interpretation of republicanism does not assume that elements such as civic virtue and political participation are intrinsically valuable (as suggested by the Aristotelian view of the polis in ancient Greece), but rather that they are instrumental for achieving political freedom, understood as independence from arbitrary power. Defenses of this instrumental view can be found in Spitz (1995), Dagger (1997), Pettit (1997), and Skinner (1998). Defenses of a traditional, Aristotelian interpretation of republicanism can be found in Arendt (1963), Pocock (1981), and Rahe (1992).

our independence from such arbitrary power—institutions that eliminate the *capacity* of individuals to interfere *arbitrarily* with one another.

The term "arbitrarily" plays a crucial role in republican freedom, as Pettit points out. Interferences aimed at promoting our interests—understood as those we ourselves recognize—are not arbitrary and therefore do not constitute domination (Pettit 1997: 23). Imagine someone restrains us from crossing the street. If we assume this person acts because they notice an approaching car that we have failed to see, then this interference does not count as domination since it serves our own interests as we understand them. In fact, we would likely be grateful for this intervention. The person did not interfere to impose what they think our interests *should* be, nor to promote values they consider *objectively* correct, but to protect what are *genuinely* our interests.

On the other hand, republican freedom differs from positive liberty because being free in the republican sense does not require having a mental state that allows us to identify our "genuine" desires, evolving into a virtuous state to pursue valuable goals, receiving certain resources, or participating politically in the community (Skinner 1991, Spitz 1993). Of course, in practice, access to material resources or political engagement can empower us and help us avoid relationships of domination. However, the value of these practices is instrumental: according to republicanism, these specific means do not *constitute* freedom itself. Conceptually, republican freedom does require institutions that prevent arbitrary interference with individuals' choices. Nevertheless, the most effective design of such institutions—such as the extent of wealth redistribution—is an *empirical* question.[10]

The notion of republican freedom helps explain the role of institutions characteristic of republican government. The idea is that institutions should be designed to prevent certain social relationships from becoming relationships of domination. The clearest example is the relationship between the state and citizens, where institutions serve to protect citizens from potential abuses of state power. Yet, other social relationships can pose similar dangers: employer-employee, husband-wife, majority-minority, teacher-student, and so forth. Broadly speaking, without institutions that neutralize the ability of the powerful to interfere arbitrarily with the vulnerable, the latter would be subject to domination by the former.

[10] For other defenses of republican freedom, see Viroli (2002), Maynor (2003), Laborde (2010), Costa (2016), and Taylor, R. (2017).

Republicanism thus demands institutions that protect not only citizens from the state but also every vulnerable party in relationships at risk of domination. For instance, from a republican perspective, labor law could prevent employees from being at the mercy of employers; family law could protect wives and children; constitutional law would safeguard minorities against majority tyranny; and administrative laws within academia might enshrine and protect students' rights in educational institutions (Pettit 1997: 61).

CHAPTER 3

Freedom as Social Cooperation (FSC)

3.1 Cooperation as a Constitutive Element of Freedom

This chapter aims to develop the idea of freedom as social cooperation (FSC) and contrast it with earlier conceptions, showing that it integrates their most appealing elements while standing as an autonomous view that places social cooperation at its core.

3.1.1 Freedom as a Practice

FSC is a conception of freedom that seeks to capture the way people have managed to collaborate with one another and to help each other develop and carry out their life plans. Consequently, FSC aims to explain the development and realization of life plans *within society*. This is why FSC cannot dispense with the idea of social cooperation. Social cooperation is, in fact, the essence of societies where people have been able to formulate and fulfill their projects.

According to FSC, then, freedom is neither an abstention by third parties (negative freedom), nor a certain mental or material condition (positive freedom), nor a form of independence (republican freedom). *Freedom is a cooperative practice for the development and realization of life plans.*

E. Spector, *Freedom as Social Cooperation*,
https://doi.org/10.1007/978-3-032-12217-9_3

FSC is a conception of freedom grounded in observable facts: a significant part of human history concerns how people have managed to expand their potential for cooperation and invent new ways to serve one another, thereby broadening their range of options. *FSC draws inspiration from how human beings have developed and realized life plans through cooperation.*

Observing how people have collaborated to expand their horizons is to observe what matters to them. This does not mean that every form of interaction among people is positive. Human history also includes dark chapters such as slavery and other forms of subjugation, clearly incompatible with FSC. FSC does not seek to abandon the distinction between what is and what ought to be (between facts and values). However, when we observe people helping each other to broaden their opportunities, we gain insight into what they consider important in life. If we believe that people matter, then what they value should matter too. FSC does not attempt to identify the true meaning of freedom by turning its back on what has happened. Rather, FSC draws on those human practices that have enabled people to develop and carry out their life plans.

Now, how can we identify freedom in practice if we do not have a prior notion of freedom? For example, we can enter a store and distinguish apples from other fruits because we have the concept of "apple" in mind. Similarly, it may be argued that we can identify freedom in practice only if we have a prior idea of what freedom is. But once we have this idea, its practical application becomes irrelevant for understanding the concept itself.

To be sure, we do require a prior notion to identify freedom in practice. However, this prior notion does not need to be a conception of freedom itself. It can simply be an idea about the *signs* that indicate certain individuals are free. Let us say that the sign that a group of people is free is X, where X is an observable fact that reliably indicates that these people are free. When X occurs, we can reasonably understand that they are exercising their freedom. Then, we only need to ask *in virtue of what* X occurs. Once we solve this mystery, we will understand *what freedom is.*

The following example will help express this idea more concretely. Suppose we are assigned the task of defining the internal structure of a sodium cation and a chloride anion. The problem is that we have no idea what a sodium cation or a chloride anion is. We vaguely know they are chemical components, but we have no understanding of their characteristics. We are assigned the task of defining the internal structure of these components, but since we do not know their basic characteristics, we do not even know where to find them. We cannot analyze what we cannot identify.

After some thought, we realize that we have a small but valuable clue to begin our investigation: salt contains these two components. With this information, we can recognize a sodium cation and a chloride anion in practice without even knowing what these components actually are: if we see salt, we know these two elements are present, and in this way, we manage to identify them. Once these two components are before us, we can proceed to analyze them to identify *in virtue of what* they form what we know as salt, for which we will need to delve into their internal structure. Note that the methodology we are using is from the outside in: we start with an easily observable fact and then delve deeper to uncover what we are looking for.

My thesis is an application of this reasoning to the idea of freedom. The first step is to give substance to X (the *observable* fact that indicates people are free). The second step is to identify *in virtue of what* X occurs. There, we will find our notion of freedom.

What is X about? Many philosophers from different traditions—ranging from negative to positive conceptions of freedom—have seen a connection between freedom and the practice of formulating and carrying out life plans, and here I will draw on this foundation (Taylor, C. 1979, Crocker 1980, Lomasky 1987, Spector, H. 1992, Steiner 1994, Cohen 2001, Sen 2006, Christman 2013b, among others). When we imagine free individuals, we often picture them engaged in designing and striving toward their own goals and aspirations. This picture makes sense: arguably, what makes freedom *significant* is precisely its crucial role in the elaboration and pursuit of life projects. Freedom is normatively relevant *due to* its fundamental place in the design and realization of life plans. In turn, this normative link provides insight into how we should define freedom: if what gives freedom significance is its essential role in the creation and realization of life plans, then we must define freedom in a way that honors this significance. By following this guide, we can be assured that our conception of freedom will encompass the fundamental elements that actually *ground* people's freedom.[1]

[1] When we ask what *grounds* freedom, we are not addressing a metaphysical question. In the philosophical literature on grounding—particularly concerning metaphysical explanation—some authors argue that if A grounds B, there must be a relation of necessity

When people are crafting and carrying out their life plans, then, we can confidently say they are exercising their freedom. These plans can take many forms: professing and practicing a religion according to one's conscience, establishing and nurturing personal relationships, expressing one's beliefs and opinions openly, pursuing a chosen career, engaging in creative and intellectual endeavors, and so on.[2] In fact, pluralism can aid us in this process of recognition. Philosophers like John Rawls (1993, xvii) have emphasized the importance of pluralism as a fundamental fact that political institutions must acknowledge and accommodate to ensure fairness and stability in a diverse society. Here, I take pluralism not merely as a fact to be managed by institutions, but as a meaningful indicator of people's genuine pursuit of their own life plans. Pluralism—the coexistence of various religious beliefs, philosophical perspectives, cultural traditions, and, more broadly, diverse worldviews—is not only a natural outcome but a significant sign of a society where individuals are genuinely pursuing their own paths. Homogeneity in these spheres often signals underlying social or political pressures, suggesting the presence of a central authority or rigid structures that constrain personal choice and impose conformity. Conversely, diversity suggests a landscape where personal projects thrive authentically and robustly, rather than merely existing in name.

The formulation and realization of our life projects is thus the way in which freedom is outwardly expressed: it is our X. This practice does not define the internal structure of freedom; rather, it is the manner in which freedom's existence is indicated and what makes it *normatively* significant.

between them: in every possible world where A exists, B must also exist (Trogdon and Witmer 2021: 255). However, this framework does not apply to normative definitions like the one I propose, which is not meant to capture truths across all possible worlds but depends on social and institutional contexts. Thus, I follow Fine (2012: 39–40) in holding that *normative* grounding is fundamentally different from *metaphysical* grounding. If Fine were wrong, and metaphysical grounding absorbed normative grounding, then my new task would be to show why *metaphysical grounding* does not entail *necessity*—though, fortunately, I would not be alone in this endeavor (Skiles 2015).

[2] Of course, it is not always easy to identify when people are truly formulating and pursuing their own projects. For example, women in certain societies may appear to be following their life plans, but in reality, they are often subject to legal restrictions and male guardianship. Simply noting that someone is not acting under obvious coercion or immediate threat, and may even appear content with their way of life, is often not enough to form a sound conclusion. It is necessary to consider the underlying institutions and structures at play.

Returning to the previous example, we might describe the sodium cation and the chloride anion as a common table seasoning used to enhance the flavor of food, a seasoning that appears as small, white, solid crystals that dissolve in water, distributing flavor evenly throughout the food. Here, our focus is not on the internal structure of these components, but on the observable properties that enable us to identify them in daily life; in particular, we are considering the role they play that makes them *gastronomically* significant.[3] To uncover its internal structure, we must examine their fundamental composition.

All we have so far, then, is X: a clue for identifying freedom in practice. When we see people actually formulating and carrying out their life plans, we know they are exercising their freedom. Now, we need to examine the context and uncover *in virtue of what* people design and realize their life plans. Once we solve this mystery, we will understand what freedom is.

Of course, the notion of freedom we are seeking is not the everyday meaning nor the brief, neutral dictionary definition. Rather, it is a distinctly philosophical conception, carefully shaped to advance a normative claim about how freedom *ought* to be understood and valued. While this definition is designed to resonate with our intuitions and common moral sense, its nature is argumentative rather than lexicographical. For this reason, it should not be surprising that the resulting account differs significantly from the common understanding of freedom.

Let us now go with that notion of freedom. What can we find in the environment of those who develop and carry out life plans? The first response that often comes to mind refers to basic realities such as air or the law of gravity. However, such natural conditions do not help us define the type of freedom characterized by FSC—a theory of freedom that focuses primarily on human interactions rather than the relations between human beings and their natural or physical surroundings. FSC seeks to set forth a theory of *social* freedom, so it assumes that freedom can only be promoted or violated by other human beings—much like negative freedom in Berlin's sense or republican freedom as described by

[3] However, it would be unwise to push the analogy too far. While those observable properties grant these components their utility, I do not mean to claim that "freedom is useful because it can be used to pursue life plans." The formulation and pursuit of life plans is inherent to freedom in a way that enhancing the flavor of food is not inherent to the sodium cation and the chloride anion. That these ions can be used to enhance flavor makes them *useful*; the role of freedom in designing and pursuing life plans makes it *meaningful*.

Pettit. Therefore, when we look at the environment of those engaged in pursuing life projects, we must turn to the *social* context. What exactly does this social environment consist of, and how does it facilitate the activity of formulating and carrying out life plans?

One possible answer is "non-interference": wherever people are able to formulate and carry out life plans, we can observe that no one is interfering with their courses of action. Thus, we might adopt a negative conception of liberty and define it in terms of the absence of interference from others. The problem is that the mere absence of interference does not capture everything that happens in the environment of someone who is formulating and pursuing a life plan. To be sure, when we imagine someone designing and carrying out their life plan, we assume that this person is not being interfered with by anyone. Nevertheless, as we will see, there is much more than just the absence of interference in the context of someone who is formulating and pursuing a life plan.

Another possible answer is that those who formulate and pursue life plans not only enjoy a sphere of non-interference, but also do so within the context of certain institutions that protect that sphere over time. Thus, we might adopt the republican conception of liberty. Yet, this notion remains too narrow: as I will explain shortly, although institutions that protect individuals from arbitrary interference (domination) by others do play a role, they do not capture everything that occurs in the environment of those who formulate and pursue life plans.

A different response could be that those who design and carry out life plans possess certain mental aptitudes, specific capacities, or material resources. In that case, we might adopt a positive notion of liberty. To be sure, those who formulate and pursue life plans often have these "assets." But these assets do not fall like manna from heaven. Consider how abstract—and how misleading—it is to imagine a person in a vacuum, without past or future, not immersed in any social context, developing their aptitudes and capacities alone, somehow receiving certain material resources for some reason, and then formulating and carrying out a life plan through them. This, too, fails to fully account for everything that happens around those who formulate and pursue life plans. Incomplete stories are poor stories, partly because they are unintelligible. So, what else lies behind those who formulate and carry out life plans? We vaguely know it has to do with freedom, but we need a conception that *defines* this idea. Once we have it, we will know what freedom is. To answer this question, then, let us analyze the following life stories, which are not real but are representative of reality.

Michael is 45 years old and works as a surgeon. He is married and has two children. On weekends, he plays tennis at a club where he participates in internal tournaments, and when the weather is not favorable, he and his wife attend European film screenings. Michael went to a private Catholic school for elementary and high school. One of his teachers noticed his vocation for medicine and advised him, at the age of 18, to pursue a pre-med track at the state's public university, which was considered one of the best in the country. While studying, Michael worked in the administrative department of an insurance company. It was not a particularly well paid or exciting job for him, but it helped him support himself during his studies. It was there that he met his future wife, who was also a student at the university, preparing for law school. After both finished their degrees, they got married, and two years later, they had their first child. The birth was difficult, but everything turned out well in the end.

Rachel is 40 years old and is an architect. She is divorced and has one daughter. Her divorce was not easy, but through mediation, her lawyers were able to reach an agreement. Today, she has custody of her daughter, although her ex-husband sees her on weekends. Rachel is currently working on a major architectural project, which involves designing a tower in the city center. She also practices Pilates twice a week and often goes out to dinner with her friends. Nutrition was a challenge for Rachel during her teenage years. Having struggled with anorexia nervosa, she was able to recover with the support of the medical team at a prestigious public hospital. She now considers herself fully recovered, although she continues weekly therapy with a psychologist to help manage her anxiety. Because of her active professional and social life, she has hired a trusted person to handle household chores and care for her daughter when she is away.

Alex is 30 years old, single, lives alone, and works as a musician. He plays in a rock band and also gives private guitar lessons at the local cultural center. With his band, he travels around the country performing concerts at various bars and clubs. Alex had a difficult childhood. He was born in a poor neighborhood in the south of the city, and his parents died when he was five years old. He was raised in a children's home and managed to finish elementary and high school. When he was 11, Alex found an old guitar in a closet at the home, and a teacher at his school taught him the basic chords. That was the beginning of a long journey, which solidified when he turned 18 and decided to dedicate himself exclusively to music. Today, his financial situation is modest, but he is happy because he does what he loves and can travel around the country—something he clearly could not do as a minor living in the children's home.

FSC rests on the idea that neither the mere absence of interference, nor the absence of domination, nor even the acquisition of specific skills, abilities, or certain material resources alone fully explains what it is in virtue of which people formulate and pursue life plans. The notion of intelligibility is crucial to understanding this reasoning: the activity of creating and following life plans is not fully intelligible if we explain it solely in terms of some prior conception of freedom. The story of the aspirations, achievements, and, more broadly, the lifestyle and projects of Michael, Rachel, and Alex begins to make sense when viewed within the context of social cooperation.[4]

FSC should not be confused with the familiar idea that social cooperation is merely the *means* by which people design and carry out their life plans. Generally speaking, the means to achieve specific ends can be left unspecified, and the story still retains its meaning. For example, if a friend tells us that last weekend they traveled to a nearby city to visit relatives, we can understand the story without needing to know what mode of transportation they used. The problem with excluding cooperation from the narrative of how people develop their way of life over time is that the story becomes *fundamentally* incomplete: cooperation is precisely the missing chapter needed to fully understand the account. It would be like mentioning only some characteristics of the sodium cation and the chloride anion—we would not be telling the full story of why

[4] As I mentioned earlier, the environment of these individuals also includes basic realities such as air and the law of gravity; however, these natural conditions are not part of the FSC framework, since FSC focuses specifically on the social dimension of freedom. It is concerned with the interactions among human beings and assumes that freedom can only be promoted or violated by other people. So, if those background, natural conditions have any significance for illustrating the idea of freedom, it is to show how people, through cooperation, have managed to deal with such circumstances—by building tables to prevent objects from falling, or by creating laws to address negative externalities that might pollute the air. But in the FSC approach, those natural conditions do not play any role in *defining* freedom.

salt is, in fact, salt; we would be failing to explain everything in virtue of which that substance qualifies as salt.[5]

To put it differently, a helpful way to think about your freedom is as being the main character in your own life story. As the protagonist, you have agency, make choices, and shape your narrative. However, by definition, a *main* character's story is never told in isolation: it unfolds in relation to other characters who interact with them. In the FSC framework, these "other characters" are the people who cooperate with the protagonist. Without these cooperating others, the role of the main character would lose much of its significance. The plot depends on the connections and shared endeavors that weave the fabric of our lives. We are the protagonists of our own story and, at the same time, supporting characters in the stories of others with whom we cooperate. From the perspective of FSC, cooperation is what renders freedom intelligible within a shared social framework.

The story of how Michael has formulated and carried out his life plan cannot be fully understood unless we include the framework of social cooperation within which he has operated (and the same applies to Rachel and Alex). In other words, rather than being a contingent aspect, social cooperation was inherent to the formulation and realization of his life plan. FSC holds that this chapter of the story is essential for understanding what it is in virtue of which Michael developed and fulfilled his goals. FSC is a conception of freedom that, while encompassing negative, positive, and republican dimensions, regards these as only parts of a more complex scheme of social cooperation—one that is inherent to the activity of formulating and carrying out life plans. This scheme is the variant we seek to understand such activity and, ultimately, to develop an appropriate conception of freedom.

Each person has their own story as a participant in this cooperative framework. In Michael's case, his story as a participant includes, beyond his parents, the construction workers who built the hospital where he was born, the midwife who delivered him, the producers of the food he ate as a child, the employee at the toy store where his parents bought his toys, the architects who designed the schools he attended, the public

[5] It is important to emphasize that this analogy, while illustrative, should be approached with caution, since—as I mentioned earlier—I am putting forward a normative thesis about the idea of freedom, rather than a metaphysical one, such as the kind we might have when explaining what *grounds* salt.

transport drivers he relied on to get to school, his teachers—especially the one who encouraged him to study medicine—the person who trusted him and hired him at the insurance company, the woman with whom he chose to start a family, the civil registry official who solemnized their marriage, the nurses who ensured the safe delivery of his first child, the tennis partners he plays with at the club, those who maintain the courts, and the staff who organize the European film screenings he enjoys with his wife. These individuals represent only a small part of the vast network of interactions to which Michael belongs—a network that is an *essential* part of how he formulates and carries out his life plan.

Moreover, when we examine the various branches of this network, we find that Michael should be grateful to millions of people he will never meet—for example, the worker who maintains the factory where the tennis rackets are made, which are then sold at the store where Michael chooses to buy his sports equipment. And Michael, in turn, contributes to this system as a surgeon, tennis player, European film enthusiast, and so on—contributions that may benefit people he will never know (no one knows where the money Michael spends on movie tickets ultimately ends up). If we performed the same exercise with Rachel's and Alex's lives, we would reach similar conclusions.

From the FSC perspective, freedom is a cooperative practice involving the formulation and pursuit of life plans over time. As mentioned earlier, FSC is a conception of freedom grounded in observable realities: much of human history revolves around how people have expanded their capacity for cooperation and invented new ways to serve one another, thereby broadening their range of options. FSC draws inspiration from the ways humans have collaborated to create and realize life plans. It embraces what it considers the most compelling aspects of human interaction throughout history. However, FSC is not a historical thesis but a normative one: its aim is not to replicate any *particular* social structure from the past, but to propose a notion of social cooperation that, inspired by the best human practices, embodies the idea of freedom. Thus, history is not the primary object of study here; rather, it provides valuable insights that inspire the design of a freedom conception rooted in social cooperation.

Once FSC is fully developed—a task that will extend through the end of this chapter—I will explore its explanatory power in Chapters 4, 5, and 6. I argue that FSC can also serve as a theory of liberal democracy, which should come as no surprise, given that the current liberal democratic system has, throughout history, incorporated the cooperative logic of various frameworks.

3.1.2 FSC: A Normative Conception of Freedom

We can distinguish between two types of conceptions of freedom: descriptive conceptions and normative (or moralized) conceptions. A descriptive conception of freedom is purely factual and therefore does not involve any moral stance. In contrast, a normative conception contains a moral theory, aiming to be normatively significant and, consequently, seeking to play a justificatory role in moral and political reasoning (Bader 2018: 59). A normative conception of freedom can give rise to a theory about what rights people *ought* to have, specifying which actions are morally permissible or impermissible and identifying which obstacles constitute violations of freedom.

As mentioned previously, FSC is a normative conception. In this section, I explain the moral components of FSC. In particular, I argue that this conception of freedom encompasses a notion of equality and a notion of dignity. Its potential to ground a theory of rights will be illustrated in the following chapters, where I will explain how FSC can function as a theory of liberal democracy.[6]

3.1.2.1 FSC and Equality

FSC defines freedom as a cooperative practice for the development and realization of life plans. However, it refers to a specific form of cooperation: individuals contribute to the scheme, with no single contribution

[6] Christian List and Laura Valentini criticize moralized conceptions of freedom. They argue that these conceptions fail to acknowledge that *justified restrictions on freedom* can exist—something that appears entirely plausible. Indeed, if such restrictions are justified, then by definition they are not restrictions on freedom (List and Valentini 2016). To respond to this critique, it is necessary to distinguish between two levels at which we can speak of freedom: a basic, foundational level, and a non-basic, derivative level. FSC is a basic conception of freedom: a theory about how society should be structured so that individuals can develop and pursue their life plans. From this basic conception, as we will see, specific rights and freedoms are derived (such as suffrage, freedom of expression, freedom of movement, the right to health, and so forth). At this non-basic level, FSC does allow for discussion about whether certain restrictions on these rights and freedoms are justified. For example, during a pandemic, freedom of movement may conflict with the right to health, and FSC must determine which right should *justifiably* be restricted.

being indispensable for its continued functioning, even though the *total* of all contributions is essential. When FSC refers to cooperation schemes, it alludes to schemes that are independent of particular individuals—that is, schemes whose functioning does not depend on how *specific* people behave. In other words, these schemes withstand individual behaviors. Otherwise, as I will explain in section 3.1.4, if particular behaviors could undermine the scheme, such a scheme would not be a suitable environment for developing and realizing life plans.

In this way, the conception of "cooperation" adopted by FSC implies a form of equality among people: we can speak of full cooperation only when the individuals make their contributions to the scheme, but no single contribution is necessary on its own for the scheme to continue functioning. In other words, each depends on the others to realize their life plan, meaning they rely on the entire scheme as a whole, but no one is indispensable. This does not mean that all the participants contribute equally to the scheme; only that no *individual* contribution is so important that the entire scheme depends on it.

To better illustrate the idea of depending on everyone, but on no one in particular, it is useful to distinguish between four scenarios:

1. Dependence on a particular individual whose cooperation is both a necessary and sufficient condition to achieve a certain goal.
2. Dependence on a particular individual whose cooperation is a necessary (but not sufficient) condition to achieve a certain goal.
3. Interdependence among individuals, where each individual's contribution is *separately* necessary to achieve a certain goal.
4. Interdependence among individuals whose contributions are *collectively* necessary (and sufficient) to achieve a certain goal, even though no single contribution is individually indispensable.

Let us consider an example for each situation.

1. Four students live together in a university residence. Three of them contract a severe virus. Though not fatal, it incapacitates them to the point that they cannot get out of bed for a week. The fourth student, having contracted the virus the previous year, is immune. This student takes on the cleaning, grocery shopping, and cooking duties for the week. In this scenario, there is a clear inequality:

the three sick students depend entirely on the healthy student for household chores.

2. A group of friends plans to have an Argentine *asado*, grilling meat over wood and charcoal, and serving it with salad. Some contribute by buying vegetables, others prepare the salad; some buy the meat, while others cut and season it. However, only one person knows how to cook the meat properly—building the fire from wood and charcoal and determining the perfect cooking time. Because this person is focused on cooking, they cannot attend to other tasks like shopping. Here, everyone assists the cook. If one assistant fails to perform their task, the goal remains achievable because others can cover the task. The help of one of the assistants is not strictly necessary. However, if the cook is unable to perform their role (perhaps due to an injury), the project fails. In this case, there is also inequality: although everyone has a role, one person is indispensable for success.
3. A small plane crashes in the jungle. Fortunately, all four passengers survive and must now survive until rescue. Each passenger possesses a unique skill essential for survival: one knows how to treat wounds and prevent infection, another can build and maintain shelters, a third can hunt for food, and the fourth can create fire by friction. Here, a form of equality exists: everyone is indispensable to the project's success.
4. Fifteen people pull on a rope to drag a very heavy object. All fifteen can move it without difficulty. Moreover, if one person does not participate (due to injury, distraction, or any other reason), the remaining fourteen can still achieve the goal by exerting a bit more effort each. There is no need for everyone to be equally strong; it suffices that no single absence destabilizes the effort. In this case, everyone contributes, and the sum of all contributions makes the system work, although no single contribution is strictly necessary (nor sufficient). This represents a different form of equality than in the previous scenario: not that everyone is indispensable, but that no one is indispensable—in other words, each depends on all, but on no one in particular.

Neither scenario (1) nor (2) reflects the kind of cooperation that FSC refers to, because both exhibit such inequality that the failure of a particular participant can derail the entire scheme. In both cases, there is a specific individual who is indispensable. Beyond status inequality (one person being more important than others), these schemes are essentially unstable: any reason preventing or dissuading the indispensable participant from cooperating leads to the collapse of the scheme. Applied to political society, such schemes could not provide a suitable environment for developing and pursuing life plans.

Scenario (3) does exhibit a form of equality: everyone is indispensable. However, this is not the kind of equality FSC draws inspiration from. First, although there is status equality (no one is more important than another), this equality is only possible in specific micro-situations and cannot be extended to political society, where it is impossible for everyone to be indispensable. Second, even if this form of equality were transferable to political society, it would not constitute a stable environment for developing and pursuing life plans, since the scheme would be too fragile: any factor preventing or dissuading a participant from cooperating would undermine the entire scheme.

The form of cooperation referred to by FSC is the one described in (4). On the one hand, it represents a form of equality that can be extended to political society: although it is impossible to make everyone indispensable, it is possible—with an appropriate institutional design—to ensure that no one is indispensable, or at least to come very close. On the other hand, since there are no indispensable participants, the system is resilient against individual anti-cooperative behaviors, making it more stable and, consequently, enabling it to create a context in which individuals can develop and pursue their life plans.

In short, FSC rests on a form of mutual dependence among individuals: everyone depends on everyone else to develop and carry out their life plans. This dependence on cooperation, far from being contrary to freedom, is an integral part of it—provided that by "cooperation" we understand an egalitarian framework to which all contribute, yet in which no single participant is indispensable.

The idea of depending on everyone without relying on any individual in particular seems to be implicitly embedded in the design of various social structures throughout history. Consider, for example, the forms of social organization developed during the Paleolithic era—what Friedrich Engels referred to as "primitive communism" (Engels 2010 [1884]). These were tribes that, through hunting, fishing, and gathering, worked to meet their immediate basic needs, distributing all resources obtained equally, without political hierarchies that concentrated power (Leonard

1994: 14–15, Ratner 2013: 39–42). These small communities shared both political power and responsibilities, without placing the authority to make the system succeed—or fail—in the hands of a single individual.

The evidence also indicates that the Sumerians had an institutional system which, in certain respects, tended toward the decentralization of power. They designed a complex governmental structure that included formal laws and pro-market measures, such as the establishment of means of exchange and credit institutions. Most importantly for these purposes, they established the earliest known bicameral congress around 3000 BC, in a part of the world not typically associated with practices we would today identify as "republican" (Kramer, S. 1981: 30–31).

This principle also underpinned democratic systems that flourished several centuries later in different parts of the world. In the fifth century BC, for example, Athens began to move toward an institutional system whose operation did not depend on particular individuals, abandoning concentrated power structures. Thus, the selection by lot of *strategoi* (responsible for foreign policy), *archons* (who presided over the courts), Council members (charged with drafting laws), and jurors (responsible for administering justice) was *designed to* create a cooperative framework in which no one person had the potential to bring down the entire system (Rodríguez Adrados 1993: 95–119). The only body not filled by lot was the assembly of citizens—the *ecclesia*—which met nearly once a week and regularly attracted over five thousand of the approximately thirty thousand full citizens. While participation was voluntary, this direct involvement of a broad segment of the citizenry complemented the system of randomly selected officials, creating a balanced framework that decentralized power by distributing decision-making across many hands rather than concentrating it in a few. Together, these institutions ensured that no single individual or small group could dominate governance (Pettit 2023: 94).

Similarly, in the second century BC, the ancient Greek historian Polybius (2011 [around 168–146 BC]: bk. 6) advocated this concept for the Roman Republic. In Rome, power was carefully distributed among independent institutions: while only members of the elite could hold office and serve in the Senate, their positions required approval through election by popular assemblies. The legislative process demanded not only proposals from officeholders but also the backing of the people's assemblies and the absence of a veto from the tribunes. Executive authority was likewise shared, exemplified by the dual consulship. This system found further endorsement from Cicero (1998 [around 54–51 BC]) and other Roman writers, and the idea became a cornerstone of republican thought throughout medieval and Renaissance Italy (Machiavelli 1997 [1531]). More recently, the idea of distributing real power in a way that prevents any single individual (or elite) from destabilizing the system was advanced by the European tradition led by Montesquieu (2015 [1748]) and later embraced by the Founding Fathers of the United States Constitution.

Note that this general principle is closely related to the notion of equal status. Arguably, equalizing real power is fundamental to eventually achieving equal status and abolishing hierarchical distinctions such as noble titles. Historically, noble ranks and social hierarchies have been grounded in the possession and transmission of actual political or economic power, which legitimized the superior status of certain individuals or families. By equalizing real power—through democratic systems, equality laws, or the reduction of exclusive political and economic privileges—the material foundation sustaining these status differences is weakened. This dynamic is exemplified by legal reforms like Spain's Law 33/2006, which equalizes inheritance rights to noble titles regardless of gender and acknowledges that such titles today hold only honorary and *symbolic* value, devoid of political power or genuine privileges. It is reasonable to assert that, by curtailing the effective power linked to these titles, society moves toward equalizing social status. In essence, equality in the access to and exercise of real power erodes the material and legal bases of hierarchical distinctions and noble titles, fostering a more egalitarian society in terms of status.

As I will explain in Chapters 4 and 5, it seems clear that the way we currently design and evaluate democratic institutions is guided by this general notion. Indeed, the classic principle of the rule of law appears to embody this idea.[7] The most important demand of this principle is that those in positions of authority do not exercise their power arbitrarily or purely at their discretion, but rather within clear limits imposed by public and stable rules. The law must stand above individuals, not the other way around. It seems, then, that this principle provides a clear directive

[7] This principle appears in the works of various thinkers throughout history, some of whom have shaped the modern liberal democratic system. See, for example, Locke 2003 [1689]: §§ 135–137; Montesquieu 2015 [1748]: bk. VI (chap. 1) and bk. XI; Dicey 1982 [1885]: 114; and Fuller 1958: 636–637.

on how the law should be designed: in such a way that it continues to function even when a person or group attempts to undermine it.

FSC draws inspiration from those cooperative frameworks that have allowed people to develop and carry out their life plans without anyone holding so much power as to cause the system to collapse. This is the ideal of equality embodied by FSC.

3.1.2.2 FSC and Dignity

FSC also embraces a notion of human dignity. Within FSC, dignity arises from equality. On the one hand, everyone relies on everyone else to be free, since freedom itself is a kind of cooperative practice. On the other hand, although in such a cooperative framework everyone *depends on* everyone else, no one is *at the mercy of* another, because no single participant is indispensable for the scheme to continue functioning. As noted previously, people are equals in this sense.

The consequence of this equality is that no participant can control the lives of others by threatening to withdraw cooperation. Although we rely on one another in general, each of us retains the right to say "no" to any individual. The right to say "no" is, if not the whole, then a significant part of what constitutes our dignity as human beings.[8]

In the feudal systems of Medieval Europe, if we were born as serfs, we had the *right* to protection from our lord, but we lacked many rights that we now take for granted. We lived where our lord told us to live. We advanced only as far as our lord allowed. We sold our harvest to our lord at a price of his choosing. None of this was negotiable. If we wanted to leave, we needed our lord's permission. We even bowed to greet him. In these systems, our dignity was profoundly undermined. Cooperative schemes replace dependence on the mercy of a lord with interdependence within a united yet highly functional community. Cooperation does not occur between a superior and an inferior who must pay homage, but among independent, equal individuals who design and pursue their own life plans.

Importantly, the notion of dignity FSC embodies is minimal and non-metaphysical. It does not rest on any claim about an intrinsic human essence, but on the relational status individuals hold within a cooperative scheme: a status defined by equality, which ensures that no participant

[8] I borrow the expression "right to say 'no'" from Schmidtz (2023: 126).

can pressure others by threatening to withdraw cooperation. In a cooperative framework, then, dignity belongs to each individual, since no one can demand that we work *solely* to satisfy their desires.[9] It is about each person having the humility to accept that others are not at their service. Within such a cooperative scheme, people are free by contributing to the freedom of others.

3.1.3 The Neutrality of FSC

In the previous section, I explained that FSC is a normative conception of freedom. However, this should not be taken to mean that FSC presupposes the correctness of any particular life plan. On the contrary, unlike some notions of positive freedom (see, for example, the conceptions of Marx and Hegel discussed in the previous chapter), FSC remains neutral with respect to different conceptions of the good. The only condition is their compatibility with social cooperation. Disruptive life plans that undermine the cooperative atmosphere—such as the actions of racist groups or those that simply promote chaos—should be discouraged and sanctioned. FSC is a normative conception of freedom, so it does not consider every plan worthy of being classified as an exercise of *freedom*. But as long as the life plans are compatible with social cooperation, FSC embraces them without passing judgment on their merits. FSC holds that freedom is a cooperative practice, but it refrains from making value judgments about the conceptions of the good that may arise within the cooperative framework.

To be sure, the neutrality of FSC is not absolute as it excludes ways of life and actions that are fundamentally incompatible with cooperative living. In that sense, the neutrality at stake here is not the radical or "complete neutrality" that would admit any and all actions or life plans. But this is exactly what one should expect from a moralized or normative concept: the neutrality FSC upholds is not the absence of all standards, but rather a broad and principled openness to different life plans, provided they are compatible with cooperation. This limited neutrality is not perfectionist because social cooperation, as defined by FSC, is not itself presented as a metaphysically superior conception of the good life, or a plan that must be realized for its own sake. Rather, it is simply the framework that makes it

[9] This notion of "equal dignity" is similar to the one suggested by Adam Smith (1981 [1776]: bk. III, ch. iii).

possible for individuals and groups to pursue their own diverse life plans, without assuming that cooperation is inherently a better or more valuable way to live. There is always a baseline—here, the requirement of cooperation—to distinguish admissible plans from those that undermine the framework. The neutrality associated with moralized concepts such as freedom is thus never absolute, but it is still relevant: it allows for a wide variety of conceptions of the good to flourish, provided they adhere to a basic standard—in FSC's case, social cooperation.

In fact, FSC is neutral even regarding the value of autonomy itself, if by autonomy we understand a metaphysical value that must be promoted. In this respect, Rawls's distinction between "comprehensive liberalism" and "political liberalism" is useful (Rawls 1993: 199). Comprehensive liberalism, which he attributes to thinkers like Kant, is a metaphysical view insofar as it affirms the moral superiority of the value of *autonomy*—not merely as freedom of action, but as the development of certain capacities such as creativity, critical thinking, analytical reasoning, and so forth (Kant 1991 [1797]: 239–240). Political liberalism, on the other hand, is a conception that does not presuppose the validity of any metaphysical conception of the good, not even the value of autonomy defended by some forms of comprehensive liberalism (Rawls 1993: 217, Rawls 1987: 1).

Rawls's account is a theory of justice rather than a theory of freedom, but his distinction helps clarify the extent of FSC's neutrality. It turns out that this conception of freedom does not assume the superiority of any life plan, not even any particular form of autonomy. The cooperative practice that constitutes freedom can take place, for example, among people seeking to develop the Kantian form of autonomy and religious groups who, dedicating their lives to honoring the mandates of a divine authority, are not interested in cultivating the capacities Kant valued.

From the perspective of FSC, neutrality is not a contingent feature of the cooperative practice that constitutes freedom. Rather, it is inherent to that practice. The cooperative scheme that FSC presupposes is not an entity independent of the people involved: it is the people themselves cooperating. In the FSC framework, social cooperation is the context in which individuals develop and pursue their respective life plans. Therefore, any scheme that attempts to impose beliefs asserting the superiority of certain plans over others is incompatible with social cooperation and thus with FSC. For example, if someone forces others to perform a certain prayer or observe a particular ritual, it would no longer be possible to speak of a cooperative context in which people develop and pursue their *own* life plans. A cooperative scheme is a context in which people design and realize their life plans, but this is different from using the scheme to promote a particular plan. Thus, FSC is a conception of freedom that does not assume the superiority of some life plans over others, as long as they are equally compatible with social cooperation.

Ultimately, the cooperative scheme to which FSC refers is an open scheme, in that it is not oriented toward any specific ends. In this regard, the scheme does not qualify as a *project*. A project is a closed structure: a plan specifically designed to achieve certain objectives. The cooperative scheme has a different nature. It is a structure without predetermined ends: a kind of empty vessel that people can fill according to the content of their life plans. The cooperative scheme is not a project, but a context in which people can design and carry out their projects.

3.1.4 Isolation and Failed Schemes

Every conception of freedom is defined not only by its core features but also by what stands in opposition to it. Negative freedom finds its contrary in coercion, republican liberty in domination, and positive freedom in forces that hinder values such as personal self-realization or the effective achievement of particular goals. In the same way, the nemesis of FSC is found in those circumstances where the very conditions that make cooperation possible break down. The two most illustrative cases—complete isolation and failed cooperative schemes—reveal what it means for FSC to be absent or undermined.

3.1.4.1 Isolation

As explained, under FSC, social cooperation is not merely a condition of freedom but fundamentally *constitutes* it: freedom *is* a cooperative practice for developing and pursuing life plans. An interesting question, then, is how we should interpret, from the perspective of FSC, the case of a person who lives far from modern society and in complete isolation.

First of all, it should be emphasized that living in isolation does not simply mean living far from other people. Some individuals live in remote countryside areas and produce for themselves, but still need to trade with others in order to obtain the money required to pay their taxes. And what benefits do they receive by paying taxes? Well, these people are recognized as the rightful owners of their land, and that property right is protected by the state (if someone tried to evict them, the owners could report it to the authorities). In one way or another, the owners of such land are part of the cooperative framework.

It is also important to note that living in a small, close-knit community involves forms of cooperation even if the group chooses to remain separate from wider society. Some communities—such as certain rural villages or religious groups like the Amish—engage in robust cooperation within their group, while limiting their interaction or cooperation with outsiders. Even though these communities might distrust or simply lack interest in the broader society, their internal cooperation still exemplifies the kind of social interaction that constitutes freedom in the sense of FSC—as mentioned in the previous section, every way of life that is compatible with cooperation is also compatible with FSC. What sets these cases apart from true isolation is precisely the ongoing mutual support within the group, even when the group is withdrawn from the mainstream.

So, we must imagine an individual living outside any form of jurisdiction, in a natural environment, not cooperating with anyone else, either directly or indirectly. To be sure, without social cooperation, someone living in this way would not have freedom in the sense of FSC. There would be no framework of social cooperation through which the person could interact with others and form a network to develop and pursue their life plans.

This kind of solitary existence might seem idyllic only in stories. Surviving while completely isolated is not easy. Harsh winters or summers, the lack of skilled labor to build adequate shelter, possible food shortages, natural disasters such as droughts and floods, dangers posed by the environment in general—venomous insects, diseases, parasites, and predatory animals—together with the absence of medicines, among many other challenges, can make solitary subsistence a daunting objective. But even for those who might manage to survive, it is clear that they would have little room to develop or pursue their life plans (unless the life plan consists of a very precarious subsistence). We all need help. Sustained social cooperation over time (accompanied by specialization, the division of labor, technological progress, and so on) has remedied the typical shortcomings of a life in complete isolation.

On the other hand, it would not be plausible to say that the isolated person is a slave or is oppressed. At best, this person would possess what is often called "natural" freedom, much like any other animal living alone in the forest. One could call this condition freedom, but in that case, it is helpful to distinguish between two types of freedom: natural and social. FSC seeks to capture social freedom, not natural freedom.

3.1.4.2 Failed Schemes

According to FSC, freedom is a cooperative practice for developing and pursuing life plans. As mentioned in section 3.1.2, FSC refers to a particular form of cooperation—one whose functioning does not rely on the contribution of any specific individual. If it did rely on someone in particular (for example, if only one person knew how to produce food), then cooperation in the sense of FSC would not exist, because the element of equality that defines it would be absent. Consequently, following the logic of FSC, we could not speak of full freedom either.

The underlying idea is as follows: a fundamentally flawed scheme, one that relies on the actions of a single individual or a small, self-organizing elite, cannot provide the proper environment for people to develop and pursue their life plans. Exercising this kind of freedom requires a degree of predictability and stability over time. These conditions are absent when the scheme is contingent on the participation of an "indispensable member." Under these circumstances, the scheme is extremely fragile because any reason preventing or discouraging this person from cooperating would jeopardize the entire structure.

Furthermore, this dependency compels people to adapt their life plans to such uncertainty. There are many reasons why the indispensable member may cease cooperating: incapacity (the person is willing but momentarily unable to help), extortion (the individual tries to manipulate others through threats of withdrawing their participation), alternative preferences (the person simply prefers to devote their efforts to something else), or various other contingencies, such as deciding to leave and join a different scheme. The mere *risk* of a system collapsing undermines people's freedom, as they cannot develop their life plans based *solely* on their convictions but must also consider the possibility that the flawed scheme could fail at any moment.[10] Let me illustrate this with an example.

[10] Note that my view differs from Pettit's. As I have explained, according to Pettit, the mere possibility of arbitrary interference undermines freedom, even if that interference never actually occurs (Pettit 1997: 22). By contrast, from my perspective, the risk of system collapse is *itself* a form of interference, since it compels us to change our plans in response to that probability.

Imagine living in a hazardous area prone to earthquakes, hurricanes, lightning storms, and other natural disasters. Such a context is hardly ideal for developing and carrying out your life plans, given the high probability that the environment could become uninhabitable. Likewise, you would have to adapt your plans to the likelihood of these natural events: you might have to rush your activities out of fear of an approaching tornado, avoid spending time outdoors to reduce the risk of being hurt in a thunderstorm, or take shelter when a hurricane is forecast, and so on. Ultimately, you would be forced to change your plans because of the likelihood that these events might occur.

A similar dynamic arises when a cooperative scheme depends on specific individuals. If, for instance, only one person knew how to produce food, we would all have to adapt our plans to the possibility that, for any number of reasons, this individual might stop doing so. If we were able, we would have to invest much of our time learning how to produce food ourselves (setting aside our own projects); otherwise, we might need to make other adjustments—for example, storing provisions and eating only the bare minimum, avoiding activities that are physically and intellectually demanding and require certain nutrients, or even devoting time to persuading that person not to abandon food production. This is why we are not free in such a scenario, or at least not to the degree of freedom that involves developing and realizing our life projects solely according to our convictions.

By contrast, the cooperative schemes that inspire FSC do provide the right environment to develop and pursue our life plans without reliance on any particular individual. We depend on a functioning system, but not on any specific participant—that is the "magic" of cooperative schemes. They provide the predictability and stability needed to design and follow through on our life plans without having to alter them due to fear of a potential collapse in the system.

3.1.5 Is the "Indispensable" Agent Free?

How does a failed scheme affect the agent who is indispensable—for example, the only individual who, continuing with the previous example, knows how to produce food? As already noted, such schemes do not constitute an environment conducive to others formulating and carrying out their life plans. But does the indispensable agent not retain this capacity?

There are several reasons why this agent might cease to cooperate. For instance, they might opt to extort others, attempting to control their behavior by threatening to withdraw food production. Alternatively, they could choose to produce food solely for themselves and devote the remainder of their time to other activities, or they might decide to leave the scheme entirely and join another. The rest of the participants would need to adapt their lives to these possibilities, whereas, arguably, the indispensable agent would not be similarly constrained, since to some extent, this agent is the one making the decisions. In this respect, it could be said that this agent occupies a higher status.

However, the indispensable agent might also cease to cooperate for reasons beyond their control: they might suffer a temporary or permanent injury that makes productive activity impossible, develop a physical or mental illness, or face personal or family circumstances that prevent them from fulfilling their productive role, and so on. If, for any of these reasons, the agent stopped producing, it would not only harm the other participants but also harm the agent themselves, as they too would be unable to sustain their own livelihood. The agent's ability to develop and execute their life plan would, therefore, be constrained by their own limitations.

Indeed, it is possible that this agent would wish to stop producing in order to engage in another activity they find more appealing. However, if the agent possesses any sense of social responsibility, disengaging from this role would not be easy. Setting aside the fact that the agent would still need to produce food for their own subsistence, they might feel an ethical obligation to continue producing for others. In this sense, the agent would be bound by their own capacity, making it more difficult to develop and pursue whichever life plan they desire. In summary, even within a failed scheme, the indispensable agent might also be unable to fully flourish.

In any case, as previously mentioned, FSC is a normative conception of freedom. This means that it does not merely offer an account of how to understand freedom, but also aims to argue that freedom, understood in this sense, is a *valuable* ideal. In particular, as stated earlier, FSC incorporates a notion of equality among persons (and even of dignity). Thus, even if within a failed scheme the indispensable agent possessed the power to extort others and could, in practice, live as a lord, this would not constitute the kind of freedom that FSC regards as morally valuable. In this respect, a proponent of FSC would occupy the same position as, for example, a defender of republican freedom when confronted with the question of whether someone who exercises domination over others is free. If one were to describe such an agent as "free," it would have to be clarified that it is not the kind of freedom that is morally significant according to republican freedom. The same applies here.

3.1.6 The Capacity to Become Free Versus the Fact of Being Free

At this point, someone may introduce the following objection. Imagine a dictator who has the power to force people to *cooperate*. Now imagine that such *forced cooperation* produces beneficial results: it lifts millions out of poverty, and so forth. Surely, we would not condone this practice despite the good outcomes—the dictator has *compelled* people to act against their will. We would say that the dictator has violated their freedom. If this is the case, then what matters is not merely social cooperation, but *free* cooperation. Arguably, freedom cannot be equated with social cooperation itself; rather, social cooperation already presupposes a concept of freedom.

Fortunately, the idea of social cooperation need not presuppose any particular notion of freedom; it requires only the idea of *voluntariness*. FSC defines freedom as a cooperative practice aimed at the design and realization of life plans. Thus, within the FSC framework, social cooperation is intrinsically connected to personal projects. Hence, voluntariness is an implicit condition of social cooperation in FSC—someone who is forced to "cooperate" is not truly pursuing their life plan; actually, this individual is not *cooperating* at all.

However, while *voluntariness* is necessary to exercise FSC—therefore, there is no FSC without voluntariness—it is possible to talk about voluntariness without FSC. This idea becomes clearer when we distinguish between the *capacity* to become free and the *fact* of being free.

On the one hand, a person has the capacity to become free when they have an opportunity to join a (non-failed) scheme of cooperation. On the other hand, the fact of being free occurs when the person is already part of a (non-failed) scheme of cooperation in which they develop and pursue their life plan.

The capacity to become free, then, is a stage prior to actual freedom. It is up to the individual to *decide* whether to use this capacity and join such a scheme. Since it is only a preliminary stage, the capacity to become free is not the same as freedom itself. Likewise, the (voluntary) decision to use this capacity and join a scheme of cooperation does not constitute an exercise of freedom, because one cannot exercise what one does not yet have. A person only becomes free (in the sense of FSC) once they have joined the scheme of cooperation and have begun to develop and pursue their life plan.

This reasoning is not as strange as it might initially seem. It also underlies earlier conceptions of freedom. In the negative conception of freedom, a slave who has the ability to escape from their owner is not yet free but has the capacity to become free once they overcome the interference. Similarly, in the positive conception, an impoverished individual who has the option to demand resources from the state has the opportunity to be free but is not yet free; they will become free when they have those resources and the effective possibility of realizing their aims. Republican freedom also accepts (or should accept) that a dominated person can sometimes act voluntarily. However, while *voluntary* actions are not necessarily *free* actions, FSC maintains that freedom (as understood in the cooperative practice embodied by this concept) presupposes voluntariness.

According to FSC, then, a free person is someone who (1) has the *capacity* to become free, and (2) in *fact* becomes free.

3.1.7 FSC as a Regulative Ideal

From the perspective of FSC, the vulnerability of the scheme to particular behaviors undermines freedom. However, it should be noted that the scheme can be more or less vulnerable, so freedom can be eroded to a greater or lesser extent. Imagine a scheme with one hundred participants, where only five people produce food, as they are the only ones who know how to do it. This scheme is quite vulnerable to the individual behavior of these participants. But it would be even more vulnerable if only one person knew how to produce food, because that person's potential to undermine the scheme would be much greater. FSC is not indifferent to different degrees of vulnerability. A moderately vulnerable scheme better honors the FSC ideal than a highly vulnerable one. If those were the only two alternatives, then, from the point of view of FSC, the first should be preferred. As we will see in due course, sometimes this is the situation: neither alternative is ideal, but some are better than others in terms of FSC.

The importance of the contribution also affects the stability of the scheme. It is not the same for a scheme to have only one person who knows how to make tennis rackets as compared to only one person who knows how to produce food. In the first case, uncooperative behavior by the manufacturer might prevent the tennis player from adopting that particular life plan; in the second case, uncooperative behavior by the producer could prevent the tennis player from adopting any life plan at all. For now, I will set aside this particular issue related to the importance of the contribution.

Importantly, as a regulative ideal, FSC offers a critical framework for evaluating existing systems and proposing reforms, especially in those aspects of the scheme that may undermine social cooperation. FSC helps us identify weaknesses and motivates changes that move the scheme closer to its ideal.

Chapters 4 and 5 aim to show that FSC can provide a foundation for liberal democracy, encompassing both its political and economic institutions. The role of FSC as a guiding light will become even more evident in this context, as liberal democracies are inherently imperfect and FSC can help us identify the reforms that are needed. Understanding the foundations of liberal democracy clarifies the path we should follow and the modifications we ought to make, serving as a practical guide—just as knowing the function of a knife is to cut allows us to recognize when a knife is not working properly and how it might be repaired.

3.1.8 Cooperation Is Not Self-Sacrifice

Finally, it is important to emphasize that, according to FSC, cooperation is by definition limited—it is an activity that should not demand excessive sacrifice from individuals. This reasoning is not an appeal to the principle "ought implies can," as it does not seek to condone non-cooperation on the basis that it cannot be performed. Rather, it aims to highlight an essential aspect of cooperation in the FSC framework: since cooperation is intrinsically tied to the realization of our life plans, it cannot, by definition, require overwhelming sacrifice.

According to FSC, freedom is a cooperative practice—a context within which individuals develop and pursue their life plans. If cooperation, as FSC claims, is constitutive of creating and fulfilling these plans, then it cannot be an activity that consumes a person's entire life and leaves no room to pursue their own projects. According to FSC, cooperation occurs when people assist one another in developing and carrying out their life plans, which means that they do not sacrifice themselves so that others alone may succeed. By definition, cooperation is restricted to activities that do not impose an excessive burden.

3.2 Primitive Cooperation

3.2.1 The "Primitive Cooperation" Model

The primitive cooperation model is a hypothetical scenario that aims to explain the ideal of FSC. It describes a situation analogous to what contractualist philosophers have termed the "state of nature" (Hobbes 1998 [1651], Locke 2003 [1689], Rousseau 2002 [1762]), though with its own distinct characteristics that clearly exemplify FSC. These characteristics were not arbitrarily chosen. Instead, they are plausible and familiar assumptions, where the psychology and physical capacities of the individuals and the circumstances they face are relatable to us.

First, the psychology of the individuals involved reflects a form of bounded rationality: they are generally rational agents capable of reasoning and making decisions, but not perfectly or fully rational in the idealized sense. Rather, their behavior exhibits the bounded rationality typical of real human agents.

Second, we should suppose that it is not the case that a single individual, family, or clique holds a near monopoly of power, whether for cultural, economic, or military reasons. Actually, the probability of such a society existing prior to the formation of a state is low, as Hobbes observed when he argued that, in a prepolitical society, "the weakest has strength enough to kill the strongest, either by secret machination, or by confederacy with others that are in the same danger with himself" (Hobbes 1998 [1651]: 82). The idea is that power is distributed more or less equally—not in the sense that everyone has precisely the same power, but in such a way that no one is so powerful as to dominate all the rest.

Third, since the human world has never been one of unlimited abundance, with manna falling regularly from heaven, we should also take as given that the primitive cooperation scenario exists under conditions of relative scarcity.

Finally, unlike Hobbes, I contend that this mutual dependence on one another makes it more likely that people will work together for common benefits, which is characteristic of human beings (Tomasello

2014). Contrary to the idea of a war of all against all, where life is described as "solitary, poor, nasty, brutish, and short" (Hobbes 1998 [1651]: 84), I assume that a certain range of cooperative social practices would naturally emerge (Hume 2000 [1739], Lewis 1969), at least in societies that are sufficiently homogenous and small.

In any case, beyond the plausibility of that scenario, it is important to keep in mind that, through the primitive cooperation example, I do not seek to convey a historical truth but rather to illustrate that social cooperation, grounded in familiar human dispositions and realistic conditions, forms the essential context for developing and pursuing life plans.

> The Primitive Cooperation Model: A group of 500 people lives in a natural environment. Within this group, there are different ways of life: various beliefs about the meaning of life, diverse religions with different types of rituals, differing views on interpersonal relationships, a range of habits and customs, and so on. Everyone understands that they need sufficient time and resources to develop and carry out their life plans. However, they realize that none of them would have enough time or resources if they acted alone. Although some people are more capable and others less so, no one can simultaneously perform all the necessary tasks.
>
> They then recognize that they could successfully develop and carry out their life plans if they cooperated with one another. With this in mind, they divide into groups and organize tasks accordingly. Some, for example, gather fruits and water, while others make and repair weapons for hunting. Some hunt smaller, more elusive animals, and others focus on larger game. While some build and maintain shelters, others make fire to stay warm at night and cook the food that others have hunted. Some make clothing, and others treat and care for people with health problems or injuries. The group members also take turns keeping watch during the night, so everyone can get a reasonable amount of sleep.
>
> This system of cooperation includes rules for resolving conflicts. First, no one can be coerced into participating, as no one can be forced to join a scheme without their consent. However, to honor their choice, the non-cooperator is excluded from the benefits of social cooperation, precisely because they have decided not to be part of the scheme. Second, anyone who tries to harm another can indeed be coerced because they introduce anti-cooperative elements into the system. Thus, when aggression

> occurs, others intervene coercively[11] to protect the victim and exclude the aggressor from the cooperative scheme, since cooperation is the foundation of the system and aggression fundamentally undermines it.
>
> The participants divide all these tasks among themselves, recognizing that not everyone has the same abilities—for example, some may craft better clothing than others. Each person cooperates according to their abilities.
>
> Thanks to this cooperative system, people can live fully and carry out their life plans.

3.2.2 Depending on Everyone, but No One in Particular

The primitive cooperation model illustrates how people create and pursue their life plans within a collaborative framework. Naturally, in such a precarious context—characterized by limited technological development and communal ownership—life plans are not expected to be very complex, even when they incorporate religious beliefs and other worldviews. As society evolves, life plans tend to grow increasingly sophisticated. People adjust their goals and plans in response to changing circumstances.

The primitive cooperation scenario exemplifies the kind of cooperation that FSC advocates for. In this scheme, each person depends on the other 499 individuals (because without their cooperation, no one could accomplish practically anything), yet no one depends on any single individual. Since multiple people are dedicated to each activity (some build shelters, others make clothing, and so forth), the lack of cooperation from a single individual does not seriously affect the system. Neither the inability of a participant to cooperate, nor a participant's attempt to control the other participants by threatening to withdraw cooperation, nor a decision by someone to leave the arrangement, nor any similar contingency, conditions the participants. *Although the system's functioning depends on everyone, it depends on no one in particular*. Of course, some are more

[11] According to Max Weber, this community would not qualify as a *political* society, since there is no entity exercising a *monopoly* on coercion (Appiah 2003: 222–223). In any case, my aim with this example is to illustrate the idea of social cooperation, not that of a political organization. In Chapters 4, 5, and 6, I will apply the concept of social cooperation to modern political societies.

capable than others, but the differences in ability are not so great that the viability of the joint project hinges on the performance of a single person.

The idea of decentralizing functions so that the scheme does not depend on any one individual (an essential element of FSC) should not be confused with the principle of division of labor. Adam Smith (1981 [1776]: bk. I, ch. i) concluded that the division of labor (defined as specialization) greatly increases production by allowing each person to focus their potential on a single task, thereby improving skill and avoiding the distractions involved in switching between tasks. However, division of labor is not the same as decentralization, because decentralization can exist without the specialization characteristic of division of labor. For example, if everyone engaged in all productive activities and rotated through them, no one would depend on anyone in particular; yet this would not constitute a division of labor in Adam Smith's sense.

The decentralization of the functions to ensure that the scheme does not depend on any one participant reflects the form of equality *inherent* in FSC. Specialization is extremely important because it enhances cooperation by increasing production efficiency, but specialization is not *constitutive* of FSC. The primitive cooperation scenario honors the ideal of FSC *because* the functions are decentralized in such a way that the scheme does not depend on any particular individual. The fact that specialization has *also* been adopted as a production method enriches the cooperative practice but does not define it.

3.2.3 Cooperation, Not Self-Sacrifice

It is important to emphasize, as I have already mentioned, that according to FSC, cooperation is, by definition, limited—it does not consume people's lives. In a social *cooperation* scheme (like that which governs in the primitive cooperation model), people help each other develop and carry out their life plans; they do not sacrifice themselves so others can succeed.

For cooperation to exist, the distribution of tasks must be sensitive to individuals' abilities—that is, each person should contribute according to their capacity.[12] Demanding that someone perform a task they cannot do,

[12] It is important to point out that even those who are not the best at any particular task can still contribute to the cooperative scheme, since, as I will explain in Chapter 5, they are likely to have a *comparative advantage* in certain activities.

or find extremely difficult, is not a call for cooperation but a sacrifice that would consume a significant part of their life (their time, effort, and so forth). Such a demand runs counter to the principles of FSC.

3.2.4 *First-Order Cooperation and Second-Order Cooperation*

As can be seen, in the primitive cooperation scenario, there are two forms of anti-cooperative behavior: (1) refusing to contribute, and (2) harming a fellow participant. On the one hand, if someone decides not to perform any task, the scheme can continue functioning because each activity is carried out by a *group* rather than a *particular* person; no one is indispensable. Moreover, the person who adopts this behavior cannot be coerced into cooperating (no one can be forced to join a cooperative scheme), but they are excluded from the benefits of social cooperation. More than a sanction, this exclusion is a sign of respect for their decision to withdraw from the cooperative arrangement.

On the other hand, someone who attempts to harm another (physically or psychologically) can be coerced because they introduce anti-cooperative elements into the system. Cooperation requires certainty and stability. Attacking a participant is itself an anti-cooperative act, but it is also disruptive: it inhibits the attacked person's ability to cooperate (someone under attack cannot cooperate) and damages the cooperative atmosphere of the scheme, as others will not be able to fully cooperate knowing they might become targets.

Given the potential for this second type of antisocial behavior to harm the scheme, the participants cooperate to repel such conduct. This constitutes *second-order cooperation*, aimed at protecting the environment in which first-order cooperation takes place. In other words, second-order cooperation seeks to preserve the cooperative scheme itself, even if it requires coercive measures: the participants work to guarantee the security they need to collaborate fully—that is, to carry out first-order cooperation. Thus, if someone attempts to harm another, the rest intervene (even coercively) to defend the victim and exclude the aggressor from the scheme (at least until they resumed cooperative behavior), so that the cooperative atmosphere remains intact and the certainty and stability required for full cooperation are maintained.

In turn, for these second-order activities to be genuinely *cooperative*, they must rely on the collective contribution of all participants, without depending on any single individual. In other words, the protective system must be resilient enough to continue operating even if a particular participant deserts—for instance, because they suffer an injury that prevents them from carrying out physical tasks. Assuming this resilience exists in the primitive cooperation scenario, we arrive at a truly cooperative scheme that encompasses both first and second-order cooperation. *First-order cooperation is concerned with producing and providing the goods and resources necessary for everyone to pursue their life plans, while second-order cooperation focuses on safeguarding the integrity and stability of that cooperative arrangement.*

As I will analyze in the next chapter, modern democracies also have practices of first and second-order cooperation that, though more sophisticated, are structurally similar.

3.3 FSC and Previous Conceptions of Freedom

3.3.1 FSC and Negative Freedom

As I have noted, FSC begins with the premise that our freedom depends on others. Yet, it retains the individualistic element that makes negative freedom appealing. Like the negative conception, FSC also rejects any interference aimed at imposing a particular way of life on us. In the "primitive cooperation" model, for example, each person leads a different way of life and seeks to develop it fully. In this sense, the scheme is designed to repel attacks intended to obstruct or frustrate any member's plans: if someone attempts to harm another, the others step in to protect the *private sphere* of the victim. The individualistic aspect underpinning the appeal of negative freedom is also preserved in FSC because this conception of freedom also includes "side constraints" (Nozick 1974): clear boundaries that others cannot cross without infringing on our freedom.

However, FSC is a more robust conception than negative freedom. According to FSC, refraining from obstructing others is only one among many cooperative behaviors people should adopt. Being free not only requires that others refrain from interfering with us; it also demands that they actively cooperate with us in pursuing our life plans (and that we cooperate with them for the same purpose). In the primitive cooperation scenario, if a person behaved as if alone, they would need to gather fruit, build shelter, hunt various animals, make fire, keep watch during the night, and take care of many other tasks. No one has supernatural powers, so no individual could perform all these activities alone. Even if someone could, it is clear that this person would have no time to pursue any life plan beyond mere survival—assuming they could succeed at all. In this respect, one person stranded on an island would enjoy a form of natural, negative liberty (since no human would interfere with their actions) but would not enjoy FSC, for this person could not receive cooperation from others.

To use the same example as in the introduction, popular survival series on platforms like Netflix vividly portray the challenges of isolation. These shows often place individuals on remote islands or in isolated wilderness, forcing them to survive. Often, the narrative suggests that those who choose to separate themselves from the collective struggle may face serious difficulties—such as dwindling resources, increased vulnerability to danger, or even death. These stories highlight the human need for cooperation and connection, illustrating that survival is rarely a solitary endeavor. Instead, it is a shared journey in which mutual reliance often plays a crucial role in overcoming adversity.

In modern societies, we take for granted a cooperative environment that supports and enables us to formulate and pursue our life plans. This collaborative foundation is so deeply embedded that we sometimes forget it even exists, imagining instead that the only thing we can require of others is that they simply do not stand in our way. When this cooperative foundation does not yet exist and we must organize ourselves to build it—as in the primitive cooperation scenario—the demand for non-interference is neither the most important nor the first thing we likely focus on. What is urgent instead is mutual collaboration and active engagement.

No human is truly self-sufficient; we simply do not possess superpowers. Fortunately, we do not need them. Humans possess another kind of superpower: the ability to cooperate and make arrangements with others. In the primitive cooperation model, people quickly realize that simply organizing to fend off potential aggressions is not enough for everyone to pursue their life plans. Beyond self-defense, they must undertake joint projects and cooperate to benefit one another. This enables each person to live according to their own worldview. Herein lies the fundamental difference between the negative notion of liberty and FSC.

3.3.2 FSC and Positive Freedom

FSC incorporates elements found in some positive conceptions of freedom. For instance, it emphasizes a strong relational aspect: freedom involves living within a community. In this way, FSC is similar to Marx's view of freedom, which is also shared to some extent by Hegel and Green. According to Marx, freedom is the realization of our human nature, which requires working for the common good and seeing ourselves as contributors to it (Garnett 2021: 22). Therefore, Marx too understands freedom as inherently connected to communal life.

However, there is an important difference between the relational component of FSC and the relational component found in the Marxist idea of freedom. The Marxist conception is perfectionist: it defines freedom in terms of an ideal to be aspired to.[13] FSC, on the other hand, is not a perfectionist conception. For example, in the primitive cooperation scenario, the framework in which people participate constitutes their freedom: it is the context where they can pursue their own goals and life plans. Nevertheless, freedom is not defined in terms of a specific objective to be achieved, such as "working for the common good," but rather as the realization of individual aims through cooperation. People cooperate with one another so that, in a sense, they work for the common good—but here, "common good" means that everyone can pursue their own life plans. In other words, FSC is content-neutral (this point was also noted in Sect. 3.1.3 of this chapter).

The neutrality of FSC regarding different life plans is similar to that exhibited by more modern notions of positive liberty, such as the conceptions of Crocker or Christman, explained in the previous chapter. However, while FSC defines freedom as a cooperative practice, those notions do not place the relational aspect at the forefront.[14] As I have

[13] However, not all perfectionist approaches lead to illiberal conclusions. See, for example, Raz (1986) and Wall (1998).

[14] To be sure, these authors acknowledge a relational component; however, in their views, this aspect is secondary and gains significance from the primacy of the individual. For example, Crocker (1980: 66–74) refers to social arrangements in which individuals are interconnected, but the reason for this emphasis is to highlight that these arrangements can either enhance or diminish individual freedom. In turn, Christman (2009: 172) acknowledges that certain social relations can affect individual freedom, but he argues that his proceduralist approach to autonomy fully accounts for these influences without necessitating a shift to a collectivist conception of freedom. In contrast, Taylor's position is nuanced, fluctuating between different notions. On the one hand, he argues that as

already noted, the relational aspect holds a central place in more traditional views of positive liberty, such as those of Hegel, Marx, and Green. FSC rejects the perfectionist idea of establishing a specific goal that people must achieve in order to be free, but, like in the Marxist tradition, freedom requires a shared social environment. In FSC, it is precisely the potential that people have to mutually benefit one another that enables them to be free. That is, what makes people free is their capacity to contribute to the freedom of others (strictly speaking, the exercise of this capacity through their participation in the cooperative scheme). *We all contribute to everyone's freedom through the same cooperative scheme.*

In this regard, it is interesting that FSC shares a trace of Rousseau's idea of freedom. These conceptions differ in that Rousseau understands freedom as inseparable from collective self-government, whereas FSC focuses on the realization of our life plans. Yet, the underlying logic of both conceptions is similar: *if everyone depends on everyone else, then no one is at the mercy of anyone.* Recall that in Rousseau's social contract each person yields themselves and their rights to the community as a whole. Since everyone yields to everyone else, it is as if no one yields to anyone (Rousseau 2002 [1762]: 163–164). Similarly, in FSC, mutual dependence within a successful cooperative framework is, from the standpoint of freedom, as if no one depends on anyone.

However, beyond this similarity, Rousseau's approach is incompatible with FSC. Rousseau holds that if everyone yields equally to the community, no one threatens anyone else's individuality because all are equally subject to the same terms. Yet, once we accept Rousseau's own idea of the *general will* as something that can speak with authority distinct from any individual, equality is no longer preserved: that entity becomes superior to its members and the system ends up depending on it. Arguably, this dependence is not conducive to an environment where people can pursue their *individual* projects. In the next chapter, I will return to this

people become self-absorbed and withdraw from active participation in governance, they risk enabling a "soft despotism"—a paternalistic form of state control. While emphasizing the role of community and collective governance, his primary focus here remains the protection and promotion of individual autonomy and self-fulfillment (1991: 1–12). On the other hand, Taylor contends that while traditional social orders limited individual freedom, they also provided meaning and purpose to life. For him, the modern focus on individualism often leads to a loss of this broader meaning. Here, Taylor suggests that our social relationships shape our purposes, indicating that atomism deprives us of true freedom—the ability to pursue those purposes we consider valuable (1991: 3).

point to explain why, although FSC requires a democratic system, it also demands some form of counter-majoritarian institution.

To be sure, some authors in the tradition of positive freedom have sought to link freedom with social cooperation. John Dewey (1998 [1928]: 313), for example, holds that a plausible notion of freedom must encompass not only the capacity to direct one's own actions but also openness and receptivity to others. The idea is that freedom involves the ability to develop oneself in varied and flexible ways, to change one's dispositions and character—an ability that arises from thoughtful, intelligent choice. Dewey holds that to be free requires change over time: we experience freedom only when we move from a static conception of the self to a dynamic one, transforming ourselves through internal deliberation (Festenstein 2022: 88). This element of dynamism requires openness and receptivity to others. For example, discovering and developing the ability to enjoy and play music calls for a willingness to build relationships with others—people with similar interests, role models, teachers, mentors, and so on (Levine 2020). In turn, this notion of freedom defended by Dewey supports his conception of democracy. In his view, democracy is a social ideal that refers to an environment where people open themselves to different perspectives and are enriched by diversity (Festenstein 2022: 90).

Although both Dewey's conception and FSC recognize that freedom involves social cooperation, they are fundamentally different projects. Dewey's view is grounded in a comprehensive doctrine with perfectionist elements (MacGilvray 2004, Festenstein 2010, Talisse 2011a, Talisse 2011b). His theory of freedom emphasizes the capacity for development in varied and flexible ways, including the ability to change one's dispositions and character—always guided by internal deliberation. This theory implies a metaphysical view of human development that can itself be questioned by other, equally reasonable positions. In this theory, social cooperation serves this form of development.

In contrast, FSC remains neutral regarding which form of moral development is superior. In FSC, the form of social cooperation that is constitutive of freedom refers to mutual collaboration in creating political, legal, and economic institutions that establish an environment where individuals can pursue their life plans. Some of these life plans may include the "dynamic development" that Dewey mentions, but others may prefer static ways of life that do not require changing one's dispositions or character. The cooperative framework to which FSC refers is neutral with respect to these life projects.

More recently, some authors have proposed other relational conceptions of freedom (or autonomy) that place social relationships at the center of attention. Marina Oshana (2006, 49), for example, defends the claim that personal autonomy is a social-relational phenomenon.[15] According to her, autonomy is constituted in large part by the social relations people find themselves in and by the absence of other social relations. Autonomy is not a phenomenon merely enhanced or lessened by the contingencies of a person's social situation; social relations do not just causally facilitate or impair the exercise of autonomy. Rather, appropriate social relations form an *inherent* part of what it means to be self-directed. From this perspective, two individuals may fulfill the same psychological, historical, and competency conditions yet differ in their status as autonomous beings due to variations in their social circumstances.

One way to understand the difference between FSC and Oshana's notion of relational autonomy is to recognize that they operate at different levels of analysis and emphasize distinct roles of the social context.

According to FSC, freedom cannot truly exist without cooperation. FSC portrays freedom as fundamentally constituted through our collaborative interactions with others. On this view, the social context is primarily a creative force—an enabling environment that generates and expands the possibilities available to individuals. Freedom is realized through the mutual cooperation that allows people to pursue and fulfill their life plans. In addition, as I will explain in detail in the next chapters, FSC adopts an institutional perspective, stressing the crucial role institutions play in establishing frameworks of cooperation that facilitate the emergence and distribution of resources for all and emphasizing that the continued existence of these institutions depends on ongoing cooperative practices among individuals.

[15] For similar views, see Mackenzie and Stoljar 2000.

In contrast, Oshana approaches the social context with a more cautious perspective. She focuses on how our social context and relations can act as invisible forces limiting or at least conditioning our autonomy. While she acknowledges that the social context can, under certain circumstances, form autonomous people, she particularly emphasizes its potential to undermine or constrain autonomy through structures of domination, inequality, and oppressive relationships. In short, Oshana highlights the importance of social structures but appears more focused on how these frameworks can unleash invisible forces that jeopardize autonomy, rather than emphasizing their great potential to create institutions and environments where opportunities continually arise for everyone.

In short, while FSC emphasizes the social context as an active, generative space where cooperation expands individual options, Oshana highlights the social context as a domain that can form either autonomous or non-autonomous individuals, with particular emphasis on the latter. While FSC emphasizes freedom's reliance on collaborative social life and institutional frameworks, Oshana cautions against the vulnerabilities that autonomy faces within social structures and unseen relational forces.

3.3.3 FSC and Republican Freedom

Just like the republican conception, FSC is a form of freedom that depends on the existence of an institutional system. Republican freedom requires institutions that prevent domination—that is, that eliminate the capacity to interfere arbitrarily with others' choices. Similarly, FSC requires the existence of a cooperation framework. Someone living alone on an island (or even with others but without any institutional system regulating their lives) might at most enjoy a form of natural freedom, but not republican freedom or FSC. Like republican freedom, FSC assumes the existence of an institutional scheme. To be sure, when thinking about institutions, we often imagine the complex structures of modern societies, but institutions are not limited to this. Even in the primitive cooperation scenario, institutions exist as there are rules governing behavior that help people know what to expect from one another, along with enforcement mechanisms that can be coercive.

However, there is a fundamental difference between republican freedom and FSC. Republican freedom consists in structural independence between individuals: its ideal is an institutional system aimed at ensuring that people are independent from one another, where the capacity to arbitrarily interfere with another's choices is eliminated. Thus, independence is the underlying value of republican freedom. To be sure, Pettit acknowledges that republican freedom is a social freedom which does not arise on an island but in the context of a community with institutions (Pettit 2012: 91). However, this conception still emphasizes the idea of independence. Republican freedom presupposes that there are "others," but its ideal is precisely that we do not depend on those "others." For example, Pettit acknowledges the importance of wealth redistribution and political participation in promoting non-domination. On the one hand, he argues that redistribution contributes to republican freedom because poverty *subjects* people to a form of exploitation or manipulation (Pettit 2008: 406). On the other hand, he asserts that citizen control over state decisions fosters republican freedom by significantly curbing the rulers' potential to dominate citizens (Pettit 1997: 186–187).[16] But in both cases, the goal is for the individual to gain independence.

In contrast, FSC assumes and embraces mutual *dependence*. Of course, there is an element of independence in FSC: after all, this notion of freedom implies that no one can direct our lives except ourselves. Nonetheless, the environment in which people develop and carry out life plans is, by definition, a framework of social cooperation—we all cooperate to help each other realize our projects. Whereas the republican ideal focuses on limiting the power that others hold over us, FSC emphasizes drawing closer to others to foster cooperation, on the basis that social cooperation is constitutive of freedom. Social cooperation, rather than the absence of domination, is central to FSC.

Republican freedom arises from the concern that people living together might harm one another through the exercise of domination. By contrast, FSC emerges from recognizing the importance of harnessing people's potential to work together and help each other achieve their life plans. In both conceptions, institutions play a central role in eliminating uncertainty and securing freedom. However, while republican freedom requires

[16] As explained in the previous chapter, in the republican conception, what is constitutive of freedom is *some* institutional system that prevents domination; the *kind* of institutional system that best achieves this goal is an empirical matter. That is why I maintain that republican freedom by definition includes certain institutions, while also holding that democratic institutions are necessary components—but not constitutive—of this form of freedom.

institutions designed to provide assurance that others will not interfere arbitrarily, FSC prescribes institutions aimed at fostering cooperation and guaranteeing that potential anti-cooperative behaviors will not destabilize the system—thus creating an environment in which everyone depends on one another, yet no one is at the mercy of another.

CHAPTER 4

FSC as a Theory of Liberal Democracy: The Political System

4.1 From Primitive Cooperation to Modern Societies

In the previous chapter, I explained the idea of FSC and compared it with earlier notions of freedom. To clarify FSC, I used the "primitive cooperation" example, which illustrates that social cooperation can be considered a constitutive element of the development and pursuit of life plans.

In this chapter, as well as in Chapters 5 and 6, I will use FSC to develop a theory of liberal democracy. I will show that, while FSC begins with a broad philosophical vision of freedom rooted in social cooperation, its practical implications are reflected in political and economic institutions that ensure that power and influence are shared across multiple, complementary actors.

To develop this institutional design theory, I will tell a story of how the primitive cooperation society evolves into what we now recognize as liberal democracy, without fundamentally altering the underlying structure of social cooperation. While this primitive society is hypothetical and the narrative fictional, it serves to illustrate that liberal democracy can be understood as a more sophisticated, yet still fundamentally cooperative scheme—a more evolved expression of FSC. As will be shown, while FSC offers a novel conception of freedom, its application to concrete political and economic institutions yields results that align with familiar and well-established principles, such as the dispersion and decentralization of

E. Spector, *Freedom as Social Cooperation*,
https://doi.org/10.1007/978-3-032-12217-9_4

power and influence, as well as the collaborative interaction between state governance and market forces.

Moreover, as we will see, part of the institutional framework emerging from primitive cooperation consists of various rights—such as the right to vote, property rights, and certain welfare entitlements—that help stabilize and sustain the cooperative order. These rights are not based on metaphysical assumptions about natural law nor do they exist as abstract, timeless entities separated from social practices. Rather, they develop through the ongoing interactions and practical arrangements among individuals engaged in cooperative relationships. They facilitate coordination, conflict resolution, and trust-building among participants, enabling the cooperative system to function effectively and evolve over time. From the FSC perspective, rights are understood as contingent institutional constructs that reflect the dynamic processes through which societies organize themselves and continuously reform their shared institutions, rather than fixed moral absolutes. This view situates rights as integral elements of the institutional framework that supports liberal democracy.

Ultimately, FSC not only enriches our theoretical understanding of liberal democracy but also reaffirms the political and economic institutional arrangements and rights long associated with this system. In this chapter, I will focus on political institutions; in Chapter 5, I will address economic institutions; and finally, in Chapter 6, I will analyze the role of the state as a "first-order cooperator" (as a producer and supplier of goods and services).

4.2 The Emergence of the State: Toward a Liberal Democracy

In the primitive cooperation model, the cooperation scheme included first-order cooperation—the production and provision of goods and services essential for everyone to carry out their life plans, such as food, clothing, and shelter—and second-order cooperation, which involves the protection of the cooperation scheme, thereby providing the participants with the security they need to cooperate fully.

Now suppose this cooperation scheme grows in size: instead of 500 participants, there are thousands or even millions. This could be due to more people wanting to join, or because birth rates increase. The crucial point is that the participants begin to realize that under these new circumstances, the rules of the scheme need revisiting and the structure requires refinement.

Due to the sharp increase in participants, second-order cooperative activities—the exercise of coercion to uphold the cooperation scheme—are carried out inefficiently. The participants find themselves spending too much time and energy on these tasks (monitoring, using force to deter aggression, expelling non-cooperators, etc.), diverting resources away from first-order cooperation, which involves producing and supplying goods and services. Although this investment of effort had already hindered production when the group was small, the problem now worsens dramatically: given the already decentralized nature of this coercion system, organizational costs become astronomical.

To address this challenge, the participants reorganize second-order cooperation, adopting two strategies: specialization and centralization. First, they recognize it is far more efficient if those engaged in production (first-order cooperation) are not the same individuals responsible for preserving the cooperation scheme (second-order cooperation). Indeed, each of these roles is complex enough to demand exclusive dedication. Just as it is more efficient for those who make clothing to be distinct from those who hunt animals (Smith, A. 1981 [1776]: bk. I, ch. i), it is likewise more efficient to free producers from involvement in public affairs, and vice versa. Thus, the specialization strategy, previously applied to production tasks, is extended to second-order activities.

Second, the participants realize that a *centralized* coercion system would drastically reduce organizational costs. Consequently, they forge a kind of "social contract," establishing a group of people—the state—who legitimately hold the monopoly on coercion and manage such affairs, receiving a share of the scheme's benefits in return. In this way, the state (the collective body of these individuals) becomes just another participant in the cooperation scheme, acting as an entity that cooperates by carrying out second-order activities aimed at protecting the scheme.

The emergence of the state, however, presents a challenge. The monopoly on coercion, by its very nature, stands in tension with the FSC conception of cooperation. Recall that the FSC framework conceives cooperation as a form of equality among people: cooperation occurs only when everyone contributes to the scheme, yet no single contribution is indispensable on its own for the scheme's functioning. In other words, all depend on all, but depend on no individual in particular. The problem with the monopoly on coercion is that it inherently involves an entity authorized to wield force. Thus, the scheme ceases to be cooperative in the FSC sense because crucial tasks become concentrated in the hands of a select few who act as a unified body. Consequently, the scheme's success ends up depending on the proper functioning of this elite.

Nevertheless, fortunately, the participants find a solution that makes the emergence of the state compatible with FSC. First, they ensure that the social contract, besides establishing the monopoly on coercion, clearly defines the functions of this monopoly and recognizes them both as *duties* and as *powers*. As duties, these functions are mandatory, so the state is obliged to fulfill them; as powers, they are limited and the state cannot overstep them. Moreover, to explain the state's functions in such detail, the social contract must include a description of the cooperation scheme, its foundations, and its basic principles. After all, the purpose of coercion is to protect the scheme—ensuring a predictable environment where participants know what to expect from one another, allowing them to fully develop themselves and express that fullness through their contributions to the scheme. Clearly stating the scheme's foundations and basic principles enables the state to better understand its functions, while enshrining them both as duties and as powers reflects the special responsibility resting on this monopoly. In this way, the social contract becomes what we today call a "constitution."

Second, the participants strive to ensure that the state, in addition to participating in the scheme by performing protective tasks (second-order cooperation), also functions as a cooperation scheme in itself. In other words, the idea is that the state should operate *internally* as a system of cooperation. As such, the state ought to be made up of independent institutions that cooperate with one another, in order to decentralize power and reduce society's dependence on any single institution.

To this end, the participants include two clauses in the social contract: one that divides the state's monopoly into three separate monopolies,[1] each responsible for different tasks ("separation of powers"),[2] and another

[1] Actually, the state includes more than three bodies (for example, the Central Bank). But for now, I will refer only to the state's three main branches.

[2] In this way, FSC can account for the classic principle of the separation of powers, as formulated by Montesquieu (2015: B. XI).

that grants each monopoly the means to oversee the others and, if necessary, prevent any from undermining the cooperation scheme ("checks and balances").[3]

The interaction among these three branches involves cooperative activities, but they hold a special status. On the one hand, they are not first-order activities, as they are not aimed at producing and providing goods and services. On the other hand, they are not second-order activities either, since they are not *directly* focused on protecting the environment in which citizens carry out first-order activities. Rather, these are cooperative activities directed internally within the state, with the purpose of ensuring that the state fulfills its functions. I will refer to these as "*intra-state* cooperative activities." In this way, the state as a whole remains a participant in the broader scheme fulfilling its functions, while also constituting a cooperation scheme in its own right—composed of internal institutions dedicated to preserving the state's structure and preventing any deviation from fulfilling those functions.

This form of power organization seems to better honor the ideal of FSC. Even so, citizens have reasons to believe that the complete scheme (society) will not enjoy total stability. The fact is that, although the state is divided into three institutions, each of these still holds key powers essential for the society's functioning—and, moreover, they are the only institutions with such powers. To be sure, each is controlled by the others, but these external checks may well be insufficient, and in any case, the functions they perform are so important that, when in doubt, it is better to strengthen the controls.

Given this situation, the participants decide to deepen the cooperative logic within the state. The idea is to introduce further provisions into the contract under which each of the three institutions also functions internally as a cooperation scheme. Each institution contains smaller—but relatively independent—units that carry out cooperative activities aimed at preserving that institution. These are also intra-state cooperative activities, but at a greater level of depth, crossing through the institutions within the state to achieve greater decentralization of power.

Ultimately, the state is divided into three institutions with different functions, and each of these institutions is further divided into various

[3] The concern that the branches of power should be able to check one another is clearly evident in the debates of the American Founding Fathers (Madison 1788). FSC also addresses this concern.

units, decentralizing functions even more. In this way, the operation of the state structure becomes less dependent on any single entity, and society as a whole becomes less vulnerable to abuses of power.

In summary, two distinctions must be kept in mind when examining the institutions of liberal democracy. The first is between first-order cooperation and second-order cooperation. As I have claimed, first-order cooperation is directed toward productive activities—basically, the production and provision of goods and services necessary for people to develop and pursue their life plans. These are the types of activities we typically associate with the market. In contrast, second-order cooperation is aimed at preserving the environment in which first-order activities take place. These are activities we usually associate with the state.

The second distinction is between external cooperation and internal cooperation. External cooperation may be either first or second-order, as described above. Internal cooperation, in contrast, is what the state carries out within its own internal structure: intra-state cooperative activities aimed at preserving the institution of the state and guiding it toward fulfilling its functions.

Finally, it is important to point out a difference between the general cooperation scheme (society), of which the state is a part, and the state as a cooperation scheme in its own right. As previously mentioned, the general scheme is open in the sense that it does not serve particular goals, but rather provides the environment in which people establish and achieve their goals. The state's cooperation scheme, by contrast, serves specific ends, mainly the protection of the general scheme.

4.3 Separation of Powers

The separation of powers is necessary for the state to replicate internally the logic of cooperation. It involves diversifying the power held by the state, since its concentration would make the system overly dependent on a single entity.

4.3.1 Legislative Power

The first branch, known as the "legislative power," is responsible for crafting the rules that govern the behavior of participants within the cooperative framework. These rules, or laws, must reflect the fundamental principles of the social contract (the Constitution). In other words, they are concrete regulations derived from more abstract principles, though their specific form depends on the particular society.

The legislative power is one of the three main institutions of the state, but within itself it also mirrors the cooperative logic to promote the fulfillment of its functions. Thus, this power is divided into two independent groups (two chambers), each with the authority to accept or veto the rules proposed by the other. Each chamber typically has a sufficient number of members, generally with similar powers, so that the operation of the body depends on all members collectively rather than any individual.

The representation criteria of these chambers may also vary by society. For example, the Parliament of the United Kingdom comprises the House of Lords, whose members are not democratically elected (including bishops with distinguished ecclesiastical careers and members of the economic, social, and cultural elite appointed by the King upon the Prime Minister's advice), and the House of Commons, whose members represent the people and are democratically elected.

In other societies, such as the United States or Argentina, the representation system is different. Both chambers are elected by the people, but the House of Representatives represents the citizens while the Senate represents the states. Additionally, the minimum age to become a member of the second chamber is generally higher than that for the first chamber, reflecting the understanding that the second should represent the voice of experience.

It should also be noted that some societies, such as Israel, Panama, and Sweden, have chosen not to divide their legislative power into two bodies, having instead a single chamber. This does not imply that the cooperative logic within the legislative power is absent in these countries. It still exists because the functioning of that chamber depends on multiple members who deliberate and vote. However, we can say that in these countries, the cooperative logic inside parliament is considerably less than in bicameral parliaments, where this cooperative logic is effectively doubled.

Finally, it is important to highlight that where members of the chambers are democratically elected for fixed terms, the separation of powers exists not only between different people at one time but also across time. The regular turnover of positions also honors the ideal of FSC, as it helps dissolve dependence on particular individuals.

4.3.2 *Executive Power*

The second branch, known as the "executive power," is responsible for enforcing the laws, which involves handling day-to-day management tasks such as collecting the resources necessary for the functioning of the state structure (including paying its officials) and providing and administering the public services overseen by that structure.

The head of the executive power (typically the president) is also subject to periodic renewal through popular elections. However, in the classic model of the separation of powers, the internal cooperative activity within the executive power is much less than that within the legislative power. In the executive power, different departments handle different areas (security, education, health, etc.), but all are subordinate to the centralized authority of the president. Furthermore, within each department, power tends to be concentrated in the hands of the secretary. Is there a plausible rationale for this exception to the general principle of power diversification? Perhaps, because the executive power handles daily management, it requires a dynamism that only a centralized authority can provide.

In any case, the model of an independent executive power with a president directly elected by the people is not the only possible one. In this regard, the literature distinguishes between two different systems: presidentialism and parliamentarism.

The first system envisages a president independent of the legislative power, elected by the people to serve for a fixed term, and even endowed with powers to influence lawmaking (for example, by vetoing laws passed by the legislative power) (Shugart and Carey 1992: 19). In the second system, the legislative power chooses the government (Lijphart 1999: 117) and can remove it before the constitutionally established term ends (Cheibub 2007: 34).[4] In this case, the government generally does not have lawmaking powers. Countries such as Australia, Canada, New Zealand, Italy, Israel, Germany, and Poland, among others, have opted for this system.

Presidential systems are generally more fragile than parliamentary systems. In fact, there is only one example of a stable presidential regime:

[4] There are also mixed systems, such as those in which both the legislative assembly and the president (who is independently elected) can dissolve the government, replacing cabinet members (Cheibub 2007: 38).

the United States. Latin America, where presidential systems clearly predominate, is a region marked by pronounced political instability.

Some authors argue that this difference in stability arises from the distinct features *inherent* to each system (Linz 1994). For example, presidential systems are said to be more susceptible to conflicts between the legislative and executive branches because the executive, under this arrangement, lacks incentives to build coalitions (Mainwaring and Scully 1995: 33). Since the stability of the executive does not depend on the support of the legislature, the executive may perceive that it can govern without backing from other political parties. Moreover, because the executive in presidential systems is typically centralized under the authority of a single president, it tends to resist diversity in its composition. This contrasts with parliamentary systems, where executive power is shared among multiple actors—such as a prime minister and a cabinet collectively responsible to the legislature—making coalition-building more common.

Note that, on this view, the fragility of presidential systems largely stems from the relatively low level of cooperative interaction within the executive power. If this thesis is correct, it is precisely because the executive power depends heavily on a particular individual (the president) that such conflicts arise. The limited internal cooperation in this branch ultimately destabilizes the system.

Others, however, maintain that presidential systems are not inherently less stable. They tend to be more unstable than parliamentary systems because of the *external* conditions in which these systems develop; for example, the authoritarian legacy of many presidentialist countries (Bernhard, Nordstrom, and Reenock 2001, Foweraker and Landman 2002, Cheibub 2007).

In the presidential system, the executive power is independent of the legislative power, which helps decentralize power and promotes cooperation between autonomous units. On the other hand, the executive power maintains limited internal cooperation because of its centralized internal structure.

By contrast, the parliamentary system, by subordinating the executive power to the legislature, mitigates the problem posed by the low internal cooperation within the executive.[5] However, as a trade-off, it limits the possibility of two *independent* branches cooperating with each other.

In this work, I assume a predominantly presidentialist model, but it is important to emphasize that parliamentarism can also be explained by FSC, as it is a system designed to limit the power of the branch that, under a presidentialist arrangement, shows the lowest level of internal cooperation.

4.3.3 Judicial Power

Finally, the third branch, known as the "judicial power," is responsible for interpreting the laws and applying them to specific disputes. This branch is not subject to popular vote; rather, it is granted guarantees that ensure its independence from the popular will, safeguarding the functioning of the system from being solely dependent on that will.[6] However, like the legislative power, the judicial power internally operates as a cooperative system. It does so based on two criteria of decentralization.

The first criterion is thematic specialization. Judges are assigned to distinct areas of law including criminal cases such as physical assaults, property disputes involving boundary conflicts or inheritance, commercial litigation, environmental regulation, labor and employment issues, intellectual property, administrative law, and family matters, among others. This division of labor is beneficial for a reason similar to that in the private sector: specialization allows judges to focus on a single area and thereby become more competent in resolving a certain type of conflict.

The second criterion is hierarchical. Here, the division is into several levels to which individuals can appeal if they believe a decision is wrong. These levels exist in each area where the judges operate, so each type of conflict has different resolution stages.

In this way, the judicial power functions internally as a cooperative system. Its operation depends on the contribution of all members, but

[5] In assuming that the internal structure of Parliament is truly cooperative, I am envisioning a diverse body with multiple political parties, similar to what is typically found in a proportional representation system.

[6] The importance of the system not relying exclusively on popular will was notably emphasized by Alexander Hamilton during the Federal Convention debates of 1787: "Give all power to the many, they will oppress the few. Give all power to the few, they will oppress the many. Both, therefore, ought to have the power, that each may defend itself against the other" (Farrand 1937: 282).

not on any particular individual. Thus, the institution is protected against uncooperative behavior by some of its members. Since courts focus on different types of conflicts, people may fall under the jurisdiction of one or another depending on their situation. Moreover, if a court behaves uncooperatively (e.g., issues a mistaken or incorrect judgment), other instances may correct that error. The right to appeal judicial decisions, a hallmark of liberal democracies, functions as a cooperation-enhancing mechanism by ensuring that conflict resolution is not determined by a single court alone.

Today, modern societies predominantly use two models for resolving disputes: civil law and common law. Civil law is applied in countries influenced primarily by the legal traditions of continental Europe, such as Spain, France, Germany, the Netherlands, and Portugal, as well as their former colonies. In this system, judges resolve conflicts based mainly on codified laws enacted by legislative bodies. Judicial precedents typically serve as interpretative guidance, but laws constitute the primary source.

Common law, by contrast, is a dispute resolution process based on judicial precedents (past cases). Originating in medieval England, common law currently governs the legal system of England and Wales, as well as other British-influenced societies including Ireland, Australia, the United States, Canada, and New Zealand. In these countries, common law primarily governs areas of private law, such as contracts and property, while public law—including constitutional, administrative, and criminal law—is generally regulated by laws enacted by legislative bodies.

Liberal democracies usually have a highest court, such as a supreme court. However, its hierarchy differs from, for example, the authority a president holds over secretaries. The supreme court's hierarchy lies in being the final authority to decide certain cases or interpret certain norms (in some countries, such as the United States and Uruguay, the Constitution itself; in others, like Germany and Colombia, constitutional courts perform this role). But lower courts are not subject to the supreme court's authority in the same way that secretaries are subordinate to the president, who can issue directives daily and influence departmental planning.

As mentioned, unlike the legislative and executive powers, members of the judicial power enjoy a certain degree of stability and are not subject to popular control. The idea is precisely that the system should not rely solely on suffrage. Still, as seen, the judicial power is internally decentralized: it functions depending on all members, without depending on any particular individual.

4.4 Checks and Balances

State power is not only divided among branches. Additionally, each branch has tools to control the others and prevent anti-cooperative behavior from undermining the system.

There are primarily two types of anti-cooperative behavior among those responsible for public affairs. The first is institutional anti-cooperation: for example, a legislator proposes a law that violates the social contract and could thus undermine the cooperative system—what we today call an "unconstitutional norm."

Why is this type of anti-cooperative behavior considered institutional? Because, generally, it cannot be stated with certainty that a given law harms the scheme of cooperation. In the vast majority of cases, reasonable people may disagree on whether a rule infringes the basic terms of the contract or whether it will harm, strengthen, or have no effect on the cooperative system. Except in exceptional cases, such disagreements are reasonable. Therefore, participants conclude that adopting a rigid criterion to judge officials' actions is inappropriate. Instead, it is considered better to assume good faith and allow them to perform their functions. This is why two legislators can have profound disagreements and propose radically different laws without either being removed. Likewise, two judges may reach different conclusions on a case without losing their positions. Similarly, two heads of the executive power may have managed day-to-day affairs quite differently during their respective terms without either being ousted.

However, even though these reasonable disagreements prevent categorical judgments on who harms the cooperative system, the system itself requires that any rule pass through several filters to remain in force over time. In this way, because the rule will be carefully reviewed by different groups, the likelihood that it seriously harms the cooperative system decreases. For example, if one chamber of the legislative power proposes a rule that could damage the cooperative framework, the system can still function because the other chamber has the authority to correct this error by rejecting it. If the other chamber approves the rule, the system may still function because the executive power has the authority to veto it (recall I am assuming a presidential system). If the executive also fails to veto it, the system remains functional because the judicial power can declare it invalid (a practice we now call "judicial review"). This decision may have general effects or apply only to the specific case, depending on the design of the system. Ultimately, if the judicial power does not invalidate it at any level, the rule could still be repealed by future members of the other branches who come to power through elections.

Thus, each branch is empowered to engage in ***intra-state cooperative activities*** by excluding a norm it sees as harmful. Although the subject of debate often involves reasonable disagreement and no categorical assertion can be made, if a branch objects to a norm, this norm becomes suspect and is excluded. If no branch objects over time, the probability that the norm damages the system is low.

In this way, the system is prepared to continue functioning even when some participants act non-cooperatively. Of course, there is always room for error. If a harmful norm slips through and remains in effect without being excluded by any branch, the cooperative system will suffer—either slightly or significantly, depending on the content of the norm. But this deterioration will not have been caused by any particular participant alone, since no one had the unilateral power to cause it. A genuine cooperative system is maintained by the collective, not by any individual, and only the collective can break it.

The second type of anti-cooperative behavior is anti-institutional. This includes acts such as a judge fabricating evidence to convict someone, an executive officer misappropriating public funds, or a legislator bribing a colleague to vote for a rule. The key idea is that the system should continue functioning even when individuals commit such acts. In these cases, the system protects itself by excluding those individuals. For instance, the legislative power has mechanisms to remove a judge who fabricates evidence or an executive official who embezzles funds through processes like impeachment. The legislative power also has internal procedures (an expulsion system) to expel a member of its own body if, for example, that member bribes a colleague to support a rule. The judicial power may also request such expulsion. Depending on the nature of the anti-cooperative act, exclusion of the individual may be partial (excluded only from the state structure) or total (excluded from the entire system by judicial decision for a period, e.g., imprisonment to allow rehabilitation).

Ideally, everyone cooperates, but a genuine cooperative system does not depend on all participants behaving this way. It is designed to keep functioning even if some participants fail to cooperate. Thus, the cooperative scheme endures because no single contribution is indispensable for the system's operation. The system is prepared to keep functioning even if a participant (or cohesive group of participants) refuses to cooperate.

4.5 Suffrage and Public Deliberation

When examining the separation of powers, I noted that both the legislative and executive branches are subject to periodic renewal through a majority voting system. Elections deepen the cooperative logic of governance by further diminishing reliance on individual persons, decentralizing authority by distributing power not only across institutions but also over time.

There exist various theories regarding the value of suffrage. Some argue that suffrage possesses intrinsic value (Simmons 1979, Christiano 1996). As expressed in the United States Declaration of Independence (1776), governments "derive their just powers from the consent of the governed." The principle here is that individuals who lack the ability to choose their governments are not fully autonomous. Others, however, emphasize the instrumental benefits of political choice. When people have the power to choose their leaders, political actors face stronger incentives to implement public policies that serve the populace's interests—or at the very least, do not harm them (Schumpeter 1950, Dahl 1956, Posner 2003).

FSC offers a different perspective. From this viewpoint, suffrage is one among the many institutions of the state. When people express their will as voters, they engage in an activity that is part of the broader processes within the state. The right to vote arises from the right to participate in the administration of the state.

In this way, suffrage constitutes a form of intra-state cooperation that propels the state toward the proper fulfillment of its duties. According to FSC, the value of suffrage does not lie in the incentives it creates, nor in the notion that voting makes individuals autonomous, but rather in the fact that, without suffrage, the system would become more dependent on a ruling elite. Even if power within the elite is decentralized and functions are divided, the fixed terms of office allow for decentralization of power over time as well, making the system less reliant on particular individuals.

Moreover, suffrage operates internally, within its own structure, as a scheme of cooperation governed by its own rules, which ensure that the system's functioning depends on all voters collectively, but not on any single voter individually. Through suffrage, everyone participates in choosing, but no particular person chooses alone. This is how cooperation endures. This stands in contrast to anti-democratic regimes, where a single individual (or an elite) accumulates decision-making power.

When electing public officials, the outcome depends on the votes of all individuals collectively rather than any single voter. In this way, suffrage diffuses the authority to choose officials across the electorate. Thus, suffrage can be understood as a form of cooperation through which all individuals contribute to the election process; thanks to these collective contributions, the selection of officials does not rest in the hands of any specific individuals.

One consequence of this modality is that it can continue to function even if some voters act anti-cooperatively by choosing not to vote. Of course, no cooperation scheme is indestructible: it can fail, but only due to widespread anti-cooperative behavior among participants (for example, if almost no one votes), not because of any individual's conduct.

In this regard, *compulsory* voting could safeguard the cooperative scheme when there is a widespread tendency to abstain and to rely on others to vote, thus obtaining the benefit—the decentralization of authority—without incurring any cost.[7] In the United States, for example, voting is voluntary, and in recent decades,[8] the most successful election in terms of voter turnout was the 2020 presidential election, in which 66.8% of eligible voters participated.[9]

In Chile, voting was voluntary between 2012 and 2021, after which compulsory voting was reinstated in 2022. During that period, voter turnout notably declined. For instance, participation rates were around 47% and 55% in the first and second rounds, respectively, of the 2021 presidential elections. In contrast, over 85% of registered voters participated in the 2022 constitutional reform plebiscite, a marked increase that may be attributed to the fact that voting in this plebiscite was compulsory, unlike other elections in Chile since 2012. Similarly, the second constitutional reform plebiscite held in 2023 also saw a high turnout, with over 84% of registered voters participating, and voting in this plebiscite was likewise mandatory. However, it remains difficult to determine whether

[7] From an economic perspective, the diversification of authority is a "public benefit": individuals may lack incentives to contribute to its provision because they expect others to do so, thus enjoying the benefit without incurring any cost. This concept will be examined in detail in the next chapter.

[8] https://usafacts.org/articles/how-many-americans-voted-in-2020/ (last accessed: August 5, 2025).

[9] https://www.census.gov/newsroom/press-releases/2021/2020-presidential-election-voting-and-registration-tables-now-available.html (last accessed: August 5, 2025).

the high turnout was primarily due to the mandatory nature of these votes or the significance that these particular elections held for Chile's political system.

FSC does not take a definitive stance on the obligatoriness of voting. While it is certainly desirable that as many people as possible participate in elections to decentralize power and prevent crucial national decisions from resting in the hands of a few, whether voting should be mandatory largely depends on the presence of civic awareness about the importance of exercising the right to vote. When such awareness is widespread, compulsory voting may not be necessary.

The concept of suffrage as a scheme of *cooperation* accounts for two fundamental democratic principles: universal suffrage and "one person, one vote." On one hand, universal suffrage guarantees that everyone has the opportunity to make their voice heard. FSC embraces this principle because, when implemented, it maximally decentralizes the power to elect officials (a qualified or restricted voting system would be incompatible with FSC, as it would render the system overly dependent on an elite). On the other hand, "one person, one vote" ensures that each individual's contribution is equally small, so that the functioning of the scheme does not hinge on a select few. As I have explained, participants in a scheme that honors FSC are equal in the sense that each depends on the others for the system to function—but does not depend on any particular individual.

Furthermore, since FSC is committed to decentralizing power, it also recognizes compelling reasons not to restrict political participation to suffrage alone. FSC emphasizes the promotion of broader political activism and public deliberation, resonating with the ideals of deliberative democracy (Rawls 1993, Gutmann and Thompson 1996, Nino 1996, Habermas 1998, Elster 1998). However, while deliberative theorists primarily see public deliberation as a means to reach impartial or reasoned conclusions, FSC emphasizes that deliberation also serves to further divide power by broadening participation and enabling more alternation in governance. The robustness of power's division increases proportionally with the number of people actively engaged in political life and the greater diversity of participants who can take turns in governing roles. Encouraging widespread political activism and fostering deliberation grounded in diverse perspectives ensure that voices from across society contribute meaningfully to collective decision-making, decentralizing power and minimizing reliance on any specific group. Similarly, flexible party laws that prevent the entrenchment of political establishments help sustain dynamic alternation in power, thereby preventing its concentration within a narrow elite.

In this way, suffrage as a cooperative scheme is intimately linked with vibrant democratic engagement and diverse public discourse—both vital to the health and resilience of democratic governance. Thus, political rights such as the right to vote, to be elected, as well as freedom of expression (including the right to protest), can be understood from the perspective of FSC (freedom of expression will be discussed in greater detail in Chapter 6).

Now, while FSC can account for suffrage and democratic elections, it also recognizes that relying exclusively on majority rule can be counterproductive. Much of the functioning of the state would be left at the mercy of majorities, which would undermine FSC.

The cooperative system must be structured to keep functioning even when the popular will adopts an anti-cooperative stance and makes decisions that undermine the framework—such as stripping minority groups of their status as equal cooperators and permitting aggression against them.[10] Liberal democracy addresses this concern through judicial review. The counter-majoritarian nature of the judiciary and its power to declare unconstitutional laws unenforceable can be understood as forms of intrastate cooperation that protect the state from harmful decisions made by majorities, thereby safeguarding the citizenry.

Today, judges have the authority to exercise judicial review in almost every modern democracy. We can distinguish two main models: concentrated and diffuse. The former authorizes only specific courts to exercise this power—such as a constitutional court or supreme court—while the latter allows every court to exercise it.

The concentrated system of judicial review generally prevails in European countries as well as in some outside the continent, like Colombia and Costa Rica. It is based on the theory of legal philosopher Hans Kelsen, who participated in designing Austria's pioneering concentrated system in 1920. Kelsen (1942: 185–186) argued for creating a specialized body to deal with constitutional matters, to avoid the legal uncertainty that could arise if all judges were granted this power, since they might reach different conclusions.

[10] James Madison (1787a), for example, addresses this concern.

The diffuse system of judicial review is practiced in countries such as the United States, Canada, Mexico, Brazil, and Argentina. In the U.S., diffuse review was firmly established in the landmark case Marbury v. Madison (1803),[11] where the Supreme Court affirmed that any judge confronted with an unconstitutional law must declare it unenforceable.

In any case, liberal democracies guard against the dangers of "the tyranny of the majority." The FSC framework accounts for both the importance of democracy and its necessary limitation through some form of judicial review.

4.6 Federalism

Federalism is a doctrine describing a particular way of distributing power within a political society. It defines a structure composed of bodies (sometimes called states, provinces, or communities) with considerable political, fiscal, and administrative autonomy, alongside a central body (the federal government) with limited authority over specific matters that concern all citizens. Importantly, none of these bodies holds the power to dissolve this organizational structure. As Alexis de Tocqueville (1838 [1835]: 53) put it, it consists of "small sovereign nations, whose agglomeration constitutes the body of the Union."

An important rationale for federalism—perhaps the most important—is to deepen the decentralization of power. It is no longer merely about dividing powers within the internal structure of the federal government, but also about having independent governments within the same society over which the federal government (already internally divided) exercises limited authority.

However, federalism can also be understood as a way to manage societal issues that are specific to local communities more efficiently. The idea is that smaller governments, closer to specific communities, are better equipped to handle such matters. For example, James Madison (1788) recognized the significance of federalism in reinforcing the separation of powers but also emphasized that it promoted a more efficient allocation of responsibilities. In his view, the federal government should address general matters requiring uniformity, such as regulating interstate and foreign commerce, while the states should focus on local issues, which

[11] 5 U.S. 1371803.

they can manage more effectively (Madison 1787b). Today, prominent examples of federal countries include the United States, Germany, and Argentina.

Federalism stands in contrast to unitarism. In a unitary model, a central authority holds all political power and establishes the rules governing social, economic, and political life throughout society. In other words, uniform laws and political institutions apply homogeneously across the entire territory. Today, many so-called unitary countries have a central government that retains political power but, for reasons of efficiency, *chooses* to decentralize some aspects of state administration—retaining the ability to reverse this decision if deemed necessary. Examples of this model include Chile, Israel, and Uruguay.

Nevertheless, drawing a strict line between unitary and federal countries overlooks the many nuances present in different societies. To better understand the various systems, it is likely more useful to speak in terms of countries that are more or less federal, depending on the degree of autonomy each political unit enjoys within the larger community. Ultimately, federalism is a matter of degree. For instance, both Argentina and the United States are classified as federal countries, yet in Argentina, the National Congress legislates on criminal law, while in the United States, except for federal crimes, criminal law is largely reserved for local states.

Spain offers an interesting case. The country is divided into 19 units with considerable autonomy (17 communities and two cities; in turn, several of these communities are further subdivided into provinces). Like many other countries (Italy, Portugal, Nicaragua, etc.), Spain exhibits both federal and unitary traits—often referred to as a "state of autonomies." On one hand, communities design and implement their own laws in parliaments elected by their citizens, similar to a federal system. On the other hand, these communities lack constituent power, a prerogative held by federated states in a federal regime.

Both unitary and federal regimes are compatible with liberal democracy. Nevertheless, FSC appears to favor a system that leans toward federalism rather than unitarism. As noted in this chapter, the state functions internally as a cooperative scheme, with intra-state cooperative activities aimed at maintaining the state's cooperative stance externally, thereby fulfilling its functions properly. Still, some might argue that the state remains a potentially dangerous actor within this cooperative framework, given its broad powers, which can undermine the egalitarian principle fundamental to schemes that honor FSC. Faced with this concern, federalism emerges as a plausible solution.

The federal system could be conceptualized as a cooperative framework where the different states participate—not only as governments but also including their citizens. Each state engages in cooperative activities both internally and externally.

Internally, this involves modalities like the separation of powers and checks and balances (among other political institutions such as suffrage), along with the use of coercion to preserve the local cooperative scheme (second-order cooperation), by preventing and sanctioning behaviors that could damage the cooperative environment within that territory, among other activities.[12]

Externally, the states collectively drive the country's economy through first-order cooperative activities, developing their own industries and providing goods and services that enrich society as a whole. Since each state (or province, or community) enjoys relative autonomy, the nation's functioning depends on the collective work of all these entities—not on any single one. The operation of the general cooperative framework is not contingent on the performance of any particular state but rather on the combined contributions of all of them.

In conclusion, FSC provides sufficient tools to explain why it is advantageous for a liberal democracy to lean toward federalism.

4.7 The Political System in Brief

The goal of this chapter was to explain how the primitive cooperation society can begin to evolve into a liberal democracy without undergoing *fundamental* changes—retaining its core nature as a social cooperation scheme in which individuals collaborate to develop and pursue their life plans. In particular, I focused on the political system of liberal democracy, showing that its institutions can be understood as refinements of that initial, fragile scheme.

First of all, I explained the emergence of the state within this framework. Given the marked increase in the number of participants,

[12] In Chapter 6, I explain that governments can also engage in first-order cooperative activities by providing basic goods and services, thereby complementing the private sector.

second-order cooperative activities (essentially, the exercise of coercion to preserve the cooperation scheme) start to become inefficient.

In response to this problem, the participants reorganize the practice of second-order cooperation by adopting two strategies: specialization and centralization. On the one hand, they realize it is much more efficient when those who produce goods and services (first-order cooperation) are distinct from those tasked with preserving the cooperation scheme (second-order cooperation). On the other hand, they note that a centralized coercive system would drastically reduce organizational costs.

The institution arising from these considerations is the state—established through a social contract—as an additional participant in the cooperation scheme, acting as a collective entity that seeks to cooperate by carrying out second-order activities related to protecting the scheme.

I also argued that, for compatibility with FSC, the existence of the state must not imply a centralization of power that renders the scheme wholly dependent on particular individuals. But how can this be prevented?

First, the participants make sure that the social contract, in addition to granting the monopoly on coercion, explicitly outlines the responsibilities and limits associated with this monopoly. To provide such a detailed explanation of the state's role, the social contract must also include a description of the cooperation framework, its underlying principles, and fundamental foundations. After all, coercion's purpose is to safeguard the cooperation scheme—creating a stable environment where participants understand what to expect from each other, allowing them to fully realize their potential and contribute meaningfully to the system. Defining these core principles and foundations helps the state gain a clearer understanding of its role. This comprehensive agreement is what we now refer to as the Constitution.

Second, the participants ensure that the state, besides performing protective tasks (second-order cooperation), also functions as a cooperation scheme itself—that is, operating internally as a cooperative system engaged in intra-state cooperative activities. As such, the state should be composed of independent institutions that cooperate with one another, decentralizing power so that the entire scheme becomes less dependent on any particular body.

To this end, the social contract introduces clauses that decentralize power. The first clause divides the state's monopoly into three separate monopolies, each responsible for different tasks (separation of powers). The second clause grants each monopoly tools to oversee the others (checks and balances). In this way, the state as a whole remains a participant exercising significant powers but is also itself a cooperation scheme, with internal institutions dedicated to preserving the state's structure and ensuring it remains within its functions.

The third clause establishes suffrage. This institution (comprised of all voters) is also a *state* institution. Thus, when voters exercise their right to vote, they participate in the administration of the state.

In this way, the suffrage institution also performs intra-state cooperative activities aimed at further decentralizing power and making the state even less dependent on particular interests. By guaranteeing regular terms of office and promoting alternation in power, suffrage pushes the state toward the proper fulfillment of its functions (though regulated by a counter-majoritarian power, such as the judiciary, to prevent abuses and protect minorities). Moreover, suffrage itself functions internally as a cooperation scheme, dependent on all voters but on none individually.

The fourth clause incorporates federalism, which can be conceptualized as a cooperation scheme involving various states, provinces, or communities as participants. Each local state (government plus citizens) engages in cooperative activities both internally and externally.

Internally, this includes the separation of powers and checks and balances (among other political institutions like suffrage), along with the use of coercion to preserve the local cooperation scheme (second-order cooperation), preventing and sanctioning behaviors that could harm the cooperative atmosphere in that territory, among other functions.

Externally, local states drive the country's economy through first-order cooperative activities, which involve developing their own industries and providing goods and services that enrich society at large. Since each state enjoys relative autonomy, the nation's functioning depends on the joint efforts of all of them, but not on any one in particular.

In the next two chapters, I will continue explaining how the society of "primitive cooperation" can evolve toward a liberal democracy without losing its essential trait of being a social cooperation scheme. Chapter 5 focuses on the economic system (mainly the market and the various ways it can be regulated), while Chapter 6 deals with the state's role in providing goods and services and how it complements the market.

4.8 The State as a First-Order Cooperator

Before proceeding to Chapter 5, a clarification is necessary. As mentioned earlier, from the perspective of FSC, the state's *raison d'être* is the need for a somewhat centralized entity to preserve the cooperation framework (that is, second-order cooperative activities). In the primitive cooperation model, for example, the state emerged as a group dedicated to second-order activities so that others could focus on first-order activities—the production and provision of goods and services necessary for individuals to formulate and carry out their life plans. However, today's states in liberal democracies are large, complex structures that manage extensive resources and have sufficient capacity to also undertake first-order cooperative activities, complementing those carried out in the private sector. Thus, as we will see, the state now also provides certain goods and services, such as sanitation, healthcare, education, and more. Although I will mention some of these examples in the next chapter (mainly when analyzing tax schemes), the state's first-order activities will be analyzed in detail in Chapter 6.

CHAPTER 5

FSC as a Theory of Liberal Democracy: The Economic System

5.1 The Origin of Private Property and Money

5.1.1 The Origin of Private Property

In the primitive cooperation scenario, individuals benefit from the second-order activities carried out by the officials of the fledgling state. In turn, these officials also benefit from the fact that individuals engage in first-order activities: the production and provision of goods and services, which are ultimately necessary for everyone—even the officials—to eat, dress, rest, and so forth. However, people begin to realize that the private sector's potential is not being fully harnessed due to two key issues.

The first one is that the production level of the scheme is suboptimal. In this scheme, the product of cooperation belongs to all who cooperate, without private ownership. Therefore, each person takes into account the likelihood that others will produce at a minimum level—*just enough to avoid exclusion from the cooperation scheme*—and thus receive more benefits than they contribute. If everyone fears others will behave this way, no one has the incentive to produce abundantly. From an individual perspective, no one wants to bear the significant burden of producing at full capacity and sharing the benefits when others contribute minimally yet gain without comparable effort. Since everyone reasons this way, production remains at the minimum, resulting in a relatively poor society.

This phenomenon is further exacerbated as the cooperation scheme grows larger. If the scheme is small, this coordination problem can be

E. Spector, *Freedom as Social Cooperation*,
https://doi.org/10.1007/978-3-032-12217-9_5

solved through discussion and agreement, whereby everyone commits to producing at a certain level. Because participants know each other, reputational costs for breaking the agreement can be significant. Social pressure plays an important role in such small groups. However, when the group consists of thousands or millions of people, communication and agreement costs become astronomical, while the costs of breaking the agreement become negligible.

Game theory scholars call this type of scenario the "prisoner's dilemma."[1] The irony of this situation is that although everyone would be better off behaving in a certain way (producing at maximum capacity), there are few incentives to adopt that behavior from an individual perspective because no one is sure that others will do the same. As a result, no one produces at full capacity, and overall welfare decreases.

It is important to emphasize that this outcome—suboptimal production—is not the fault of any individual participant: recall that within a cooperation scheme, everyone depends on everyone else without relying on any specific individual. Consequently, the deterioration of the system results from collective action rather than the behavior of any single participant.

One possible solution is to raise the threshold individuals must meet to remain part of the cooperation scheme. This approach narrows the definition of "cooperation": the participants who do not produce at a certain level will no longer be considered cooperators and will be excluded from the scheme—losing access to its benefits.

However, this approach is highly costly in terms of monitoring. Differentiating between various levels of production is far more complicated than simply identifying who does and does not produce at all. Moreover, each activity is fundamentally different from the others, so imposing a single production threshold across all activities would be insufficient (for example, there is no universal standard that could apply equally to treating and curing a sick person and to manufacturing hunting weapons). It would be necessary to establish a distinct production threshold for each type of activity, resulting in tremendously high logistical costs.

[1] The name of the dilemma comes from the fact that the example originally used to describe its logic involved two prisoners accused of a crime, who were held separately and had to choose between confessing and not confessing. The situation was set up so that both would have been better off not confessing, but from an individual perspective, each had incentives to confess (Kuhn 2019).

The second issue is that consumption tends to be supra-optimal. Although production is limited, participants in the scheme continue to demand goods and services, as they need them to carry out their life plans—food, clothing, shelter, and so forth. Incentives to produce beyond the minimum are weak, while incentives to consume remain steady. As a result, demand far exceeds supply, leaving many individuals dissatisfied.

For these reasons, participants decide to abolish the system of collective ownership and include the right to private property within the social contract, giving rise to a market economy. This means individuals own the goods they produce, thereby gaining the right to enter into contracts and exchange those goods for others (let us assume, for the moment, that in the absence of money, a barter system operates). This adjustment to the scheme reduces monitoring costs, resolves the problem of suboptimal production, and addresses the issue of excessive consumption.

First, the market economy lowers monitoring costs because it is no longer necessary to investigate who is producing and who is not—or who produces more or less—in order to exclude the latter from the system. Those who produce nothing are automatically excluded: without anything to offer on the market, they cannot engage in exchanges and consequently cannot extract benefits from the scheme. Those whose production is scarce receive benefits proportional to their level of contribution—those who produce little can only acquire little. Accordingly, the state does not monitor production levels; instead, it concentrates on protecting participants from various forms of aggression—including safeguarding private property—and potentially providing certain basic goods and services (a topic to be discussed in the next chapter).

Second, relatedly, the market economy solves the problem of suboptimal production because participants now have strong incentives to produce at a high level: the more they produce, the more exchanges they can make, and the greater the benefits they enjoy. Each person understands that others reason in the same way, so everyone ends up producing at a high level.

Third, the market economy addresses the problem of supra-optimal consumption because increased production brings supply closer to demand. Of course, it is possible that, for some reason, a resource becomes scarce. But the cause will not be a lack of production incentives. Suppose, for instance, that a rare infection decimates local bee populations, causing a significant scarcity of honey—an essential resource for food. The advantage of a market economy lies in the presence of a price system (which does not necessarily imply the existence of money, since we are still assuming a barter system). Prices communicate information about the relative scarcity or abundance of resources, and people adjust their consumption accordingly. Thus, if honey becomes scarce, its price rises, encouraging individuals to moderate their consumption and purchase it only when strictly necessary (Hayek 1945).

5.1.2 *The Origin of Money*

Once a market economy is established, people realize that they can make it more efficient. Although exchanges already occur in this system, individuals notice that far more transactions could take place if they abandoned the barter system and adopted a common denominator when buying and selling goods and services. Let me explain this point.

Suppose a person wants to buy corn and has some fruit to offer in exchange. To complete the trade, this person must find someone who not only wishes to sell corn but also wants to buy fruit. Finding such a match can take a considerable amount of time, a valuable resource that could be devoted to other tasks.

Participants soon recognize how inefficient the barter system is. Gradually, a certain element—likely small and easy to handle—emerges as a common denominator in daily transactions. Buyers and sellers begin to use this element as a standard for pricing and conducting exchanges. In doing so, transaction costs are significantly reduced. This is precisely the function of what we call money: it holds no intrinsic value but simply represents the goods and services we can buy and sell. In other words, money is merely a medium of exchange, created to save time and streamline trade.

This explanation illustrates why the wealth of an economy lies not in the amount of money circulating, but in the goods and services produced. Suppose people decide that a certain type of stone will serve as the medium of exchange. If, for some reason, production of goods and services ceased, this medium of exchange would lose its value. It would be absurd to think that under such circumstances people would become wealthier simply by acquiring more stones.

Indeed, if a central authority hoarded a vast quantity of these stones and flooded the economy with them without regard to the volume of goods and services produced, there would be an excess of stones relative to available goods, causing the stones to lose value—a phenomenon known as "inflation."

As an example, the so-called "price revolution" that took place in Western Europe during the late 16th and early 17th centuries involved a massive increase in prices triggered by an influx of precious metals from the Americas. These metals, generally used as mediums of exchange, did not make Europe richer; they merely caused prices to rise (Hamilton, E. 2000).

Strictly speaking, inflation is the decline in the value of the medium of exchange caused by its excessive supply (in modern societies, this is often due to excessive monetary issuance). While prices of some products may rise in any economy, a generalized increase in all prices is not coincidence; it reflects that the money in circulation loses value because its supply surpasses the volume of production.

Inflation is harmful because although all prices rise, they do so at different rates. If every price—including wages, which represent the cost of labor—increased uniformly, inflation would be neutral and would not harm anyone. However, inflation is not neutral: money enters the economy through different channels and at varying speeds, distorting relative prices. Consequently, some prices rise more than others (typically, wages lag behind), and even those that increase by the same percentage do so at different speeds. As a result, many individuals inevitably suffer significant losses.

In sum, money is a tool designed to facilitate trade. As a mere medium of exchange, the amount of money circulating does not make a society richer. True wealth lies in the goods and services produced—which money is only a representative of, serving as a common denominator to help buyers and sellers connect more easily.

5.2 Anti-Cooperative Behaviors and Criminal Law

In the primitive cooperation model, two types of anti-cooperative behavior could arise: the first was failing to contribute to the scheme (for example, not working or working only minimally); the second was acting against another participant.

Regarding the first behavior, participants needed to ensure that anyone choosing not to contribute, or contributing only minimally, would be excluded from receiving benefits. This was not so much a punishment as a sign of respect for their decision to leave the cooperative arrangement. However, as society became more numerous, the monitoring costs—the costs of verifying the contribution made by each person—became too high.

As I have already noted, the advantage of a market economy (which presupposes private property) is that non-contributors are automatically excluded from benefits, thereby reducing monitoring costs. The market allows us to enjoy its benefits only if we offer something others want and can access. In other words, the market requires that we do our part, at least if we wish to reap its advantages. But if we do not wish to, the system is not threatened because we are not indispensable. It is important to point out that goods and services can be offered not only in the private sector but also in the public sector. For example, a lawyer applying for a position as a court clerk is offering a product and attempting to make a contribution. In some sense, therefore, they are participating in the market.

The second type of anti-cooperative behavior warrants a different analysis. This behavior consists of aggressive acts against participants, threatening their physical or psychological integrity (in market economies, such behaviors also include attacks on property, such as theft, robbery, fraud, scams, and so forth). This kind of conduct is indeed problematic, as the aggressor injects anti-cooperative elements into the scheme. Cooperation requires a certain degree of certainty and stability. Attacking a participant is inherently anti-cooperative, but it is also disruptive, impairing the victim's ability to cooperate (a person being attacked cannot cooperate) and undermining the cooperative atmosphere: others cannot fully cooperate knowing they may become targets. For this reason, in the primitive cooperation model, participants carried out second-order cooperative activities: if someone tried to attack another, the others intervened (even coercively) to protect the victim and excluded the aggressor from the scheme (at least until they regained a cooperative attitude), thereby maintaining the cooperative atmosphere and the necessary certainty and stability needed for participants to cooperate fully.

In modern societies, these second-order cooperative activities are the responsibility of the state, and offenders serve their exclusion periods in penitentiary institutions. From the perspective of FSC, criminal law should be understood primarily as a mechanism to preserve and enhance the cooperative arrangements that form the foundation of social and economic life. On this view, criminal law's primary function is to protect the cooperative framework that allows individuals to engage with one another productively and peacefully.

According to classical criminal law doctrine, crimes do not harm only the victim but constitute an attack against society as a whole; thus, society, represented by a prosecutor, brings the accusation (although the victim, having been *especially* harmed, may play a special role as a complainant). This is why criminal law is considered a branch of public law: certain behaviors impact society as a whole, and society (through a state prosecutor) occupies the role of accuser. FSC captures this component of criminal law by recognizing that anti-cooperative behavior directed at harming a participant shatters the cooperative atmosphere of the entire scheme.

Much has been debated regarding the philosophical justification of legal punishment. FSC aligns with at least two such justifications. The first holds that the purpose of punishment should be the re-education and eventual social reintegration of the offender (Lacey and Pickard 2021: 271). FSC could fully embrace this thesis. In a system based on FSC, the scheme, through the state, excludes the criminal *because* they have behaved anti-cooperatively. If this is the case, it suggests that the state should make efforts to help the excluded individual regain a cooperative attitude. Once regained, there is no reason to maintain exclusion; indeed, excluding someone who has restored their cooperative stance wastes their potential to enrich the cooperative scheme.

The second account holds that punishment is justified by its social pedagogical effect: reinforcing respect for norms, consolidating trust in the law, and calming the community's legal conscience by confirming conflict resolution (Roxin 1976). FSC also embraces this rationale. Indeed, it can be expressed in FSC terms: excluding the aggressor from the scheme serves to remind all participants of the importance of respecting the terms of social cooperation and conveys the certainty and trust essential for full cooperation.

Significant attention has focused on so-called retributionist theories, which argue that offenders should be punished because they morally deserve it (Cottingham 1979). Unlike retributionist theories, FSC shifts attention away from *condemning* individuals and toward preserving and enriching the cooperative scheme itself. FSC does not justify punishment as a form of moral desert or backward-looking blame (Kelly 2018); rather, it views exclusion and sanctioning as practical measures designed to protect the stability and trust necessary for cooperation to thrive. The purpose is forward-looking: to restore a cooperative environment where all participants can contribute confidently and productively. By prioritizing the maintenance and enhancement of social cooperation over moral retribution, FSC rejects the notion that punishment is about "paying back" or inflicting deserved suffering. Instead, it focuses on encouraging offenders to regain a cooperative attitude and reintegrate as active contributors, thereby enriching the social fabric rather than perpetuating cycles of blame and resentment.

In short, from the perspective of FSC, criminal law, as a second-order cooperative practice, aims to preserve the cooperation scheme. This preservation is accomplished by encouraging offenders to regain cooperative attitudes and by reaffirming to all participants the terms of social cooperation so they have the confidence necessary to continue cooperating.

5.3 Government Financing of Public Expenditure

5.3.1 State Funding Mechanisms

As we can see, the society of "primitive cooperation" has evolved considerably since its original form. Politically, it now features a constitution, a state with separation of powers and checks and balances, suffrage, and presumably a federal structure. Economically, it operates a market economy where private property is protected (I will elaborate further on the institution of the market in the next section).

In this section, I explore the mechanisms through which those acting on behalf of the state (public officials) receive compensation for their duties, as well as the resources they need to fulfill their functions. The state essentially relies on two primary revenue systems: taxes and public debt. There is also a potential third system—monetary issuance—in countries where central banks are authorized (even if implicitly) to finance certain government programs through currency creation. Alongside explaining the basic structure of these three systems, I examine the design they should have to uphold the ideal of FSC.

5.3.2 *Taxes*

The primary means by which the state raises resources is through contributions made by all participants in the scheme. The proper functioning of the state is essential to maintain the scheme, and those contributions are indispensable to the state's proper functioning. From the FSC perspective, therefore, those contributions foster social cooperation; moreover, making those contributions is itself a form of cooperation, since they represent the recompense granted to officials for performing their duties as well as the resources enabling them to carry out their tasks.

If people fail to make these contributions, the cooperation scheme will sooner or later collapse. For this reason, the scheme itself should be designed to encourage such contributions. In this regard, two fundamental questions arise when designing the contribution mechanism:

1. Should contributions be voluntary, or obtained through state coercion?
2. How should the burden of making these contributions be distributed?

The first question concerns whether the use of state coercion is necessary to collect the funds required for the state to function properly. We know the state holds a monopoly on coercion, but is it necessary to employ coercion itself to raise the money needed to finance this coercive monopoly?

The second question assumes an affirmative answer to the first. If contributions are compulsory, under what conditions should individuals contribute more, and under what conditions should they contribute less?

5.3.2.1 *Mandatory or Voluntary?*

To address this question, it is useful to draw two distinctions. The first distinction is between small groups and large groups. The second distinction concerns two types of benefits the state can provide. Economists differentiate between public benefits and non-public benefits.

Public benefits are those that, once provided, benefit everyone without excluding those who did not contribute to their financing (Musgrave 1959). Consider, for instance, security, which in my vocabulary is a second-order activity. It consists in the state's provision of protection that enables people to live safely in a neighborhood, city, or country (for example, through the police and armed forces). Security is regarded as a public benefit because once an area is protected, non-payers cannot be excluded from enjoying that protection—they cannot, for example, be expelled from the neighborhood. The same logic applies to street cleaning, a first-order activity. Once the service is delivered and the streets are clean, all residents benefit regardless of whether they contributed financially. This reasoning likewise applies to environmental quality. Importantly, up to this point I have examined second-order activities performed by the state; the first-order activities undertaken by the state will be analyzed in the next chapter, although, as can be seen, some examples are given here to illustrate the distinction between public and non-public benefits.

The state commonly provides public benefits because they would not be efficiently produced through market mechanisms. Indeed, few would be willing to produce a good that can be consumed without payment: beyond the lack of profitability, it would be rational to wait for someone else to provide it and free-ride on their effort.[2] Since everyone thinks this way, the good is either not produced or underproduced, failing to meet demand. Ultimately, this leads to a prisoner's dilemma, as explained at the beginning of this chapter.

Non-public benefits are those that can be specifically targeted to those who pay for them, excluding non-payers—such as the provision of healthcare and education (which, in my vocabulary, are considered first-order activities). Sometimes the state provides these benefits for reasons of equality or other moral considerations. They are not public benefits because it would be entirely possible to exclude someone from a hospital or school if they have not paid.[3] Nevertheless, the state often provides

[2] Strictly speaking, this lack of incentives becomes even more evident when, in addition to the impossibility of excluding those who did not contribute to financing the good, the good can be consumed infinitely as long as it is provided—that is, one person's consumption does not diminish another's ability to consume it (Samuelson 1954).

[3] It could be argued that goods such as healthcare and education are public benefits, given that their advantages are not experienced solely by students in a school or patients in a hospital. We all benefit from a more educated and healthier society. For example, a better-educated population could promote economic prosperity, which would ultimately benefit everyone, regardless of how much each individual has invested in their own education. Similarly, a healthier society could benefit all of us because the fewer people infected with a contagious disease, the less likely it is that any one of us will become infected, regardless of our personal investment in health.

these goods on the premise that they are basic rights, meaning access should not depend on citizens' economic power.

From these two distinctions emerge at least four possible scenarios:

(1) a small society where the state produces only public benefits;
(2) a large society where the state produces only public benefits;
(3) a small society where the state produces both public and non-public benefits;
(4) a large society where the state produces both public and non-public benefits.[4]

Whether raising funds to finance the state requires coercion will depend, in part, on which of these scenarios we find ourselves in.

A Small Society Where the State Produces Only Public Benefits

If we imagine a scheme with few participants, it is not unreasonable to think that these contributions could be voluntary, even when it is not possible to exclude those who do not pay for the benefits (that is, even if we assume the state produces exclusively public benefits). After all, in small groups, people may have incentives to cooperate: potential disdain from their peers, and the resulting personal sense of shame, could exert effective social pressure.[5]

Moreover, even assuming there is no social pressure, individuals would likely realize that in small groups it is unwise to abstain from making

It is true that education and healthcare (along with other goods, such as social assistance to vulnerable groups) have a public dimension. However, although I will not analyze this issue in detail here, I believe their non-public dimension predominates—namely, the fact that patients and students can be excluded from hospitals and schools if they do not pay the fees. The consequence of a public benefit is that there are no incentives for these goods to be produced through market processes. The existence of many private schools and hospitals suggests that the non-public dimension of these goods is more significant.

[4] I do not analyze other possible scenarios, such as governments that produce only non-public benefits, since these would be quite far removed from what occurs in contemporary societies. The cooperation schemes I envision are intended to correspond to what happens in modern democracies, as ultimately the goal is to assess the extent to which FSC can justify their institutions.

[5] For an analysis of the influence of ethical and social norms, see Sugden (1984) and Young (1998). My point is that the emergence of these types of norms is much more likely in small groups.

these contributions. In small groups, interactions involve the same people repeatedly—in other words, individuals "cross paths" again and again. If a person chooses not to contribute, their inaction will be noticed by their peers and will earn their distrust, which will affect how those peers behave in the future. When the game is repeated indefinitely, it may be advantageous for a participant to cooperate to signal their willingness to continue cooperating as long as others do the same. If everyone reasons similarly, cooperation might emerge spontaneously (Axelrod 1982).[6]

Ultimately, if there is an established pattern of behavior consisting of making these contributions, then, *assuming no single contributor is indispensable for the scheme to continue functioning*,[7] a form of cooperation compatible with FSC will arise: each person depends on the contributions of others, but since each individual's contribution is relatively small, no one depends on any particular person. If someone behaved antisocially and stopped contributing, it would not seriously jeopardize the scheme.

To be sure, from the FSC perspective, those who abstain from cooperating should not enjoy the public benefits provided by the state. As I have noted, there is nothing wrong with choosing not to cooperate. But it is indeed a choice: to forgo the benefits that cooperation entails. Thus, if someone decides not to contribute, they can legitimately be deprived of those benefits. However, in this case, excluding them from the benefits is not possible (or is extremely costly) precisely because these are public benefits.

In any case, this impossibility does not pose a major problem in this scenario. Recall that, since this is a small group, cooperation is likely the general rule. There would be few cases of antisocial behavior, and the scheme could attempt to address them in various ways; for example, by trying to persuade those individuals of the importance of cooperating. The important point is that when a pattern of cooperation exists, isolated instances of non-cooperation do not threaten the overall scheme.

A Large Society Where the State Produces Only Public Benefits

In a large society, things can be different: social and ethical norms that promote contributions rarely extend uniformly across all subgroups.

[6] See also Taylor, M. (1976); Axelrod (1980); and Schotter (1981).

[7] Admittedly, if the society is too small, this scenario is improbable because each contribution becomes essential. I am imagining a relatively small society, but with enough participants to sufficiently disperse influence.

People can form bounded communities of like-minded individuals—including groups whose members mutually legitimize non-contribution—so significant pockets of low willingness to cooperate may persist.

But what about the repetition of interactions? Does the same game not get repeated? In large societies, people do not necessarily cross paths again, which reduces the incentives to cooperate in individual interactions.[8] Moreover, when society is large enough, non-contributors can hide in anonymity. It is as if they were not part of the game: they can stand aside, waiting for the game to yield benefits they then enjoy without participating (recall that we are still imagining the state provides only public benefits, so it cannot exclude those who do not contribute).

In a small society, assuming the game is repeated indefinitely, individuals have incentives to send a signal that they are willing to cooperate so the other player understands and decides to cooperate in future interactions. The goal, of course, is to obtain the benefits of cooperation in each encounter. Since everyone reasons this way, ongoing cooperation emerges. In contrast, when there are thousands or millions of participants, the individual considers that they can opt out of the game and remain anonymous, without having to forgo the benefits.

For these reasons, in a society of thousands or millions, voluntary contributions could lead to minimal or no revenue, because the established pattern of behavior that might arise in small societies does not exist. In a large society, each person has an incentive to abstain from contributing, hoping that others will do so instead and that they can benefit free of charge. Since everyone—or at least the vast majority—reasons this way, revenue would be negligible, and the entire cooperation scheme would be at risk (since basic goods like security could not be financed). In this scenario, the use of coercion may be the only tool to increase revenue and thus preserve the cooperation scheme.

State coercion is a way to restore the general practice of contributing, thereby putting the scheme back into operation. There will surely be some isolated free riders, but as they are isolated, the scheme could continue functioning (including the sanctioning of these free riders). Once again, a cooperation scheme is at work where everyone depends on everyone else, but yet no one depends on anyone in particular.

[8] It is true, however, that some authors have provided evidence that cooperation can emerge even in large groups where interactions do not necessarily repeat between the same individuals. For example, see Bowles and Gintis (2011: 3).

A Small Society Where the State Produces Both Public and Non-Public Benefits

If the society is sufficiently small, then we find ourselves in a scenario similar to the first one. With social pressure combined with repeated interactions among the same individuals indefinitely, cooperation could emerge without the need for coercion. When cooperation arises spontaneously, the distinction between public and non-public benefits becomes irrelevant: since people generally contribute, the inability to exclude the few free riders from public benefits is not a major problem.

Of course, in this case, it would be advisable to try to persuade non-cooperators through non-coercive means. Even today, there are communities that strive to manage themselves without using physical force. For example, in the forests of the Democratic Republic of Congo, there is a pygmy people called the Mbuti. This group lives by gathering and hunting, activities they perform jointly. They share common religious and moral beliefs, as well as a language. When someone behaves antisocially and refuses to cooperate, others try to encourage them to change their attitude through non-coercive methods. These may include persuading the person by reminding them of their obligations, explaining the importance of cooperation for survival, or even gently mocking their antisocial behavior (Appiah 2003: 221–222).

In summary, in small societies, spontaneous cooperation could emerge without the need for coercion.

A Large Society Where the State Produces Both Public and Non-Public Benefits

This scenario is the most complex, yet also the most relevant, as it generally applies to contemporary democracies. Modern societies tend to have millions of inhabitants. Likewise, democratic governments typically assume responsibility for providing both public benefits (such as security) and non-public benefits (such as housing for vulnerable groups).

Regarding public benefits, the same analysis applied in the second scenario remains valid. The use of the state's coercive power is likely necessary to increase revenue collection. Voluntary contributions do not seem to be a viable option. First, given the large size of society, it is reasonable to assume that cooperation would not emerge voluntarily. Second, the nature of public benefits provides no incentives to cooperate, since these goods can be enjoyed by both contributors and non-contributors alike.

The matter of non-public benefits (healthcare, education, recreational spaces, etcetera) requires special consideration in large societies. Indeed, individuals' incentives may vary depending on how the system is designed. If the state were to grant these benefits to everyone regardless of contribution, the outcome would be similar to that of public benefits—coercion would again be necessary. Conversely, if the state excluded those who do not contribute (for example, denying access to public healthcare to those who do not help finance it), incentives for voluntary contributions might increase.

In practice, however, such exclusion mechanisms are only feasible if contributions are designated for specific uses. In modern democracies, the earmarked contributions are the minority. Generally, people contribute to a common pool, which the state and local governments then use to finance goods and services without linking specific contributions to specific benefits. In any case, a system of voluntary contributions earmarked for specific purposes appears conceptually feasible, although it entails certain challenges.

First, it would be unclear how to distinguish between different types of contributions. When contributions are mandatory (taxes), the state determines the source of funding—such as income tax, sales tax, commercial transaction tax, or capital gains tax. For instance, if a museum is financed by a specific tax, and an individual evades that tax, it is technically possible for the state to deny that person admission to the museum. In contrast, if people can choose whether or not to contribute, the source of their funds becomes less relevant: it does not matter if a contribution comes from salary, inheritance, or investment income. Ultimately, all these resources fall into one category: personal wealth. What happens if someone makes only a relatively small contribution? Which goods or services might they be denied? Should the state refuse them treatment at a public hospital? Should it deny them access to a public library? Or exclude their children from a public school? Such a system risks being riddled with arbitrariness.

Perhaps, with a sufficiently sophisticated design, the above problem could be addressed. For example, there might be a procedure through which individuals choose which goods or services they wish to support, much like donors supporting specific charitable causes or neighborhood improvements. Indeed, regarding the contribution amount, the state could issue guidelines based on people's purchasing power; for instance: "If you earn X amount per month, contributing W amount to the health system would be sufficient to use this service; contributing V amount to the education system would be enough for access to that service," and so on. Thus, individuals would enjoy only those goods or services to which they contributed at the specified level. Like tax systems, voluntary contribution systems could also be progressive.

However, a caveat is necessary. It seems reasonable that certain state goods and services should be available to people regardless of whether they helped finance them. Public education, for example, primarily benefits children. It does not appear appropriate to deny access based on the parents' decision not to contribute. Furthermore, educating children so they can become productive participants in the cooperation scheme is important for maintaining the scheme itself. Excluding some children would damage the system and thereby harm its participants (this is where the earlier observation that education carries a public benefit component becomes relevant).

The justice system is another example of a service that should be provided to everyone regardless of their financial support. For instance, if someone who chose not to contribute to the justice system is hit by a driver, it would be problematic for the state to deny them judicial and administrative resources to file a lawsuit. Using the justice system selectively to benefit some but not others, for any reason, conflicts with the very idea of society. Can we speak of a cooperation scheme when citizenship is fragmented over something as fundamental as the application of civil and even criminal law? To some extent, living in society implies being governed by the same basic rules, and those concerning the justice system are among the most important.

Moreover, even when contributions are earmarked for specific uses and exclusion mechanisms function effectively, it is reasonable to assume that wealthier individuals would have little interest in voluntarily contributing to, say, public health or education systems, since they can obtain these goods on the market by purchasing services privately. If only those with limited means contribute voluntarily, it will be more difficult for the state to provide quality goods. The provision of goods such as education and healthcare has a redistributive component: the system is designed so that everyone must contribute regardless of who consumes which goods.

In short, in this scenario, a voluntary contribution system directed at financing non-public goods and services faces several drawbacks. I do not intend to dismiss this possibility outright, but perhaps these challenges have influenced governments to rely more on coercive power to collect the necessary resources to finance these state-provided goods and services.

Coercion and Cooperation: Are They Contrary Concepts?

According to FSC, freedom is a cooperative practice aimed at the development and fulfillment of life plans. Is coercion compatible with freedom understood in this way?

Coercion exercised within the cooperation scheme (that is, second-order cooperative activities) operates on two levels. At the first level, coercion is intended to preserve the cooperation scheme by repelling anti-cooperative attitudes that would undermine the cooperative atmosphere of the system. At this point, I hope to have shown that far from being in conflict with FSC, this form of coercion makes it possible. Indeed, the practice of cooperation requires a certain degree of certainty and stability, a particular environment that coercion can help establish.

At the second level, coercion is aimed at collecting the necessary resources to sustain this coercive scheme (these are the taxes discussed above). If a system of voluntary contributions proves ineffective in raising those resources, and therefore the collection process needs to be coercive, then we can assert that this form of coercion is also compatible with FSC. After all, freedom cannot exist without cooperation; cooperation cannot persist without the exercise of coercion; and without coercive resource collection, the coercive system cannot be maintained.

5.3.2.2 The Distribution of the Burdens

The conclusion of the previous section was that there are good reasons to believe that, at least in large societies (such as modern liberal democracies), the contributions necessary for the proper functioning of the state structure should be mandatory. This implies that the state may collect resources by exercising its coercive power. I now intend to offer some considerations on how, from the perspective of FSC, the burdens of making these contributions should be distributed.

First of all, it is necessary to distinguish the question "how should the *burdens* of making these contributions be distributed?" from the question "how should the *resources* raised through those burdens be distributed?" Consider, for example, the notion of "social justice." For present purposes a precise definition of that ideal is not required. A vague notion will suffice: suppose that by "social justice" we mean an equitable form of wealth redistribution.

A state can practice social justice in the way it collects resources, and it can practice social justice in the way it distributes those resources.

These are two different dimensions of social justice. Thus, a government that only levies taxes on the middle class is not practicing social justice in the first sense, since it is exempting the upper class from paying taxes. Nevertheless, if that government uses the collected resources to distribute wealth equitably, it is practicing social justice in the second sense. Conversely, a government that distributes the burdens of paying taxes equitably but then does not distribute wealth equitably is practicing social justice in the first sense but not in the second. Those who regard social justice as a valuable ideal will, of course, maintain that the state should practice social justice in both senses. My point is that the two senses are conceptually distinct.

This distinction clarifies the aim of this section. I will focus here on the question: "How should the burdens of tax payment be distributed?" By contrast, I will leave for Chapter 6 the question of how the collected resources should be distributed or into which goods and services they should be translated (although I have already made some general remarks in the previous section when I discussed whether contributions should be coercive and introduced the notion of public and non-public benefits).

The activity of paying taxes shares a similarity with the act of voting. In the previous chapter, I argued that, from the perspective of FSC, suffrage is a form of intra-state cooperation. When individuals act as voters, they participate in the management of the state. The right to vote arises from the right to participate in state administration.

Similarly, from the FSC point of view, tax contribution is also an institution of the state, so it is also a form of intra-state cooperation. Thus, by paying taxes, participants take part in the internal administration of the state—though, unlike voting, paying taxes is considered more a duty than a right.

Likewise, as with suffrage, the tax scheme should also (if it is to honor FSC) operate *internally* as a scheme of cooperation in which everyone depends on everyone, but on no one in particular. As I have said, suffrage operates internally in this way because it is supported by the votes of all, but by no individual vote in particular. The tax scheme should be designed in the same way. In other words, each participant's contribution should add to the scheme but should not be indispensable for the scheme's functioning. Otherwise we could not speak of cooperation (at least not cooperation in the FSC sense), since the element of equality that characterizes it would be absent: the functioning of the scheme would be conditioned on the correct performance of a single participant. If, for example, that participant decided to move to another society, the scheme would be profoundly harmed.

The idea, then, is that the functioning of the state structure should depend on there being a tax scheme to which everyone contributes, but it should not depend on any particular taxpayer. Thus, each person depends on there being people who contribute to the scheme, but because everyone contributes a relatively small part, the system does not depend on any specific contributor. The contribution size may vary according to various criteria; however, from the FSC perspective, it is preferable that no individual contribution be disproportionately large, so that the functioning of the scheme does not depend on a single taxpayer or, likewise, on a very small group of taxpayers.

From a legal standpoint, taxes are usually classified into two types: direct and indirect. A direct tax is one that a person or organization pays straight to the government, such as income tax or property tax, without involving any exchange of goods or services. This tax is applied by taking the taxpayer's economic capacity into account; for example, their wealth, monthly earnings, or receipt of income. An indirect tax, by contrast, is collected when someone buys a product or service, with the seller acting as the intermediary who passes the payment on to the government. This tax is applied by considering the *exercise* that the taxpayer makes of their economic capacity; for example, sales tax, value-added tax, taxes on property transfers, or other legal acts that involve the circulation of wealth.

At the same time, in economic terms, a distinction is commonly made between progressive and flat tax systems. Progressive taxes apply increasing percentage rates to the tax base as the base itself grows. For example, individuals with low incomes might pay a 10% tax on their earnings, those with middle incomes 20%, and those with high incomes 30%. This structure exemplifies a progressive tax system, which can be applied to both individuals and corporations.

By contrast, flat taxes apply a constant percentage rate to the tax base, irrespective of its size. For instance, a 15% value-added tax charges the same rate on all goods purchased, regardless of their price.

The distinction between direct and indirect taxes is independent of the distinction between progressive and flat taxes. This means that we can have progressive direct taxes, where, for example, higher incomes are taxed at higher rates; flat direct taxes, where a uniform rate applies to all incomes; progressive indirect taxes, where the tax rate increases with the value of the economic activity; and flat indirect taxes, where the same tax rate applies regardless of the amount involved in the economic activity.

Now, it is important to point out that, beyond whether taxes are direct or indirect, all taxes ultimately fall on wealth (there is no way for the taxpayer to settle them otherwise, at least if private property is protected). If the state establishes a 10% tax on the purchase of food, lawyers will say it is an indirect tax on consumption, but what actually happens is that the taxpayer pays out of their wealth.

From this perspective, we can understand why, although indirect taxes can be progressive or flat with respect to their tax base (which is a specific economic activity), they are regressive in terms of their impact on the taxpayer's wealth. For example, if the tax on purchasing bread is 5% of its price, everyone pays the same amount of money since the price is the same for all. However, as income decreases, this tax represents a larger percentage of that income. In other words, people with lower incomes pay a higher proportion of their earnings in this tax. This characteristic underlies the regressivity of indirect taxes: although the tax amount paid on bread is identical for all taxpayers, it constitutes a different share of each individual's income.[9]

Direct taxes, on the other hand, are flexible enough to be regressive, neutral, or progressive. Regressive direct taxes are those where the percentage of income paid in tax increases as income decreases. In practice, no country adopts this type of tax.

Neutral direct taxes are flat taxes, where the tax rate is the same for all income levels. In this case, individuals with lower incomes pay less money overall (for example, 20% of 100 is less than 20% of 1000), but the percentage remains constant. Countries like Armenia, Estonia, and Hungary use this system.[10]

Progressive direct taxes are those where the percentage of income paid increases as income rises. Most countries have this type of tax, including Canada, Finland, New Zealand, Belgium, Germany, Italy, and Greece,

[9] What if the tax on purchasing bread were not a flat 5% for everyone, but instead decreased in line with the taxpayer's purchasing power? The tax would no longer be regressive. However, the reason is precisely that such a tax would no longer be indirect in the *full* sense, because it would *directly* consider the taxpayer's economic capacity.

[10] See https://worldpopulationreview.com/country-rankings/countries-with-flat-tax (last accessed: August 16, 2025).

among many others (of course, many of these countries also have indirect taxes).

Which system best aligns with the ideal of FSC? According to the FSC framework, freedom is fundamentally rooted in social cooperation. However, "cooperation" here does not refer to just any mutually beneficial interaction—for instance, the alliance between a slave and their master to defend property. Rather, it denotes a practice of genuine mutual collaboration aimed at the development and realization of individual life plans. In this practice, each person depends on others collectively, but without relying on any single individual in particular.

If, as FSC asserts, social cooperation is constitutive of freedom, then cooperation must be the context in which individuals develop and carry out their life plans. Cooperation, in this sense, is necessarily limited, meaning it does not completely absorb the person's time, effort, or capacities. Therefore, the distribution of tax burdens should be sensitive to the inequality of resources that participants acquire through the system.[11] The burden of making contributions must be proportional to the resources possessed by the contributor; otherwise, if the state imposed a heavy burden on someone with little, it would not be a request for cooperation but rather a sacrifice that would consume a significant part of their life—something that no reasonable notion of freedom could demand.

The difference between cooperation and sacrifice is also illustrated by the primitive cooperation model. As I pointed out in Chapter 3, in that scenario, participants do not demand too much from those with lesser cooperative capacity because they understand that such a demand would require self-sacrifice rather than cooperation—and this requirement is incompatible with the idea of freedom.

Given these considerations, it is reasonable to assert that indirect taxes do not uphold the ideal of FSC. These taxes are regressive in their impact on the taxpayer's economic situation: as previously noted, the percentage of income paid toward these taxes increases as income decreases. Consequently, as a taxpayer's income declines, their contributions shift from being *cooperative* to becoming a form of sacrifice, ultimately imposing an excessive burden on those with lower incomes.

[11] This holds true even when a person's life plan is to live modestly, with limited resources. Indeed, there is no guarantee that their perspective will not change in the future. That is why it is always better to have more resources rather than fewer, so one has the ability to review and change their life plan if necessary.

Of course, one could imagine an extremely low indirect tax that leaves sufficient room for everyone—including those with lower incomes—to pursue their life plans. In this case, the tax might better align with the FSC ideal, but the trade-off would be its practical irrelevance as a revenue source. Alternatively, exempting individuals below a certain income threshold could eliminate this tension; however, the reason is precisely that this approach introduces an element of direct taxation by *directly* considering taxpayers' limited economic capacity. Beyond these nuances, the fundamental issue remains: an *indirect* tax that *genuinely* aims to raise revenue does not, in principle, align with the FSC concept of cooperation.

Direct taxes are more effective in distributing burdens in a manner consistent with FSC. In particular, both flat and progressive direct taxes (which can apply to individuals and/or companies) align with FSC, though the latter appears to better honor this conception of freedom.

A flat direct tax applies the same percentage rate to all income levels. This does not mean everyone bears the same tax burden. Those with lower incomes bear a lighter burden: although the rate is the same, it results in a smaller amount of money as income decreases. In this sense, the system appears sensitive to resource inequality and thus recognizes that it is inappropriate to demand significant sacrifices from those with fewer resources. Nonetheless, while those with lower incomes carry a lighter burden, it is still true that they spend a larger proportion of their income meeting basic needs, leaving them with fewer resources to develop and pursue their life plans. Therefore, it is reasonable to think that the flat tax, though somewhat consistent with FSC, does not best honor this ideal. The burden on those with fewer resources should be even lighter to allow them more resources for personal development. This is where progressive direct taxation becomes especially relevant.

The purpose of a progressive direct tax, then, is to alleviate the tax burden on those with lower incomes (who spend a greater proportion of their money on meeting basic needs) so that they can retain more funds to better develop and carry out their life plans. In this way, the progressive tax appears to honor the idea of a system in which participants cooperate to realize their respective projects, with the demand to cooperate calibrated according to each person's capacity.

It is necessary to clarify, however, that progressivity must be such that it does not undermine the essential element of cooperation in FSC: that everyone depends on everyone else without depending on any one individual in particular. The burden should fall on those who possess the most, but not to the extent that the entire system relies on the contributions of a small, wealthy group. Each participant's contribution should add to the system, but it should not be indispensable for the system's functioning. Otherwise, the element of equality that characterizes FSC would be absent: the operation of the system would depend on the proper performance of that participant (or, equivalently, a small elite). In addition to making the state's functioning dependent on their contributions, placing an excessive burden on them would *actually* incentivize withdrawing those contributions. These elites have the ability to move from one society to another, taking their resources to whichever offers a better business climate.

The idea, then, is that the functioning of the state structure depends on a tax system to which everyone contributes, but it should not depend on any particular contributor. Thus, each person depends on the presence of contributors, but because everyone contributes a relatively small share, the system does not depend on any single contributor. Contributions may vary in size based on different criteria, but from the FSC perspective, it is preferable that no individual contribution be large enough to threaten the system's stability. Ultimately, the tax system must balance sensitivity to those with less economic capacity with the need to avoid excessive dependence on a few individuals upon whom the entire system relies.

Much has been debated about the effectiveness of the progressive tax in reducing inequality, among other positive consequences (Moyes 1988, Piketty and Saez 2003, Pickett and Wilkinson 2011: 247, Oishi, Schimmack and Diener 2012). Here, the focus is somewhat different. My defense of progressive taxation is grounded not in its implications for material equality, but in its capacity to achieve an appropriate balance between two elements that are essential from the FSC perspective: first, ensuring that the demand for cooperation does not become a demand for *sacrifice*, as such a shift would contradict genuine cooperation; and second, preserving the viability of the cooperative system by preventing it from relying on a small number of contributors.

Finally, it should be noted that, up to this point, when I have referred to progressive direct taxes, I have mainly been talking about those levied on the income of individuals (and sometimes businesses). However, income is not the only taxable base to which these taxes can apply. Some have advocated for a progressive wealth tax, arguing that wealth is a better indicator than income for measuring a person's economic status. It happens that many people possess significant wealth but, for various reasons, currently have little or no income (Saez and Zucman 2020). At present, countries such as Spain, Norway, and Switzerland impose this type of tax.

A wealth tax, as a direct and progressive tax, upholds the ideal of FSC as long as it does not place the entire burden on a narrow economic elite upon which the system ultimately depends. As mentioned earlier, a scheme that levies taxes solely on millionaires may seem appropriate from a social justice perspective, but it conflicts with the FSC principle because the system becomes vulnerable to the behavior of this elite (for example, if they were to leave the country, the scheme would collapse). Of course, the system should not lie at the opposite extreme—being insensitive to the situation of the most disadvantaged—because such a demand would no longer be one of cooperation but rather a sacrifice akin to immolation. To honor FSC, the wealth tax, like any direct and progressive tax, must strike a balance between sensitivity to those with less capacity to cooperate and the need to avoid placing the burden on a few individuals upon whom the entire system depends.

5.3.2.3 Taxes and Federalism

So far, I have assumed that the cooperative scheme is governed by a central authority that establishes a tax system for everyone. Now, let us imagine a federal system, where each unit—whether province, state, or community—has the power to decide its own tax system.

Previously, I argued that FSC recognizes the importance of federalism as a way to distribute political power. A federal system consists of distinct units with considerable political, fiscal, and administrative autonomy, alongside a central body (the federal government) with limited authority over issues of common concern. In a federal system, neither the central body nor the units can alter this structure.

In a federal tax system, each local authority has its own tax regime. This means that each unit independently decides which types of taxes to impose, determines the level of the tax burden, and assumes responsibility for tax collection. The general principle is that taxes are regulated by each local authority, except for a few taxes set by the central government to ensure the proper functioning of the overall cooperative framework—for example, funding the branches of government, national defense, and preventing practices that could jeopardize the entire system, such as illegal immigration, drug trafficking, and human trafficking. Depending on the system, the federal government may also finance national education and healthcare institutions.

We can conceptualize a federal tax system as a cooperation scheme where the local governments are the participants. Each government designs its tax system and offers it to society as an option under which people can live, enriching the range of choices available. Thus, each local government participates in the scheme, but *none of these participants is indispensable for the system's operation*. This means that if a government engages in anti-cooperative behavior—such as imposing excessive taxes or unfairly distributing burdens—its citizens can move to other units (Tiebout 1956). This would be far more difficult if all taxes depended on a central authority that behaved anti-cooperatively.[12]

Moreover, the ability of citizens to move between different tax regimes ensures that no jurisdiction strays too far from the ideal of social cooperation, as doing so would cause it to lose too many contributors. On one hand, a local government would avoid implementing a system that forces the less wealthy to *sacrifice* by shouldering an excessive tax burden, since these individuals would migrate to more reasonable regimes. This would leave only the wealthier residents, who, despite paying higher taxes due to a smaller tax base, would face a shortage of available labor to sustain their economic model. This disincentive to impose undue burdens on the less well-off fosters social cooperation, because, as explained earlier, sacrifice is incompatible with genuine cooperation.

On the other hand, a local government would also avoid a system where only the wealthy pay taxes, making the entire tax structure dependent on their contributions. This is because the wealthy could also relocate, severely reducing the tax revenue. This disincentive to impose taxes exclusively on the wealthy promotes social cooperation, because the system's stability cannot depend on a small elite; otherwise, genuine cooperation breaks down.

Therefore, governments have incentives to adopt tax systems consistent with social cooperation, where burdens are sensitive to those with fewer resources but do not rest *solely* on the richest, which would make the system dependent on them. It is plausible they would settle on progressive direct taxes, differing in details like tax amounts, exact rates, or penalties

[12] Of course, they could emigrate to other countries, but that is much more difficult.

for non-compliance—or even proportional direct taxes, which, as argued, are also compatible with FSC's concept of social cooperation.

Is it feasible for a local government to impose *indirect* taxes within a federal system, given the incentives for people to leave? The answer is yes, and it happens frequently. For instance, U.S. states, operating under a federal tax system, typically include consumption taxes. As noted earlier, these taxes are regressive, meaning they place a heavier burden on less wealthy individuals. I previously argued that for these people, such contributions constitute a sacrifice rather than genuine cooperation—an argument that referred to indirect taxes imposed by the federal government, not local ones. So, if these taxes are regressive, how do they persist at the local level, where less affluent residents could move to areas with more favorable tax policies?

The quality of public services, better job opportunities, or greater prospects for advancement are some reasons why someone might choose to live in a place even if the local government imposes indirect taxes. While the regressivity of these taxes is a disadvantage, other benefits may outweigh it, leading individuals to conclude they are better off staying. Are indirect taxes incompatible with FSC when applied locally?

To be sure, it is not clear that those residents are forced to make a sacrifice for the system. They are not forced because it is their choice, and it is not a sacrifice if they accept the system's legal framework (with its advantages and disadvantages) as offering a promising future. Rather than a sacrificed person, we see someone moving to a place where they believe they can flourish. If this proves untrue, they can move again. The tension between regressive taxes and FSC arises when a central authority imposes them, forcing the less well-off to contribute in that way. In a federal system, in contrast, they can choose based on their life plans.

In short, to honor the FSC ideal, a federal tax system does not require all local taxes to be direct (though it does require all federal taxes to be direct). Local tax systems will probably be reasonable in the sense that they will be neither *deeply* regressive nor entirely dependent on an economic elite. Otherwise, as argued, they would lose too many taxpayers. There is no cause for concern if some local governments impose occasional indirect taxes without reaching extreme levels. If, despite this, people "vote with their feet"—that is, by choosing to remain in that territory—it indicates that the area still provides opportunities for full development under that tax system. In that case, such taxes are part of an institutional scheme that is compatible with FSC.

The conclusion is that a federal tax system is a cooperation scheme dependent on all local governments but on none individually: if a local government acts anti-cooperatively—by adopting a tax system too far removed from social cooperation—the overall cooperative scheme can still function because citizens can move to other jurisdictions. Moreover, the ability to vote with one's feet encourages local governments to avoid tax systems that stray too far from social cooperation—ideally variants of progressive or proportional direct taxes, though some may also include indirect taxes without threatening FSC, as explained earlier.

5.3.2.4 A Higher Tax Burden Does Not Necessarily Mean Higher Revenue

The state needs resources to function. So far, I have explored one of the three ways the state can raise these resources: taxation. In this section, I aim to examine the relationship between taxation and revenue collection.

Typically, those who believe the state should raise more resources than it currently does advocate for increasing the tax burden. However, in economics, the relationship between raising taxes and increasing revenue is debated. Economist Arthur Laffer, for example, argued that higher taxes do not always lead to higher revenue.[13] The idea is that tax rates influence people's incentives to work, save, invest, and produce, which directly affect tax revenues.

Imagine a state imposes a 0% tax rate. In this scenario, people have maximum incentives to work and produce, but the government collects no revenue. Conversely, if the tax rate is set at 100%, individuals have no incentive to work or produce, again resulting in zero revenue.

The optimal tax rate for maximizing revenue lies somewhere between 0 and 100%. The exact point depends on societal factors and remains debated. Beyond this optimal rate, increasing taxes no longer raises revenue because higher rates reduce incentives to work and produce. If the state is taxing at or beyond this point, increasing taxes will not generate more revenue; in fact, it may reduce it (Tucker 2009: 323).

[13] At a famous 1974 meeting, Laffer explained this idea to officials of U.S. President Gerald Ford's administration (see Wanniski 1978). Although Laffer's idea has faced criticism for assuming conditions that may not hold in practice, it remains valuable because it prompts us to consider that the relationship between higher tax burdens and increased revenue may not be straightforward and requires case-by-case analysis (Gahvari 1989).

5.3.2.5 *Paying Taxes Is Not the Only Way to Contribute (Nor Necessarily the Most Important)*

Thomas Edison is often credited with inventing the light bulb. He was among those who profited by helping others see what they were doing, especially at night. Today, our life expectancy is several decades longer than in Edison's time, and the light bulb—enabling, for example, surgeons to see clearly during operations—is one reason for this improvement in health and longevity.

Suppose Edison had given every cent he ever earned to a tax collector, all in the name of benefiting society. Even if he had given away every penny he made from the light bulb, it would not compare to the enormous benefit of having the light bulb itself. Edison's invention transformed society by extending productive hours, enabling nighttime work and activities, and sparking a vast electric lighting industry that forever changed the economy and daily life.

As you have likely noticed, I am not referring only to Edison. Any competent car mechanic might be doing more for their community by repairing thousands of cars—which, for instance, enables a surgeon to arrive on time for an operation—than by paying taxes on their services. Today, we can turn on a light almost without cost and see after the sun sets. We can fly across the Atlantic Ocean. We can speak with someone on the other side of the world. If asked where Edison grew up, we could provide a detailed report in two minutes using the Internet.

We may not be Edison, but we can do things Edison could hardly have imagined. Thanks to the cooperation of millions of people who wake up every day intending to contribute to their communities in countless ways, today we enjoy far more freedom than geniuses like Edison ever did (Johnson, Lusch, and Schmidtz 2019: 200–201).

5.3.3 *Public Debt*

Sometimes, governments approve budgets that involve spending more than they collect through taxes. A budget is a plan for expenditures over a specific period, usually one year. When, in a given year, tax revenues exceed spending, there is a surplus. Conversely, when government spending exceeds revenues, there is a deficit. Public debt is the accumulation of deficits over time. Therefore, a government can run a surplus in a given year while still carrying accumulated debt from past deficits.

Public debt can be divided into two types: domestic debt and external debt. Domestic debt is owed to the country's own citizens, typically consisting of bonds, bills, and other debt instruments held by individuals or businesses. External debt is contracted by a government with foreign institutions or countries. Among these lenders are the International Monetary Fund, the World Bank, the Inter-American Development Bank, and the Inter-American Investment Corporation. Usually, such loans are made—and must be repaid—in the creditor's currency. Debt obligations may be short or long term, with fixed or variable interest rates. Generally, the greater the risk of default (i.e., failure to meet payment obligations), the higher the interest rate required.

My objective is to analyze external debt from the perspective of FSC. While I do not analyze domestic debt directly, some conclusions will also apply to it.

FSC defines freedom as a cooperative practice for designing and realizing life plans. In this framework, everyone contributes and helps create the context in which people develop. Contributions need not be equal, as individuals have different capacities and can contribute only up to certain limits. Nonetheless, although contributions differ, none should be so large that the operation of the scheme depends on it.

As can be seen, reciprocity is inherent to FSC: everyone contributes to the scheme that constitutes everyone's freedom. As the scheme deviates from this scenario, cooperation loses its purity, and FSC diminishes. Suppose some participants are forced to direct some of their contributions not toward enriching a common freedom scheme, but *solely* toward increasing the freedom of others. This represents a departure from FSC. If this tendency deepens, and participants must direct all their contributions toward others' freedom, the scheme ceases to be common freedom and divides into two distinct schemes: one of serfs and one of masters. As the scheme moves away from FSC toward the opposite extreme, what began as a cooperative common scheme gradually splits—like a water droplet slowly dividing into two—until two schemes emerge, one of which must labor for the other.

Moreover, every cooperation scheme is by definition stable over time, even as participants renew across generations. This raises questions about what behaviors by current participants might jeopardize the scheme by harming future participants. The same principle applies: if future participants are forced to direct some of their contributions solely toward increasing current participants' freedom, the scheme deviates from FSC.

These reflections are important for understanding the conditions under which borrowing from international actors might constitute anti-cooperative behavior toward future participants. In this regard, it is important to distinguish two dimensions of external public debt: (1) the mechanism by which the state contracts external debt, and (2) the use of funds and mode of repayment.

Regarding the first dimension, the mechanism that best honors FSC is one giving voice to all sectors of society. Accordingly, the legislative branch, as the most representative body, should approve borrowing. Indeed, to enhance democratic legitimacy, the rules could require a qualified majority—for example, two-thirds of votes—in the legislature to approve international debt, although most societies require only a simple majority.

Regarding the second dimension, two distinctions are useful: (1) debts payable in the short term versus long term, and (2) projects that strengthen *only* current participants' freedom versus projects that strengthen freedom for current and future participants.

From these distinctions arise four possible scenarios: (a) current participants incur short-term debt to finance projects strengthening *only* their own freedom; (b) current participants incur short-term debt to finance projects benefiting current and future participants; (c) current participants incur long-term debt to finance projects strengthening *only* their own freedom; and (d) current participants incur long-term debt to finance projects enhancing freedom for current and future participants.

Scenario (a) seems straightforward. Suppose a democratic government mismanaged resources, squandering funds on unprofitable activities and running out of money for current expenses such as energy subsidies, public employee salaries, pensions, etc. Consequently, society, through its representatives, decides to incur debt with an international institution to cover these expenses; the debt, including interest, is to be paid in full within five years. If society repays on time, the cooperation scheme remains stable. Current participants absorb both the benefits and costs of borrowing. In practice, since funds finance current expenses rather than investments, repaying the debt (including interest) will be difficult (current spending does not generate wealth). However, that relates to borrowing prudence rather than FSC compatibility. Setting that aside, this mode aligns with FSC.

Scenario (b) involves current participants incurring short-term debt to finance a project that enhances freedom for both current and future participants. For example, investments in productive infrastructure—such as building roads, bridges, and tunnels—can lower transportation costs and stimulate economic growth. Although this project expands opportunities for both current and future participants, only current participants bear the costs because they must repay the debt quickly. However, the benefit to future participants does not destabilize the cooperation scheme, as current participants have voluntarily chosen this repayment mode—perhaps out of a social commitment to creating better opportunities for the future. Thus, this mode is also compatible with FSC.

Scenario (c) occurs when current participants incur debt to strengthen only their own freedom but refuse to shoulder all costs. Therefore, they borrow long term—say 50 years—to share costs with future participants who will pay part of the debt despite not directly benefiting from the loan. This destabilizes the cooperation scheme. As noted, reciprocity is inherent to FSC: everyone contributes to the scheme defining everyone's freedom. Cooperation is inherently mutual. As the scheme strays from this scenario, cooperation loses purity and FSC fades. This happens in (c): future participants are forced to contribute solely to increasing current participants' freedom. Thus, the scheme deviates from FSC.

Finally, scenario (d) represents a form of borrowing compatible with FSC, like (a) and (b). Here, current participants incur long-term debt so that both current and future participants share repayment costs, funding projects that enhance freedom for all—for example, infrastructure investments that lower transport costs and create more wealth, or funding science and technology programs whose benefits accrue over time. Although future participants have not explicitly approved the debt, since funds target projects expanding options for all and ultimately strengthen the scheme, this borrowing is a contribution, not a burden—and can be considered welcome.

In summary, the only form of borrowing that conflicts with FSC seems to be scenario (c), where current participants borrow to strengthen only their own freedom but shift repayment costs onto future participants.

As explained earlier, domestic debt is owed to a country's own citizens—typically individuals or companies. Governments may prefer domestic to external debt for several reasons. First, operating in local currency is easier as it avoids dealing with constant foreign currency fluctuations and cross-border transfers. Also, banks find local debt simpler: domestic issuance and creditors operate in a common language, reducing communication costs.

Broadly, the same reasoning for external debt applies to domestic debt. Its compatibility with FSC depends on current participants not imposing repayment costs on future participants unless projects also enrich the conditions in which future participants will live and expand their opportunities.

Finally, public debt is not the only practice that can affect future generations. Other behaviors, like environmental pollution or depletion of natural resources, can have similar effects. While not explored here,[14] the creation of state institutions aimed at minimizing such practices can foster cooperation between present and future generations. Being internal state institutions, their cooperative activities would qualify as intra-state, aimed at guiding the state in its role as a second-order cooperator that preserves the cooperation scheme *over time*.

5.3.4 *Monetary Issuance*

5.3.4.1 *The Monopoly on the Supply of Money*

Having already analyzed taxes and public debt, I now turn to monetary issuance. Strictly speaking, the state's authority to issue money (through the central bank) did not originally arise as a means to finance the state apparatus and government programs, but rather as a way to monopolize the money supply. However, as we will see, some legal systems today consider financing social programs to be one of the objectives of monetary issuance. This is why I include in this section an analysis of the central bank and its role in defining monetary policy.

At the beginning of this chapter, I explained that in a market economy, money can emerge spontaneously to facilitate commercial transactions. Money serves as a common denominator—a good representing everything that can be bought and sold—which helps avoid the high transaction costs inherent in a barter economy.

Today, in most modern societies, governments (1) designate a specific type of currency as legal tender and as the mandatory medium of exchange, and (2) retain the exclusive authority to issue that currency, maintaining a legal monopoly over it.

The first measure involves the state granting legitimacy to a single type of currency. "Legal tender" means that its nominal value is certified by

[14] For a detailed discussion, see González-Ricoy and Gosseries 2016.

the state on each unit and that this value must be accepted when settling debts. "Mandatory use" means that individuals cannot legally demand payment in any currency other than the designated legal tender.

Interpreted in the best possible light, this measure aims to ensure that money retains its status as a "common denominator," thus preventing the problems inherent in a barter economy. One could think that if there were hundreds of currencies through which trade could occur, we would return to a scenario where time and energy would be wasted searching for a trading partner who values the same currency as we do. Some might think that, in such a scenario, transaction costs would rise again, thereby hindering commercial activity (I will later analyze whether this reasoning is plausible).

The second measure is based on the idea that if anyone were allowed to issue the currency designated as legal tender, that currency would lose its value—essentially ceasing to exist in any meaningful sense—due to inflationary effects. To prevent this, societies typically grant a legal monopoly over the issuance of legal tender to a single entity: in the United States, this is the Federal Reserve; in Chile and Argentina, the Central Bank; and for European countries using the euro, the supranational European Central Bank. Throughout this text, I will use the term central bank generically to refer to all these institutions.

5.3.4.2 The Structure of the Central Bank

The central bank is one of the institutions that make up the state. Recall that the state consists of institutions that carry out intra-state cooperative activities (internal cooperation) aimed at preserving the state structure and ensuring it fulfills its functions properly. This means that the state itself is a cooperative system, with internal institutions that cooperate among themselves to direct it toward achieving its goals (and these institutions also engage in further internal cooperative activities at an even deeper level). Earlier, I referred to the three main branches of government (legislative, executive, and judicial). The central bank is a relatively new institution but currently performs functions of great importance, such as defining the government's monetary policy. For this reason, it deserves independent analysis.

As a state institution, the central bank carries out intra-state cooperative activities to help preserve the state structure and guide it toward fulfilling its functions. As an independent institution, the central bank sets limits to the political ambitions of the government. For example, an excessively expansionary monetary policy (issuing too much money) may yield short-term political gains by initially stimulating economic growth. Therefore, it can be tempting for the government in power to adopt such measures as elections approach, even though they may raise inflation expectations in the medium and long term, thereby compromising the country's economic future. The central bank's objective is to design a responsible monetary policy, free from political ambitions, and thereby help the state properly achieve its goals, with economic stability being one of its primary aims.[15]

On the other hand, it should be noted that in its interactions with other state institutions, the central bank not only sets limits; it is also constrained by other state entities. For example, mandatory accountability of the central bank to congress is a practice adopted by many democracies.

Furthermore, the central bank *aspires to* function as a cooperative system internally, with its various bodies collaborating closely to guide the institution in fulfilling its aim. Let us consider a few examples.

The United States Federal Reserve was established in 1913. According to regulations set forth by the Federal Reserve itself, its objectives include stabilizing prices, controlling long-term interest rates, promoting the soundness of financial institutions and the stability of the financial system as a whole, and maximizing employment.[16]

Bearing these objectives in mind, the Federal Open Market Committee (FOMC), an internal body of the Federal Reserve, formulates monetary policy. The main monetary policy tools at the Federal Reserve's disposal are (1) open market operations, (2) the interest rate the Federal Reserve pays on bank reserves, and (3) the reserve requirement ratio.

The voting members of the FOMC consist of the seven members of the Board of Governors (appointed by the president and confirmed by the U.S. Senate), the president of the Federal Reserve Bank of New York, and four presidents of the remaining Federal Reserve Banks, who serve on a rotating annual basis according to established regional groups. The FOMC meets eight times a year, and decisions are made by simple majority.

[15] The relationship between central bank independence and financial stability has been well documented. See, for example, Fraccaroli, Sowerbutts, and Whitworth 2020.

[16] https://www.federalreserve.gov/aboutthefed/fedexplained/who-we-are.htm (last accessed: August 17, 2025).

Meanwhile, the institution responsible for issuing euros for those European governments using the currency (the "Eurozone") is the European Central Bank (ECB), established in 1998. According to its own regulations, the ECB's primary objective is price stability in the Eurozone, defined by its Governing Council as inflation close to 2% over the medium term. It also aims to *contribute* to the stability of the financial system, while clarifying that the primary responsibility for financial stability lies with individual governments.[17] Unlike the Federal Reserve, the ECB does not have *social* objectives such as maximizing employment.

The ECB is composed of four bodies: the Governing Council (responsible for *defining* monetary policy), the Executive Board (responsible for *implementing* monetary policy), the General Council (which promotes the enlargement of the Eurozone, since not all European countries use the euro), and the Supervisory Board (which plans and executes the ECB's supervisory duties).[18]

As can be seen, the Governing Council is the primary decision-making body. Its mission is to define the Eurozone's monetary policy and, specifically, to set the interest rates at which commercial banks can borrow money from the Central Bank. Decisions are made by simple majority.

The Governing Council is composed of the six members of the Executive Board (the President, the Vice President, and four other members) along with the governors of the national central banks of the 21 Eurozone countries. In turn, the members of the Executive Board are appointed by the European Council, which is an *external* political body that includes the heads of state or government of the EU member countries. This appointment is done by a qualified majority vote, and the Executive Board members serve non-renewable terms of eight years.[19]

As can be observed, central banks can adopt at least two positions regarding their objectives. The first, which we might call a "narrow mandate," holds that the central bank's exclusive function should be to preserve the currency's value and promote financial stability. The second, or "broad mandate," holds that the central bank should also pursue social

[17] https://www.ecb.europa.eu/pub/pdf/other/ecbhistoryrolefunctions2006es.pdf (last accessed: August 17, 2025).

[18] https://www.ecb.europa.eu/ecb/orga/decisions/html/index.en.html (last accessed: August 17, 2025).

[19] https://www.ecb.europa.eu/ecb/orga/decisions/eb/html/index.es.html (last accessed: August 17, 2025).

goals, such as promoting employment and even social equity. While the European Central Bank clearly operates under a narrow mandate, the Federal Reserve leans toward a broad mandate. In Latin America, we also find examples of both approaches, as illustrated by Argentina (broad mandate) and Chile (narrow mandate).

On one hand, the Central Bank of Argentina was established in 1935. Within its internal structure, the body that defines monetary policy is the Board of Directors, which is supervised by another entity, the Internal Audit Office (Sindicatura). The Internal Audit Office's role is "to oversee the Central Bank's compliance with the provisions of the Organic Charter and other applicable regulations, reporting to the Board of Directors, the Executive Branch, and the National Congress on this compliance."[20]

The Board of Directors consists of a president, a vice president, and eight directors. Decisions are made by a simple majority of the ten members. The president, vice president, and directors are appointed by the Executive Branch with the Senate's approval, also by simple majority. They serve six-year terms and may be reappointed. Currently, the Central Bank of Argentina sets as its objectives the promotion of monetary stability, financial stability, employment, and "economic development with social equity."[21]

On the other hand, the Central Bank of Chile, founded in 1925, is governed by a Board of five members. The Board makes decisions on monetary policy, financial regulation, and exchange controls by simple majority. Members are appointed by the President of the Republic for ten-year terms, subject to Senate approval by simple majority.[22]

Additionally, the Central Bank of Chile has internal control bodies that oversee the institution's adherence to its functions: the General Manager, the Auditor, and the Comptroller.[23]

The Central Bank of Chile's objective is to safeguard the stability of the currency—that is, to maintain low and stable inflation over time—as well

[20] https://www.bcra.gob.ar/Institucional/Autoridades_Detalle.asp?Nombre=Sindico (last accessed: August 17, 2025).

[21] https://www.bcra.gob.ar/Institucional/Carta_Organica.asp (last accessed: August 17, 2025).

[22] https://www.bcentral.cl/contenido/-/detalle/ley-organica-constitucional-del-banco-central-de-chile-ley-n.c2b0-18.840-3 (last accessed: August 17, 2025).

[23] https://www.bcentral.cl/web/banco-central/el-banco/gobierno-corporativo/personas (last accessed: August 17, 2025).

as to promote the stability and efficiency of the financial system, ensuring the normal functioning of both domestic and international payments.[24] It does not consider social goals such as employment promotion or social equity.

I do not intend here to develop a theory on whether a central bank should adopt a narrow or broad mandate. Rather, my interest lies in offering observations on which internal structure of a central bank may be more effective in guiding it toward proper functioning. Since I remain neutral on whether the narrow or broad mandate is preferable, I define "proper functioning" as the central bank's tendency to fulfill the objectives it has been assigned, whatever those objectives may be.

For a central bank to truly operate as a genuine cooperative system, monetary policy decisions should be made collectively by the entire decision-making body rather than by any individual member or any organized faction. If the decision-making body became dependent on a particular faction, the bank's proper functioning would rely on that group's performance, which is incompatible with FSC, regardless of how well that group performs.

My analysis begins with two distinctions. The first is between large decision-making bodies and small decision-making bodies. The second is between heterogeneous decision-making bodies and homogeneous ones. By "heterogeneous," I mean bodies whose members represent different sectors (for example, different political parties, or even different countries, as is the case with a supranational central bank that sets monetary policy for several countries). It should be clarified that these distinctions are not black-and-white in practice. Bodies can be more or less numerous, and more or less heterogeneous. Nevertheless, these classifications serve to illustrate the point.

Based on these two distinctions, three possible scenarios arise: numerous and heterogeneous bodies, numerous and homogeneous bodies, and small and homogeneous bodies. A possible fourth scenario is small and heterogeneous bodies, although a body with few members cannot, in itself, be very heterogeneous.

In any case, it is the numerous and diverse bodies that best represent FSC. These bodies are least likely to be dominated by a stable coalition—that is, the system's proper functioning is less likely to depend on the

24 https://www.bcentral.cl/web/banco-central/el-banco/gobierno-corporativo/funciones-del-banco (last accessed: August 17, 2025).

performance of a particular group. While regularly renewing members helps to dilute concentrated power, it has its limits: a new member may well inherit the interests of their predecessor. Therefore, mere rotation of power cannot fully address the shortcomings of a small or homogeneous body.

Take the European Central Bank as an example. First, its decision-making body, the Governing Council, is relatively large, comprising 27 members. Second, this body is quite diverse: six members belong to another organ of the Central Bank (the Executive Board), while the remaining 21 are governors of the national central banks of the Eurozone, each representing a different country.

In this context, the formation of a stable, organized group dominating the system seems unlikely (though not impossible). Because the decision-making body is large, a coalition of just two or three members would be insufficient to control the system; a significantly larger coalition would be required and would need to remain intact over time to maintain dominance.

Furthermore, it is a heterogeneous body, with members representing different countries. Stable coalitions dominating the system are possible but less likely than when officials represent no specific interests beyond those of "the nation." When many individuals represent different countries—assuming those countries can exert political pressure on their representatives—stable coalitions become less probable because it is unlikely that the interests of, say, ten countries will remain fully aligned over time. If no one dominates the system, then the system does not depend on any single individual or organized group.

Still, it must be emphasized that although such coalitions are less likely, they are not impossible. It could happen that different representatives, each acting on behalf of their respective countries, are influenced by the same interest group—for example, the agricultural sector within each country. If these agricultural sectors maintain aligned interests over time, which is plausible, they could form a stable coalition dominating the system.

To address these risks, the central bank should strengthen its internal cooperative functions through supervisory bodies empowered to oversee the proper functioning of decision-making bodies. Central banks typically have internal entities responsible for these oversight roles. For example, as mentioned earlier, the Central Bank of Chile has a complex supervisory structure composed of three distinct bodies. In most modern societies, central banks also interact with other state institutions, such as the parliament, to which the central bank is systematically accountable.

I do not intend here to delve into the specific designs of decision-making bodies within central banks. Rather, my goal is to emphasize the importance of these bodies being sufficiently large and heterogeneous to minimize the risk of capture by particular interest groups. Ideally, the system would function as a genuine cooperative scheme, relying on everyone but on no one in particular. If any member were to act non-cooperatively—for example, by advocating policies that could trigger hyperinflation—the system could still function properly because the other members would veto such proposals. Crucially, given the system's size and diversity, it would be difficult for that member to gather enough support to push through their proposals. While ideal institutions may not exist in reality, we should nevertheless strive to approximate this ideal as closely as possible.

As can be seen, as a body becomes more homogeneous and/or smaller, the cooperative scheme deteriorates and FCS diminishes. This does not mean that smaller or more homogeneous bodies always produce worse results. FSC is a conception of freedom that aims to function as a theory of liberal democracy, rather than as a theory on how to guarantee price stability or financial stability. It is not impossible for a small and homogeneous body to achieve good results (even one person, making good decisions, could satisfactorily meet the central bank's goals). However, such a scenario would be far from the ideal of FCS, since the country's monetary policy would depend on the performance of a single individual.

5.3.4.3 Is the Central Bank Necessary?

Central banks are mostly known for setting their countries' monetary policy. However, this is not their only function; indeed, some authors argue that monetary policy was not the original purpose for which central banks emerged. Charles Goodhart (1988: 7), for example, claims that the *raison d'être* of central banks lies not in their monetary role but in "micro functions": essentially, generating and maintaining confidence in the banking system by monitoring banks and providing them with a source of reserves and liquidity.

The question addressed in this section is whether such a monopoly as exercised by the central bank is necessary or whether the same functions could be fulfilled by different entities within a decentralized scheme. From the perspective of FCS, this question is especially important. Recall that, in principle, the concept of monopoly conflicts with the ideal of FSC because, by placing certain functions in the hands of a single entity, the entire scheme becomes dependent on that entity's performance. Of course, once we accept that a certain monopoly is strictly necessary, FSC provides tools to ensure that such a monopoly does not threaten the cooperative scheme. For instance, when analyzing state structure, I referred to intra-state cooperative activities that guide this monopoly toward fulfilling its functions properly. However, this form of institutional design only becomes relevant once we have accepted that the monopoly is strictly necessary. Is this the case for the central bank?

Regarding the generation of confidence in the banking system, central banks are not the only alternative. For example, in the United States, primarily between 1857 and 1907, private clearinghouses emerged across different regions, playing a significant role in maintaining confidence in their respective banking systems by providing liquidity support and coordination during financial panics (Timberlake, Jr. 1984). Each clearinghouse grouped different banks, charging a capital fee for membership and subjecting them to periodic audits.

During crises, clearinghouses played a crucial role by issuing "loan certificates," which banks received in exchange for pledging assets as collateral. These certificates could be used as a form of currency to settle obligations with other financial institutions. By transferring this burden, banks were better equipped to meet public withdrawal demands and maintain liquidity during periods of financial stress.

The clearinghouse did not disclose which banks were requesting loan certificates, thereby preventing panic-driven runs on individual institutions. If a bank could not repay the loan certificates following the panic, it was subject to orderly liquidation. Should the amount owed exceed the value of its collateral, the losses were proportionally absorbed by other clearinghouse members according to their capital shares. Additionally, the indebted bank risked expulsion from the clearinghouse (Gorton 1985: 280–281, Ossa 1992: 19). The distinctive feature of clearinghouses was that they fulfilled some central bank functions competitively, without monopoly powers.

With respect to monetary policy, its definition and formulation are currently regarded as the central bank's primary functions. As explained, monetary policy may vary depending on the institution's goals. Some countries establish a narrow mandate for their central banks, limiting monetary policy to financial objectives—primarily price stability. Others adopt a broad mandate, allowing the central bank to pursue additional social objectives, such as promoting employment or supporting programs aimed at meeting broader societal needs.

If we assume the central bank should achieve social goals, then the debate over whether monetary policy should be state-established or left to the market loses relevance. The market consists of millions of people making dispersed decisions, not serving *particular* objectives. Social goals must be pursued by a centralized entity, which in our societies is the state. Therefore, conceding that monetary policy must serve social goals implies accepting that the money supply must be state-controlled. Perhaps this was one reason some governments have promoted these central bank functions: to leave no doubt about the institution's necessity.

I will set aside the social function adopted by some central banks and assume a narrow mandate, whereby the sole aim of monetary policy is price stability. Is it necessary to monopolize the money supply to achieve this goal?

Generally, economists agree that markets are the most efficient mechanism for resource allocation. However, many make an exception for money, arguing that the money supply must be heavily regulated and even monopolized. The key question is: what would happen if anyone could freely issue legal tender currency? One possible outcome is that the money supply would become excessively large, causing the currency to lose its value, resulting in astronomical inflation.

However, imagining a currency as legal tender is inappropriate when evaluating what would happen in an open currency market. In such a market, there would be no legal tender; private actors could issue their own currencies but would have no guaranteed users and would need to compete to attract them (Hayek 1978: 19–20). In turn, attracting customers is not achieved by creating a product destined to lose value over time; rather, people must find the product—in this case, that particular currency—attractive and trustworthy. So, if we decide to open our own bank, we could issue a currency—let us call it *pepitos*. For people to find this currency attractive and become our clients, we need to assure them that the currency will maintain its value. Thus, our "monetary policy" would be responsible for this assurance.

Pepitos do not exist, but successful examples of free banking systems and decentralized money supply have existed. The experiences of 19th-century Canada and 18th- to 19th-century Scotland serve as clear examples. Likewise, today there are non-state currencies such as Bitcoin, which are increasingly used in domestic and international transactions. The fact that buyers and sellers use (and trust) non-state currencies prompts us to reconsider the necessity of a currency monopoly.

Previously, I explained that money emerges to reduce transaction costs: in a barter system, finding a buyer or seller is difficult; money appears as a common denominator that facilitates exchanges. So far, I have assumed this reasoning supports the monopolization of the money supply: if money is a common denominator, there should be only one type; having many currencies would increase transaction costs, as people would choose different currencies, effectively returning us to a barter-like system.

However, this reasoning is questionable. Money, as an instrument to reduce transaction costs, is more a general concept than a specific good. It refers to any good practical to use as a medium of exchange and ideally capable of maintaining its value over time. Suppose we decide to sell a cellphone for a value X (for example, X defined in terms of a certain amount of gold). We care little whether the buyer pays with 10 *pepitos* (as long as 10 *pepitos* equal X) or 20 *juanitos* (as long as 20 *juanitos* equal X). What matters is that the currencies are sound and retain their value—these qualities ensure their survival in an open currency market.

Is a central bank truly necessary? When adopting a narrow mandate that limits its role exclusively to financial objectives, the answer is not straightforward. Alternative models—such as a competitive system of clearinghouses combined with an open currency market—represent viable options worth considering.

5.3.5 Conclusion

The state arises from the need for a centralized authority capable of carrying out second-order cooperative activities, thereby preserving the environment in which individuals produce goods and services. However, given the state's nature as a monopoly, it can only be compatible with FSC if its internal bodies engage in intra-state cooperative activities that guide the state toward the proper fulfillment of its functions.

To perform its functions, the state requires financing. In this section, I have examined the main mechanisms available to the state for revenue collection: taxation, public debt, and, in certain cases, monetary issuance. The conclusion is that FSC is not inherently incompatible with these financing mechanisms, but it does impose specific conditions to ensure they preserve a cooperative orientation.

First, the tax system must avoid placing an excessive burden on those with the least resources so as not to transform *cooperation* into *sacrifice*, while also ensuring it does not rely solely on contributions from an economic elite, thereby preventing dependence on them.

Second, to preserve the element of reciprocity essential to cooperation, public debt should be structured so that it does not benefit only current participants by imposing costs disproportionately on future ones.

Finally, the internal structure of the central bank must embody a strong cooperative logic. This includes broad and diverse decision-making bodies and oversight organs, ideally subject to control by other state institutions such as the legislature, to ensure the central bank remains properly oriented toward fulfilling its functions with a cooperative spirit.

5.4 Market as a Scheme of Cooperation

5.4.1 The Market and Dispersed Knowledge

When we hear the word "institution," we often picture a building or some other physical structure. However, this image is misleading. Institutions (or conventions, as David Hume called them) are invisible frameworks composed of codes of conduct or sets of rules—whether written or unwritten—that enable people to know what to expect from one another, thereby creating predictability. Institutions can be political, such as the three branches of government; social, like friendship or religion; legal, such as family law or traffic regulations; or economic, like the market.

Before beginning the analysis of the institution of the market, it is important to clarify what kind of institution we are dealing with. We can distinguish between two types of institutions.

The first type includes institutions designed to enable their members to collaborate in achieving one or several concrete goals. What makes these institutions intelligible is the attainment of defined objectives; without such goals, they would have no reason to exist. For example, the judiciary falls into this category as a network created to resolve disputes between individuals. Similarly, other political institutions—such as the legislative and executive branches—fit this classification, as do some social institutions like religion, which seeks to provide an environment where followers may practice their faith.

The second type includes institutions that are not organized around having their members fulfill defined objectives. The quintessential example of this type is the market. For instance, Robert Nozick (1974: 150–164) understood the market as an environment where people can pursue a wide range of goals, from creating a software company to founding a non-governmental organization dedicated to helping indigenous peoples. I will elaborate further on this characteristic of the market in a later section. For now, it suffices to emphasize that market participants are not necessarily aligned toward achieving defined objectives.

Given this characteristic of the market, it would be inappropriate to refer to this institution in the same way we refer, for example, to the institutions of the state. Some people debate whether the provision of certain goods or services, or even their prices, should be regulated by the state or "by the market." The idea that the market can "regulate" is mistaken because it suggests that it consists of people organized to achieve a specific purpose. The market is millions of individuals freely making exchanges and decisions about their own lives, thereby pursuing millions of diverse goals. To claim that the market has regulatory capacity is to misunderstand its nature. The goods or services transferred through the market, as well as their prices, are the result of the actions of millions of people, but not of a *plan* organized by them. Interestingly, markets are products of human *action*, but not of human *design*.

The market is the environment in which individuals engage in first-order cooperative activities related to the production and provision of goods and services. In earlier sections, I explained why private property and the market are a far more effective source of wealth generation than the old model of collective property characteristic of the primitive cooperation system. However, the market economy can also be understood by contrasting it with another model: a "centrally planned economy," where production, investment, prices, and wages are determined by the government (consider, for example, the economic model of the Soviet Union). As I will explain in detail later, this system is incompatible with FSC because all economic activities are concentrated in a single body, leaving participants in the scheme dependent on its proper functioning.

Of course, the fact that, for economic reasons, centralized planning tends to perform poorly exacerbates the problem. As Friedrich Hayek (1945) argued, markets transmit information that enables the satisfaction of needs and preferences far more effectively than any state economic plan. Hayek distinguishes between two types of knowledge. The first is scientific knowledge, which can be expressed through generalizations and thus easily communicated to others. However, Hayek emphasizes that most of the knowledge required to generate wealth is not captured by explicit generalizations but is instead embodied in decisions based on local and changing circumstances, to which individual agents have unique access. This second type of knowledge—knowledge of "the particular circumstances of time and place"—cannot be *formulated* and therefore cannot be communicated to others.

Note that Hayek does not deny the merits of economic planning; his point is that such "planning"[25] is only possible in the *decentralized* form that takes place in a market economy, which presupposes property rights. Even assuming that the planner could *process* all relevant information to allocate resources efficiently, they cannot *obtain* that information. This is not merely a technical difficulty, perhaps temporary, related to methods of information gathering: that information cannot even be formulated in a way that can be communicated. Hayek seems to be referring to a type of knowledge that Gilbert Ryle (1946) calls "knowing how," in contrast to "knowing that."

"Knowing that" refers to a type of propositional knowledge. "Knowing how," on the other hand, refers to a type of practical knowledge. An example of practical knowledge is knowing how to ride a bicycle: no one acquires that skill by reading a book filled with sentences that express true propositions about the movements of a good cyclist. Hayek seems to point to this distinction between "knowing that" and "knowing how" when he writes that the gains obtained in the market depend on information about "the particular circumstances of time and place." For example, sandwich vendors outside a soccer stadium make decisions (what ingredients to use, where and when to set up shop, what drinks to offer, and so forth) based on past experiences, guesses about the preferences of that specific crowd, information about input prices, and so on—none of which can be fully expressed in any set of propositions. Of course, this reflection applies to any other agent in the market (Pincione 2015: 2461–2463).

Governments that have attempted to centrally plan the economy have failed spectacularly. For example, from 1958 to 1962, China experienced a catastrophe of historic proportions known as the Great Chinese Famine. During this period, the communist government controlled the vast majority of social resources and monopolized production and distribution, making individuals heavily dependent on this apparatus. The

[25] However, we must be careful with this expression, since, as I clarified earlier, it is not correct to say that the market "regulates" or "plans."

government dictated which types of crops to plant and where, as well as how the resulting products were distributed. The consequence was a massive food shortage that caused the deaths of an estimated 30 to 45 million people due to famine.

5.4.2 *The Role of Prices*

What mechanism does the market use to transmit knowledge that cannot be expressed in propositional formulas? According to Hayek, it is precisely the prices that emerge in the market that serve as the vehicle through which knowledge of particular circumstances of time and place is communicated. Prices are, ultimately, a form of language.

What is language about? While artificial languages, such as computer languages, are deliberately constructed, most languages are natural. They emerge spontaneously through social interaction. Language is an ongoing, dynamic process through which people adapt to one another. No single person designed the process by which languages evolve; instead, they develop collectively and continuously over time.

Like language, prices are a form of communication. As we offer a good or service, it gains a price. Like language, prices allow people to form mutual expectations. Prices help people coordinate in complex ways as they individually decide what to produce or consume. Thinking that an authority needs to decide what the price of corn should be is like thinking an authority needs to decide what sound people should make when referring to corn. No one needs to decide. Coordination emerges spontaneously.

Price signals enable people to respond to information they do not directly possess. Prices fluctuate—they can rise or fall for many reasons—and these changes alert us to react appropriately even if we are unaware of the specific causes behind them. In other words, price changes inform us that something significant is occurring, allowing us to adjust our behavior accordingly without needing to know all the details.

Imagine the price of a good increases. The reason might be that production costs have risen, or that the good has become more essential in a particular location—leading to increased demand and higher prices—or perhaps political unrest has made the product harder to obtain, causing scarcity and price spikes. We do not need to know the exact cause of the increase. What matters is that this price rise conveys critical information: the good is becoming relatively scarcer, and therefore we should economize its use.

Conversely, imagine the price of a good decreases. This might be due to increased production creating strong competition, the discovery of a cheaper substitute, or a drop in production costs. Again, we do not need to know the specific reason; the falling price signals abundant supply, warning that it may not be wise to start producing that good. For example, to decide whether to offer carpentry services in Madrid, one checks how much carpenters earn. If prices have plummeted, it indicates an oversupply, and the market likely does not need another carpenter.

As these examples show, prices guide us on how best to contribute to society. If we wish to contribute, we must provide something others value. Checking prices—assuming they are undistorted by government intervention—reveals the most effective way to do so.

If prices represent a form of communication, governments have good reason not to control them. Price controls—minimum or maximum—are state-imposed restrictions that limit price fluctuations. Minimum prices aim to keep prices above a certain level to protect producers, while maximum prices seek to cap prices to protect consumers.

In simple terms, if prices transmit vital information, price controls distort this information. Prices fluctuate in response to market changes affecting supply and demand, reflecting people's preferences. When the government sets prices, it interferes with this natural communication, often resulting in false signals.

For instance, when the market price of a good falls, it indicates that demand at higher prices could not be met—perhaps because consumers lack the money or prefer substitutes. Continuous price drops signal that entering that market may not be profitable. However, if the government prevents prices from falling, the good remains artificially expensive despite low demand. This false signal encourages overproduction, leading to surpluses and waste. During the Great Depression, minimum price supports for agricultural products led to the disposal of massive food quantities because consumers could not afford the inflated prices.

Conversely, if prices are high, it indicates scarcity relative to demand, signaling potential profits to new producers. When governments cap prices to prevent increases, prices remain artificially low despite scarcity. This misleads consumers into overconsumption and discourages suppliers from entering the market, resulting in shortages. For example, in 2003, the Argentine government imposed maximum electricity prices to protect consumers, but the artificially low prices conveyed false information, boosting consumption and ultimately causing widespread power outages.

5.4.3 *The Market as a Form of Social Cooperation*

In 1959, Vice President Richard Nixon showed Soviet Premier Nikita Khrushchev a model of a six-room American house. Khrushchev and the Soviet press ridiculed it, suggesting it was a lie. Western journalists, stunned, realized that Khrushchev was not joking. Khrushchev was not a laborer but a high-ranking official of the Soviet Union. Yet somehow, even he had been deceived by communist propaganda. Everyone realized that the Soviet Union was so incredibly misinformed that even its leader, Khrushchev, had no idea that such a lifestyle was possible for average Americans. The model house Khrushchev thought impossible was sold for $14,000. It had been built to be affordable for typical steelworkers at that time.

In a centrally planned economy, such as the Soviet Union, the planner cannot know whether to order a factory to produce plastic or metal shovels, gold or aluminum wire, or leather or canvas shoes. Planners must guess what to produce and where to send it. People stand in line for hours to receive whatever is distributed that day. Perhaps they go home with a plastic shovel. If it is useful, they may trade it (on the black market) for canvas shoes, which might have been distributed to someone else on another day. The fundamental fact remains that a factory producing plastic shovels will neither know nor care if it is producing something useful. There is no incentive to worry since there will be no paying customers anyway, except in the black market.

The Soviet GDP per man-hour in 1987 was less than a third of that of the United States. In 1800, when 95% of workers were farmers, many countries could not feed all their citizens. Today, some of those countries, which employ less than 2% of their workforce in agriculture, produce food in excess. Most people now living in these countries are completely freed from the chains of hunger and no longer need to worry about food production. Many strive to make lasting contributions to literature, art, or technology. Historically, commercially advanced societies have produced not only goods and food but also artists, poets, and inventors. It is no coincidence that cultural centers have often coincided with commercial hubs: Athens in ancient Greece, Venice and Florence during the Renaissance, and New York today (Johnson, Lusch, and Schmidtz 2019: 66–67).

A centrally planned economy is fundamentally at odds with the concept of equality underlying FSC. Centralizing economic power makes us dependent on the proper functioning of a single participant—in this case, the state bureaucracy. It is unnecessary to assume that the government harbors ill intentions; nor is it essential to emphasize that under such a system we would be subject to the goodwill of the state, as a proponent of republican freedom might argue. Even if, by some extraordinary circumstance, we could be certain that the government always acted with the best intentions and maintained that goodwill over time regardless of circumstances, we would still lack freedom in terms of FSC. We would be compelled to shape our lives based on the likelihood that the government can fulfill these good intentions. The fact that, for economic reasons, this likelihood is extremely low—and that the government's performance as a centralized planner is virtually doomed to fail—exacerbates the problem. Thus, even under morally ideal conditions, people's freedom would rest on a very fragile foundation.[26]

The market, on the other hand, is deeply divided, as it consists of thousands or even millions of people working independently; everyone's contribution is essential, but the contribution of any particular individual is dispensable. In other words, the market is, *in principle*,[27] sufficiently decentralized so that we all depend on everyone else without depending on anyone in particular. No one is obliged to make their contribution since no one can be forced to belong to a cooperative scheme. However, the antisocial behavior of some people who abstain from contributing does not endanger the system. For example, if a supermarket raises prices, we can shop elsewhere; if a clothing brand starts producing low-quality products, we can choose another; if we want to fly abroad, we are not dependent on a single airline; if we want leisure activities, we have hundreds of options, ranging from natural science museums to heavy

[26] On the other hand, note that I do not assert (nor dismiss) that this situation leads to a lack of freedom through social causation mechanisms (Hayek 1944, Friedman, M. 1962: 7–17). This is a well-known proposition and will not be analyzed here. The link I affirm here is constitutive. In a centrally planned economy, people lack freedom because they *depend on* the proper performance of a particular group of people: there is no genuine scheme of *cooperation*.

[27] Later, in Sect. 5.5, I will analyze the problem of monopolies.

metal concerts; if a sports club is full and cannot accept more members, dozens of other clubs will welcome us. Ultimately, we rely on the talents and abilities of others, although, since so many people participate, we do not depend on anyone in particular.

The idea that the market is a form of social cooperation may seem strange, but appearances can be deceiving. In fact, social cooperation is the fundamental activity of the market. Let us think about our own reality. There is almost nothing we can do without the assistance of millions of people we will never meet. Suppose we want to do something simple enough not to require anyone's help—for example, prepare a pizza. We would start by making the dough. How would we do it? We would need to buy flour from a store. But remember, we want to prepare the pizza without anyone's help. Therefore, we must grow the grain and mill the flour ourselves. How would we do that? We could buy a plow, but to prepare the pizza without anyone's help, we would have to build our own plow. And, of course, if the plow is made of metal, we would not want anyone else's help digging up that ore—we would do it ourselves, with our own hands. We could not even use a shovel because that, too, would require metal to make (Johnson, Lusch, and Schmidtz 2019: 1).

Fortunately, we belong to a cooperative scheme. We cooperate with others, and others cooperate with us. If we want a pizza, we can work for a few hours to earn a wage. We benefit someone who needs our work, and in return, we benefit by receiving remuneration. Then, we can use that wage to reward thousands of strangers around the world who carry out thousands of activities culminating in delivering a pizza—activities no one living could have done alone. We can order a pizza that will be in our hands in ten minutes, instead of making it without anyone's help, which might take more than ten years. We spend an hour ordering and enjoying a pizza, and in the remaining ten years, we have the freedom to, for example, study a degree, graduate, start a business, fall in love, get married, and even have children. Relying on the abilities of others allows us to develop and carry out our own plans. And by contributing to this scheme, we are benefiting not only people close to us but also people we will never meet: if, for example, we dedicate ourselves to making nails, we will never know where the next nail we produce will end up or who it will help. We might sell many nails to many wholesale buyers, who in turn might resell them. Perhaps some will end up as part of furniture in a home, benefiting a young couple. Others might become part of wheelchairs, helping hundreds of patients in a hospital.

Ultimately, when this type of interaction occurs among millions of participants across a wide range of products, it results in a vast network of cooperation, enabling each of us to design and pursue our own life plans.

5.4.4 *The Market Is Not a Zero-Sum Game*

The popular idea that the market is incompatible with social cooperation likely stems from the mistaken belief that the market is a zero-sum game. What is a zero-sum game?

In society, people have two main ways to get what they want. The first is by harming others—for example, stealing. The second is by benefiting others—for example, trading. In other words, we bring services that others desire to the market and offer them at prices they can afford. In doing so, we aim to benefit our fellow citizens and, consequently, improve our own situation.

A zero-sum game is an interaction where one person's gain comes at the expense of another's loss. When there is consent and the goal is entertainment, zero-sum games can be exciting—for example, sports or card games like poker. In other cases, zero-sum games signal societal decay: theft, fraud, and scams are zero-sum games that harm people; when repeated, they show that institutions are failing. For instance, if we steal $10 from someone, we gain $10 and our neighbor loses $10. The total wealth change from this interaction is zero: adding "10" (our gain) and "-10" (their loss) results in "0." Hence the term "zero-sum game." We only improve our situation because someone else is worse off.

A positive-sum game, by contrast, is an interaction that creates net gains, meaning value has been added. Using a familiar metaphor, in positive-sum games, the pie grows. Trade is a positive-sum game: all parties involved benefit from the transaction. If we buy a cellphone for $200, it means the seller values the $200 more than the phone, and we value the phone more than the $200. As a result, both of us are better off than before. Progress arises not from harming others, but from benefiting them. That is the "magic" of trade.

What is the relationship between trade and the market? The market is the context in which trade occurs. When we think of traders, we usually imagine people with a clothing business or other product on a busy avenue. But any voluntary exchange qualifies as trade: from buying a hot dog at a football stadium to paying university tuition. When these simple transactions are multiplied by billions, we can predict that society will be much richer and everyone will be better off. We find a cooperative scheme built by everyone, but whose functioning does not depend on anyone in particular. The essential activity in the market is cooperation, not competition, because in the market we do not progress if we do not think about what others need or prefer. In fact, at its best, the market is characterized by people being so eager to serve one another that they actively *compete* to do so (Johnson, Lusch, and Schmidtz 2019: 3).

5.4.5 *Equality of Opportunity?*

Once we understand that the market is a positive-sum, cooperative game, we are in a position to see why the popular ideal of "equality of opportunity" suggests a mistaken characterization of the market.

This ideal holds that a person's future should be shaped more by their choices than by the circumstances they are born into. A key implication is that every child deserves a quality education, regardless of their family's socioeconomic background or financial means. If everyone truly starts from an equal footing, then any social or economic inequalities that emerge later are justified because they reflect each person's merit—their talents and effort—rather than factors beyond their control, like family background. Thus, it is fair for some people to be wealthier than others only if their greater wealth is a result of greater talent and harder work.[28] However, these differences are unfair when they result from some people starting "further ahead," meaning they were lucky enough to have wealthier parents or to grow up in a more privileged environment. The starting line must be equal for everyone.

This ideal is widely accepted. Nevertheless, we must be careful in interpreting it because it lends itself to confusion about the nature of the market. The problem is that, as it is usually portrayed, it suggests that life in society is necessarily like a race. In a race, winning means getting ahead and leaving others behind, so one person's gain means others' loss. Fortunately, society does not have to come to this.

Life in society may or may not be a race, depending on how its rules are defined. If the way to progress is by harming others, then it is possible that society will end up resembling a race. If the way to progress is to

[28] According to an even more ambitious conception of equality of opportunity, not even different talents can justify socioeconomic differences, since talents are also undeserved (Rawls 1999: 86–87).

trade, then society is quite different from a race. When institutions are properly designed, the main way to progress is by benefiting others.

In a genuine market economy, personal progress does not mean leaving others behind in a race. Instead, it means reaching out to others and offering a good or service they need or want at a price they can afford. In such a system, you cannot advance by focusing solely on yourself; you must consider the other person's perspective, empathize with their needs, and find ways to make their life easier. This is how modern economies function, and the results are far better compared to societies that suppress the market economy, where life can truly feel like a race, with ordinary people scrambling to the supermarket just to get what little remains.

The goal of society should not be to rank people's relative performance as if life were a competition, but to create a safer, more livable environment where individuals can develop and pursue their life plans cooperatively; where no one needs to win and no one is doomed to lose; where everyone depends on one another, but no one is at anyone's mercy.

It is important to note that this is not a rejection of the ideal of equality of opportunity itself, but rather a critique of one particular interpretation that necessarily frames life as a race. While this ideal may encourage thinking in terms of competition, it does not depend on that metaphor. Even if we acknowledge that the market is not a zero-sum game and benefits all participants, we can still argue that it does not benefit everyone equally. This inequality would be unjust if we reasonably assume that everyone ought to have a roughly equal chance to access various social or economic positions.

In the next chapter, I develop a theory based on FSC explaining why the state should guarantee everyone the possibility to access goods and services such as housing, health, and education, among others. The resulting theory preserves the spirit of the ideal of equality of opportunity, although its foundation will not be to equalize conditions at a supposed starting line where the race begins, but rather to incorporate all people into the social cooperation scheme.

5.4.6 *The Market: Do Only the Best Benefit?*

FSC rests on the idea that freedom is a cooperative practice. People can develop and carry out their life plans because they receive cooperation from others. For cooperation to exist, then, people have to make their contribution to the scheme. This is the element of reciprocity that characterizes cooperative schemes. This does not imply that a centralized authority should verify that people's contributions are equally important. The type of contribution a person makes should depend on their capabilities—and even their preferences, as I will explain. In fact, demanding too much from people without considering their abilities would turn cooperation into self-sacrifice. As I have already pointed out, by definition, cooperation is an activity that does not consume a large part of one's life.

Moreover, it is doubtful that there is such a thing as more important and less important contributions. People develop and carry out life plans by virtue of the *whole set* of contributions made by everyone, without it being clear that some can be distinguished as more or less relevant. For example, a surgeon who operates on patients and saves lives apparently makes a greater contribution than someone who repairs cars, cleans houses, or stocks supermarket shelves. However, the surgeon can devote time to practicing medicine because there are other people who carry out those supposedly less relevant tasks. Arguably, society is a complex network of interactions that constitute the environment in which people develop and carry out life plans; a network that must be considered as a whole, because each contribution depends, in turn, on the others. Therefore, it cannot be said that one is more important than another.

If this reasoning is correct, individuals should be allowed to contribute according to their own preferences. Since individuals benefit from the network of contributions as a whole, rather than from any specific contribution, there is no justification for forcing anyone to make a particular kind of contribution merely because it is deemed more important.

A common belief is that, in a market economy, only the best succeed. This misconception likely arises from the false notion that markets are defined by competition rather than cooperation. If the market were purely competitive, it might make sense to think that only the best prevail while those lacking particular skills are doomed to failure.

However, as I argued earlier, the core activity in the market is cooperation, not competition. Here, I aim to directly challenge the notion that those who are not the best at anything are destined for poverty. My argument rests on the well-known theory of comparative advantage, but to understand it fully, one must first grasp the concept of opportunity cost.

5.4.6.1 Opportunity Cost

Opportunity cost is the loss incurred by choosing one course of action over another. In other words, it is the benefit foregone when one alternative is chosen instead of another. For example, if we have two options, A and B, and choose A, our opportunity cost is the benefit we would have gained by choosing B—and vice versa.

Consider two job offers: one paying $2000 per month and the other $1500 per month, assuming all else is equal (same tasks, hours, etc.). By choosing the $2000 offer, our opportunity cost is $1500 per month—the benefit foregone from not taking the other job. This cost is worthwhile since choosing the $1500 offer would have a higher opportunity cost of $2000 per month.

Opportunity costs are inevitable because we cannot do everything and must make choices. Suppose we want to earn both salaries; we could accept both jobs if schedules permit. However, this also comes with a significant opportunity cost: no time for rest, family, or hobbies. Opportunity costs are not only monetary—they include any valuable activity we forgo by choosing a different course of action.

Opportunity costs are often hidden. Accountants include production costs like materials, transport, and taxes in financial statements but do not reflect missed opportunities. Yet, these costs are crucial when making decisions.

Finally, recognizing opportunity costs and the finite nature of time reveals that nothing is truly free. For instance, if someone offers free ice cream in the park, standing in line means sacrificing time that could be spent playing soccer, studying, or working. Once opportunity cost is considered, even "free" ice cream has a cost.

5.4.6.2 The Theory of Comparative Advantage

The theory of comparative advantage was developed by the British economist David Ricardo (1817). Although originally formulated to explain the benefits of free trade between countries, this theory also helps dispel the myth that, in a market economy, those who are not particularly skilled at any activity are destined to fail.

First, it is important to distinguish between two types of advantage: absolute and comparative. Absolute advantage is the ability to produce more or better goods and services than anyone else. In contrast, comparative advantage is the ability to produce a certain good or service at a lower opportunity cost than others. The key insight is that we can benefit even if we do not have an absolute advantage, because in a market economy, people's commercial activities are driven not by their absolute advantages but by their comparative advantages.

LeBron James is probably the best basketball player in the world. Yet it is easy to imagine that if LeBron wanted to be a shelf-stocker at a supermarket, he would also be the best at that. He is very tall and strong. He has long arms. Therefore, if absolute advantage is what matters, LeBron would outperform anyone in that job.

Now consider Peter, a 20-year-old who wants to get his first job to finance his university studies. He sees that a supermarket is looking for a shelf-stocker to work in the mornings. LeBron may be much better at stocking than Peter, so LeBron has an absolute advantage. Should Peter be discouraged by this? No, because even though Peter does not have an absolute advantage over LeBron, he does have a comparative advantage. And comparative advantage is what matters. But what does this mean?

Peter can do the stocking job at a lower opportunity cost than LeBron. Peter attends university in the afternoon and usually has mornings free. It is true that he will not have much time to study at home during the day, but he can make time at night to study for a couple of hours each day. On weekends, he can spend time with friends, family, and other activities.

LeBron's situation is different. For him, the opportunity cost of working as a shelf-stocker is astronomical because he would have less time to train, his level of play would decrease, and he could lose billions of dollars in career earnings and endorsements. Peter has an overwhelming advantage over LeBron regarding the supermarket job, but this is a comparative advantage (Johnson, Lusch, and Schmidtz 2019: 96).

Now suppose Bill Gates is the best software developer in the world. Our friend John is also a software developer, though not as good as Bill. Imagine John is applying for a highly paid job at a major company. Of course, Bill would be a much better candidate for the position because he has an absolute advantage. But John does not need to be better than Bill to succeed. In fact, since John is not better than Bill, he has a comparative advantage, because the opportunity cost of taking this job is much lower for him. Bill cannot spend time working at this company, even though the job is well paid. He would lose millions of dollars because he would have to give up other activities.

Finally, imagine a small law firm with a lawyer, Linda, and an intern, Robert. The intern is responsible for organizing materials, handling court paperwork, and similar tasks. Of course, Linda is a better lawyer than

Robert, who has not yet graduated. But Linda would also perform better than Robert at the intern tasks. Thus, Linda has an absolute advantage over Robert in both activities. However, both benefit from specializing according to their comparative advantages and disadvantages. Let me explain.

Suppose Linda, as a lawyer, produces the equivalent of $175 per hour, but if she devoted herself to intern tasks, she would produce the equivalent of $25 per hour. Robert can produce the equivalent of $0 per hour as a lawyer, since he lacks the qualifications, but he can produce the equivalent of $20 per hour performing intern tasks. Although Linda is better than Robert at both activities, by performing intern tasks she would lose $175 per hour in potential legal work. Her opportunity cost of doing intern tasks is high. Therefore, it is advantageous for her to focus on practicing law and hire an intern. Robert's opportunity cost is lower than Linda's. Regarding the intern position, Robert has a comparative advantage over Linda. Thanks to this comparative advantage, Robert benefits as the intern position gives him the opportunity to gain valuable work experience.

As mentioned earlier, the theory of comparative advantage can also apply to international trade. Many criticize trade liberalization because they argue that countries without any outstanding advantages would be excluded and, having nothing to offer, would not create jobs for their people. They then advise these countries to close off and produce everything they need themselves; even if the products are not high quality, at least people would have jobs.

However, this reasoning assumes that absolute advantages are what matter. Actually, international trade, like local trade, can function based on comparative advantages. For example, in recent years, India has become the main provider of call center services for the North American market, even though the English proficiency of these employees is generally low. North American companies could offer better call center services with native English speakers. However, the opportunity cost of providing these services domestically would be high, as they would have to forgo other more profitable activities. Therefore, they choose to hire services from India, which benefits from this trade because these people have a lower opportunity cost.

Thanks to the theory of comparative advantage, we can conclude that in a market economy, even those who are not highly skilled at anything can benefit and find their place in the cooperative scheme. Of course, this does not mean that people should resign themselves to being shelf-stockers or legal interns. As I will explain in Sect. 5.5.3.2, social mobility is essential for individuals to find work that is fulfilling. This section aimed only to illustrate that even individuals at the initial stage of entering the workforce—who may not yet be highly skilled at any particular task—can find their place from which to contribute meaningfully.

5.4.7 *The Market and Neutrality*

Another common criticism of the market economy is that, far from being neutral, it corrupts human beings by promoting selfishness and greed. The reflections made in Sect. 5.4.1 are particularly relevant here. Thinking of the market as an institution serving certain predetermined goals is a misunderstanding of its nature. Similarly, it is mistaken to view the market as an institution that promotes particular character traits (even if we assume that this is not its purpose, but merely an incidental outcome).

The market is essentially chaotic: millions of people making decisions about their own lives every day, with millions of different goals—from entrepreneurs developing new software to benefactors working for the common good, including doctors, philosophers, artisans, musicians, psychologists, and so on. In fact, the market does not only include monetary transactions but encompasses any kind of agreement based on the consent of the parties involved. This includes groups voluntarily organized to defend social causes, such as Black Lives Matter and Me Too, as well as communities that choose lifestyles independent of profit motives, like the kibbutzim in Israel. It would be an enormous coincidence if this vast and diverse array of interactions—which we will never fully know—were all geared toward promoting just one or two traits, such as selfishness and greed.

It is not even clear that *monetary* transactions embody selfishness and greed (Darwall 1999: 145). Unlike a system based on force, such as feudal regimes, in a market economy people usually collaborate with one another in developing and carrying out life plans. It means recognizing that it is wrong to use others to pursue our ends and that it is wrong for others to use us to pursue theirs. So, if we want others to collaborate with us in achieving our goals, we must humbly approach them and offer our own cooperation so that they can also achieve their goals. That is all that commercial exchange in a market economy is about. It is not obvious how selfishness and greed can be identified in such interactions.

Now, perhaps we are considering the weakest version of this criticism of the market. Maybe the stronger version is not that the market lacks neutrality because it promotes selfishness and greed, but that it lacks neutrality because it is a social structure that constantly shapes our lives toward certain activities. For example, in a recent and interesting work, Waheed Hussain introduces an objection to the market economy based on its supposed authoritarian character. According to the author (2023: 134), a market economy is not a neutral system that simply provides people with certain rights and options. It is a social control mechanism that shapes people's activities according to production and consumption patterns (Hussain 2023: 136). Supply and demand systematically change over time, *influencing* people to produce one good or another and shaping the set of options available to each *individual* consumer.[29] This process unfolds bypassing individuals' judgments about whether the different supply and demand equilibria are justified (Hussain 2023: 118). Therefore, the market structure can be considered authoritarian (Hussain 2023: 135).

However, it is not clear how an impersonal process like the market can be authoritarian. A de facto president could be considered authoritarian if they take measures not approved by the citizenry. A parent could be considered authoritarian if they impose totally arbitrary rules on their children. But the market is not an agent making deliberate decisions.[30] In what sense, then, is it authoritarian?

To be sure, when we live in society, to some extent, others' choices can shape our own scope of action. Supply and demand express the preferences of the entire population (including ourselves), and it is true that no one asks us whether the current equilibrium is justified. Living in

[29] The word "individual" is important because it would not be accurate to say that the supply of goods *shapes* the set of options available to the *entire* group of consumers, since it is precisely the group of consumers (the demand) who determine, with their aggregated preferences, which goods will be offered.

[30] Hussain acknowledges that the market is not an entity making decisions, but an impersonal process made up of millions of people. In fact, he disagrees with those who hold large corporations responsible for market oppression of individuals: "… this personalized view of moral subordination obscures the fact that *corporate officials themselves (and even corporations) may be morally subordinated to a significant degree in an advanced market economy*…. Standing behind all of these particular actors is an *impersonal* process of social coordination that works through market competition" (emphasis in original) (2023: 159). Even so, he continues to maintain that the market is authoritarian.

society partly requires accepting that the world does not need to ask our permission to function. Impersonal processes like the market are schemes that, in FSC terminology, depend on everyone but depend on no one in particular. Therefore, they do not need our individual judgment to function.

Ultimately, an impersonal process like the market, formed by the preferences of millions of people, does not require an individual judgment to approve or reject its operation. There is no *single* person designing the market. Thus, there is no *single* person who needs to approve it.

In fact, it is strange that an impersonal process like the market could *limit* our scope of action as much as the author suggests. Precisely because there is no central authority making decisions about people's lives, competitive markets tend toward enormous diversity, both in the products offered and in the lifestyles people adopt. Some entrepreneurs and traders choose to cater to majority tastes, but others succeed by identifying small niches and offering goods and services to minority groups (groups with a minority religion, a minority political ideology, a minority sexual orientation, or any other minority lifestyle). It is not clear how an environment where people have such different lifestyles can be a social control mechanism. If it were, there probably would not be people inside that mechanism denouncing it for exercising "social control."

Of course, what has been said here does not rule out the need for market regulation in certain cases. In the next section, I will explore some of these regulations. However, from the perspective of FSC, the reason for these regulations is not that the market itself is authoritarian, but rather the need to correct some flaws that, in particular circumstances, can make the market overly dependent on certain individuals or corporations. FSC does not criticize impersonal schemes for being authoritarian; on the contrary, FSC proposes measures to depersonalize schemes when they become dependent on someone in particular, because this dependence threatens freedom. According to FSC, depersonalizing cooperative schemes is the key to freedom.

5.5 Market Failures as Threats to the Cooperation Scheme

5.5.1 *Second-Order Cooperation Is Not Limited to Protecting Property Rights*

So far, I have distinguished three forms of cooperation. First, first-order cooperation involves the production and provision of goods and services that typically—although, as I will analyze in the next chapter, not exclusively—occur in the market. Second, second-order cooperation comprises state activities aimed at using coercion to preserve the environment in which first-order cooperative activities take place (for example, the security of individuals involved and the protection of their property rights). Finally, intra-state cooperation occurs within the state itself, where its institutions interact to drive the state toward fulfilling its functions.

In this section, I will again focus on second-order cooperation, but not on activities related to security or property rights protection. Instead, I will concentrate on those aimed at regulating the market. These state activities are also considered second-order because their purpose is to maintain the environment necessary for first-order cooperation through the use of coercive measures. In particular, I will discuss three forms of second-order cooperative activities: antitrust regulations, labor regulations, and union-related activities.

5.5.2 *Monopoly*

It is plausible to consider that certain economic regulations could help ensure the full enjoyment of FSC. Essentially, the idea is that the government should prevent the concentration of economic power that unfettered markets might produce—a concentration that could result in monopolies. A monopoly exists in the provision of a certain *type* of good or service when there is only one supplier for that specific good or service. It is common to believe that a market economy often leads to the concentration of economic power, which results in monopolies controlling the supply of goods and services. Is that really the case?

First of all, recall that the emergence of a monopoly conflicts with FSC, since in such a case the provision of a good or service depends entirely on a single supplier. This condition diverges from a genuine cooperative scheme, where individuals design and pursue their life plans relying on collective cooperation without depending on any single individual. Typically, the consequence of a monopoly is a price increase. Of course, the severity of this situation depends on the type of good or service in question. It is not the same, for example, to have a monopoly on water as to have a monopoly on tennis rackets. It is reasonable to think that, in the first case, people's ability to realize their life plans would be much more affected. While one might switch to paddle or ping-pong without tennis rackets, without water, practicing any sport at all becomes impossible.

In any case, it is clear there is a tension between the existence of a monopoly and FSC. If this monopoly results from the concentration of power in a market economy, then there appears to be a strong reason for state intervention in this realm. However, some reflections are in order.

On the one hand, the very notion that markets tend toward monopoly is far from obvious. In markets where the entry of competitors—whether internal or external—is not legally barred, monopolies are exceptional. Fortunately, monopolies are very difficult to sustain without laws protecting monopolistic firms from competition. The constant pursuit of higher profitability by investors practically guarantees that investments will flow into sectors of the economy generating the greatest returns (and where there are one or few firms and high demand, there are usually large profits). Competition will predictably increase, and prices will fall (Pincione 2015: 2421).

As I explained in Sect. 5.4.2, in a market economy, prices serve as signals that convey information about the relative abundance or scarcity of a given product. A high price for a good or service indicates that it is scarce compared to demand. This price signals to potential competitors that it might be profitable to start offering that good or service, given its scarcity. For example, under a legal framework protecting intellectual property, software programs exhibit monopolistic characteristics. Yet it is precisely these characteristics, and the resulting higher prices they enable, that make investing in the development of alternative software worthwhile. Generally, in a market without legal barriers to entry, the extraordinary profits typical of a monopoly provide an incentive for technological progress, which ultimately undermines the monopolist's dominance (Pincione 2011).[31]

[31] On competition in the software industry, see Friedman, D. 2000: 259.

In this way, a company competes not only with actual rivals but also with potential ones. A monopoly might arise from being the best provider of a particular good and offering it at an affordable price. In such instances, the firm may technically qualify as a *monopoly*, yet ironically be unable to *act* like one because if it were to excessively raise prices or degrade product quality, it would become more vulnerable, prompting new competitors to emerge and attempt to unseat it.

In past centuries, merchants and entrepreneurs often needed government permission to open businesses in many sectors of the economy, especially in Europe and Asia, with monopoly licenses granted to those who paid the government directly for these rights. However, by the late eighteenth century, economic development had revealed an important lesson: monopolistic practices could be profoundly harmful to society as a whole. Consequently, there was growing advocacy for freeing the economy from monopolies and similar forms of government control. Today, for instance, true monopolies are rare at the national level in the United States, although certain forms of government regulation at the state level—such as laws limiting the number of taxis permitted to operate—effectively constrain competition, artificially raising fares and reducing taxi availability (Sowell 2015: 148–149).

In markets where legal barriers or government restrictions do not impede the entry of new competitors, market forces tend to exert pressure on monopolies, thereby creating opportunities for new ventures to challenge their dominance. For instance, the computer industry was once dominated by gigantic machines occupying thousands of square meters and requiring astronomical production costs. However, with the advent of microchips—smaller, more affordable components—smaller computers emerged, capable of performing the same tasks. These lower production costs allowed medium and small-sized companies worldwide to enter the market. Consequently, not even a national monopoly could forestall competition.

On the other hand, even if a monopoly emerges and remains stable over an extended period within a market economy, this does not mean that it faces no competition from other goods or alternatives within the broader economy. For example, in Spain, when a high-speed train began operating between Madrid and Seville, the share of passenger traffic shifted from 33% by rail and 67% by air to 82% by rail and 18% by air. Clearly, many people viewed air travel and rail transport as alternative ways to get from one part of the country to another. Both modes of transportation had to compete equally with all airlines and all railway companies traveling between cities. Even goods that are very different from one another can serve the same purpose. For instance, corn and petroleum come from different industries, yet both can be processed into raw materials that serve as the basis for producing plastics (Sowell 2015: 167).

In fact, even goods that serve very different purposes can act as economic substitutes. For example, if a single company were to produce jet skis, it would need to set a price that makes those jet skis more attractive to consumers than cars, air travel, dining out, or any other alternative spending options. If priced too high, the company would quickly lose its market. We define a monopoly as a market condition in which a single supplier exclusively offers a particular type of good. However, goods from different categories often compete with each other. For example, if a chocolate monopoly were to raise prices excessively or produce poor-quality chocolates, young consumers might stop buying them and start choosing candy instead.

Beyond these considerations, I do not intend to dismiss entirely the possibility that *genuine* monopolies may arise in a market economy. Several years ago, such monopolies existed in some countries where regional telephone companies held exclusive control before the advent of the Internet and mobile phones. Today, similar monopolistic conditions persist in the provision of essential services like electricity and water supply. In these contexts, FSC is fully compatible with—and may even necessitate—the establishment of antitrust agencies, as commonly found in modern democracies.

Ideally, these agencies aim to address the rare monopolies that may arise in the market, if any. For example, in the United States, the Federal Communications Commission (FCC) regulated the prices charged by AT&T, which held a monopoly on long-distance communication services for many years. In fact, if truly independent, these agencies could act as watchdogs over the state itself, which sometimes tends to adopt measures that block new competitors from entering the market in order to favor businesspeople with political connections, often in exchange for campaign financing, among other things.

It is important to emphasize, however, that poorly designed antitrust agencies can exacerbate the problem by becoming instruments for powerful interests seeking to establish or preserve monopolies.

In principle, both economically powerful groups and the government itself—along with para-governmental organizations such as unions or professional associations heavily regulated and funded by the state—have incentives to invest time and resources to ensure that legislative or judicial discretion works to their advantage. The specific forms this investment takes—whether through votes from workers in regulated industries, financial contributions to election campaigns, various forms of corruption, and so forth—depend on the particular political regime, including the stringency of bribery penalties and the likelihood of detection and punishment (Pincione 2015: 2420).

Antitrust agencies are often established in response to popular demand. However, once created, media attention tends to shift elsewhere, and the public often forgets about their existence. Meanwhile, the companies regulated by these agencies allocate significant time and resources to lobbying efforts aimed at influencing government policies to enact regulations that protect them from new competition.

In the United States, for example, railroad regulation was initially justified by the industry's monopoly status in certain regions. When the rise of road transport began to challenge this dominance, the Interstate Commerce Commission (ICC) did not concede that regulation was less necessary. Instead, it sought and obtained expanded authority from Congress to limit the operations of road carriers. This intervention ultimately hindered the growth of a more efficient and often more affordable transportation sector for certain types of goods (Sowell 2015: 158–159).

Without proper institutional design, using political power to counterbalance economic power may prove counterproductive in combating power concentration (Stigler 1971). To mitigate this risk, antitrust agencies—like other state institutions—should operate internally as cooperative systems.

I do not intend to provide a detailed analysis of how antitrust agencies should be designed. At a minimum, they should adhere to the principles of separation of powers and checks and balances that govern other branches of government, ensuring internal accountability and preventing excessive concentration of authority. This means they must have a clear legal framework guaranteeing their independence within the state structure. Such a framework could also require that its members, besides being highly experienced professionals, gain approval from all or at least the vast majority of political forces. For instance, the statute could mandate appointment by qualified majorities in one chamber of the legislature. With simple majorities, a dominant political force in the legislature could appoint members who intend only to defend that political force's interests. Qualified majorities (or even unanimity) reduce this risk.

Moreover, the legislature could oversee the agency's operations; for instance, it could be authorized to summon agency representatives to provide explanations if irregularities are suspected. Even absent suspicions, these representatives could be statutorily required to submit annual reports to legislators, detailing the monopoly cases investigated and the measures implemented.

In any case, the logic remains consistent: as state entities, antitrust agencies engage in intra-state cooperative activities that support the state's fulfillment of certain functions; namely, second-order cooperative activities aimed at preserving the first-order cooperative environment by protecting it from monopolies and abusive practices. Moreover, to prevent antitrust agencies from ultimately serving interest groups with strong lobbying power, it is crucial that they operate internally as cooperative systems—independent of particular individuals and receiving collaboration from other bodies, such as legislative audits.

5.5.3 The Labor Market

If a monopoly is an economy with only one seller, a monopsony is an economy with only one buyer. In a monopoly, the sole seller has the power to set prices. Conversely, in a monopsony, it is the single buyer who holds the power to determine prices. Economists predict that in a monopoly, prices will rise above competitive levels, whereas in a monopsony, prices will fall below competitive levels. For example, in the labor market, if only one employer is hiring workers—which means the employer acts as the only buyer of labor—the price of labor will probably be low. This situation, often described as monopsony power, can lead to miserable wages and poor working conditions.

In modern societies, labor markets are not monopsonies, as there are typically multiple employers. However, many argue they do exhibit characteristics of an oligopsony: few employers compared to the number of job seekers. The consequence of an oligopsony is similar to that of a monopsony—low wages or poor labor conditions.

Marx famously argued that the labor market exploits workers, who accept any wage as long as it is better than starving (Marx 1977 [1867]:

ch. 6). Assuming that the labor market in each sector is an oligopsony, Marx's reasoning holds true. In this scenario, while the supply of labor (from the workers' side) is fully competitive, there is little competition among employers who demand labor. As a result, employers have the power to set wages, and workers have no choice but to accept what is offered. Modern labor laws in democratic societies are fundamentally aimed at addressing this imbalance.[32]

Labor law is the product of the political and social activism of the working-class movement. Although the earliest uprisings began in seventeenth-century Europe, it was not until the nineteenth century that the movement was able to organize itself effectively and achieve significant influence (Spector, H. 2006: 1119). During this period, socialist ideologues provided the intellectual foundation that allowed the movement to flourish. For example, in England, Robert Owen inspired the founding of the Grand National Consolidated Trades Union in 1834; in Germany, Ferdinand Lassalle established the General German Workers' Association in 1863; and the following year, Karl Marx helped to create the First International (Abendroth 1972: 15–26, 32, 33, 40).

The emergence of American labor law was also influenced by socialist ideas. For example, Walton Hamilton, one of the leading labor policy experts in the first half of the twentieth century, advocated for the socialization of corporate property. He supported social reforms that included, among other measures, social control over commerce (Hamilton, W. and May 1923: 68, 119).

In terms of FSC, labor law can be defined as another form of second-order cooperative activity by the state (aimed at correcting imperfections where first-order cooperative activities take place). It consists of a complex set of restrictions on the freedom of contract in labor markets. To be sure, if the number of people seeking a particular type of job were equal to or less than the number of available positions, labor rights would be unnecessary, as the labor market would be fully competitive on the demand side—that is, the side of employers who demand or seek to hire workers. At least in the labor market, there would be a genuine cooperative framework in which employers would offer well-paid jobs, and employees would depend on them collectively, rather than on any single

[32] In any case, although labor law is founded on addressing a problem identified by Marx, he believed that labor law can, at best, limit exploitation but never fully eliminate it. See Atienza 1982: 28–29.

employer. If one employer offered a worker a very low wage or poor working conditions, it would be relatively easy for that worker to find a better offer elsewhere. Thus, an anti-cooperative attitude by any one employer would not disrupt the system.

On the other hand, in an oligopsony—or, even more so, a monopsony—employees become dependent on a particular employer. Such an employer can pressure workers to accept miserable wages or unhealthy working conditions, knowing that finding another job would be difficult. As mentioned earlier, labor law often operates under the assumption that the labor market functions as an oligopsony.

Following Henry Farnam's classification, labor legislation can be divided into three categories: worker protection rules, which include limits on working hours and requirements for safety and health conditions (now also covering prohibitions against sexual and moral harassment in the workplace); redistributive rules aimed at influencing terms of exchange, such as mandatory payment in legal tender, minimum wage laws, wage controls, compensation for wrongful dismissal, and social security guarantees; and permissive legislation, which facilitates the creation of institutions for collective worker action and collective bargaining (McCurdy 1998: 190–191; Spector, H. 2006: 1120).

FSC defines freedom as a cooperative practice for the development and fulfillment of life plans. As participants in this cooperative framework, we are equal in the sense that each person depends on others to develop and carry out their life plan—that is, on the entire scheme—but does not depend on any one individual, so no single participant is indispensable. It seems obvious that, in a cooperative system like the one we are envisioning, wages and work are crucial components in the realization of life plans. Let me explain why.

5.5.3.1 Wages

Wages are crucial because they provide the means through which people can obtain the resources needed to fulfill their life plans. In the primitive cooperation scenario, individuals made their contributions and, in return, received the resources necessary to carry out their projects. Making a contribution was the prerequisite for benefiting from others' contributions, in a context where property remained largely collective and money did not exist, despite the presence of a division of labor.

In modern cooperative schemes, which include private property and a market economy, money—as a medium of exchange—is analogous to the resources people needed in the primitive cooperation scenario to realize their life plans. Individuals can hardly develop and carry out their life plans if they receive extremely low wages or none at all. Redistributive labor legislation—such as minimum wage laws and compensation for wrongful dismissal—plays a crucial role in preventing such undesirable outcomes. Additionally, collective worker action, especially through collective bargaining, can contribute significantly to improving wages.

It is important to emphasize that these measures are not valuable in themselves but are aimed at achieving a specific goal. Their actual success depends on empirical evidence. For instance, research indicates that minimum wage laws can reduce employment opportunities for the least-skilled workers—such as young people without experience, who contribute less productivity to a company. The reasoning is straightforward: if an employee produces output valued at $100 per month, but the minimum wage law requires the company to pay $200 per month, the company is likely to lay off the worker to avoid incurring losses. Evidence shows that the vast majority of those negatively affected by such labor legislation are low-skilled individuals, including young people trying to enter the workforce and gain experience. Dozens of studies compiled in 2006 by the National Bureau of Economic Research, covering the United States, European countries, Latin America, the Caribbean, Indonesia, Canada, Australia, and New Zealand, conclude that minimum wage laws lead to job losses among the least-skilled workers (Neumark and Wascher 2006).

Similarly, additional measures such as mandatory severance pay can protect current employees, but may discourage new hiring due to the increased costs employers must bear, potentially harming the unemployed. It is important to remember that not all employers are large corporations. In most cases, they are small and medium-sized enterprises with limited resources, for whom any added cost could deter them from expanding their workforce. Some countries—such as Sweden, Denmark, and Switzerland—have chosen to keep dismissal costs low, either by requiring low or no severance pay or by granting employers broad discretion to justify dismissals.[33] In exchange, workers have unemployment insurance funded by their own contributions during employment, often

[33] EPLex database, at https://eplex.ilo.org/en#browse-by-country-section (last accessed August 21, 2025).

significantly supplemented by the state and employers, thereby spreading the financial burden of dismissals more broadly.

The upshot is that any form of labor legislation should undergo careful empirical analysis to ensure it is not counterproductive relative to the goals it aims to achieve. FSC's commitment to labor law is conditional: it depends on whether these rules help strengthen the cooperative framework and assist individuals in designing and fulfilling their life plans. If these rules fail to meet this standard, FSC's commitment to such institutions weakens.

5.5.3.2 Work

Work is also crucial in realizing life plans, but in a different sense. It is not merely important because it provides a livelihood—that idea adds little beyond what has already been said about wages, which are the result of work. Rather, developing and fulfilling our life plans requires that we see our work as an integral *part of* those plans. In modern societies, work occupies a significant portion of our time. The types of tasks we perform and the people we interact with in the workplace form an important part of our lives (Smith and Deranty 2011). Therefore, if work were excluded from our life plan and regarded solely as a *means* to fulfill it, we would end up dedicating a substantial amount of time to activities we perceive as disconnected from our true self. The means to pursue our life plan would overshadow the plan itself. Ironically, the means would become an obstacle.

Marx addressed this issue extensively, arguing that wage labor alienates workers. The core idea is that work is alien to the worker—it is not an expression of their true nature or essence. In performing labor, the worker does not freely develop their physical and mental energies. Work, in itself, does not satisfy a need but serves merely as a means to fulfill a basic necessity—subsistence, according to Marx's critique of capitalism. Consequently, through their work, the worker does not affirm their own identity but instead negates it. While working, the individual does not experience a true sense of self; rather, this feeling of authenticity arises only outside of labor, perhaps when they are at home with their family. Based on this reasoning, Marx concluded that wage labor is forced labor (Marx 2018 [1844]: 598).

Adam Smith, for his part, argued that monotonous and simple jobs have a detrimental effect on workers by dulling their social and intellectual skills. He referred to tasks related to pin manufacturing, suggesting that such work ultimately brutalizes workers (Smith, A. 1981 [1776]: bk. V, ch. i). While Smith did not explicitly express concern about work diverting us from our life plan, he used this example to explore whether the state should provide education to citizens to counteract such dulling effects. Much of his reasoning, however, aligns with Marx's argument: it is reasonable to believe that spending at least eight hours a day cutting or sharpening wire is unlikely to be part of most individuals' life projects and instead functions merely as a means of subsistence.

Can the government play a role in ensuring that work is not merely a means to an end but also an integral *part* of individuals' life plan? Certain labor rights appear designed to advance this goal—such as limits on working hours, health and safety regulations, and prohibitions against sexual and moral harassment in the workplace. These protections, often supported and enforced through collective worker action, contribute to creating safer and more pleasant work environments. While these measures alone are insufficient, they are arguably necessary conditions for workers to view their jobs as fundamental components of their life aspirations. Without such minimal safeguards, it seems impossible for work to be seen as anything other than an unpleasant necessity—a cost one must bear to achieve other ends.

As I explained earlier, if the number of people seeking a particular type of job is equal to or less than the number of available positions, labor rights become less relevant because the labor market is competitive on the demand side. In this scenario, employees depend on employers collectively, but not on any single employer. If one employer offers a job with low wages or poor conditions, workers can relatively easily find better opportunities elsewhere. Thus, an uncooperative attitude from any one employer does not significantly disrupt the system.

Conversely, in an oligopsony—or, even more so, a monopsony—workers do depend on specific employers. Such employers can coerce workers into accepting low wages or unsafe working conditions, knowing the difficulty of finding alternative employment. As noted, labor law seems to be predicated on the assumption that the labor market functions as an oligopsony.

Certain labor rights, then, appear to be a necessary condition for integrating a person's work with their life plan. This is not sufficient, but it is as far as labor law can contribute in principle.[34] The missing element extends beyond labor law and concerns the broader economic and social system. Fundamentally, for a worker to regard their job as an extension of their life plan, the work environment must provide a space where they can express their convictions and pursue their projects. Crucially, the nature of the work itself must align with the individual's particular life plan.

Someone who has studied law will naturally seek employment in a law firm, a court, or another legal institution—whether independently or as part of an organization—where they can apply their knowledge and advance professionally. A fashion designer will pursue opportunities that allow them to express their aesthetic sensibilities. A doctor may aspire to establish a private practice or work within a public or private hospital. A restaurant owner will shape their establishment according to their vision, inevitably reflecting their personality and projects. An educator might seek roles at elementary, middle, or high schools, or at the university level, or even become a private tutor. These career choices are shaped by each individual's unique aspirations.

In this respect, the principle is straightforward: the richer and more diverse a society, the more likely it is that individuals will *eventually* find work that enables them to achieve personal fulfillment. The term "eventually" is deliberate, as it is common for people to undertake jobs that do not closely align with their life plans. Even in the wealthiest societies, a young person's initial job—such as a teenage shelf-stocker in a supermarket—is often unrelated to their long-term goals. Nevertheless, such experiences impart fundamental skills—such as discipline and teamwork—that facilitate future progress and, if the system rewards effort and merit, lead to employment more aligned with their aspirations.

Certain jobs naturally attract people more than others because they engage and develop a person's innate or acquired abilities. Rawls's "Aristotelian principle" offers valuable insight here: the most fulfilling activities are complex ones that stimulate a person's capacities. According to Rawls, enjoyment increases with the complexity of the activity, as complex tasks satisfy the desire for variety and novelty while allowing for ingenuity and inventiveness. Moreover, complex activities provide the pleasure of surprise and the chance to develop a personal style—making it unlikely that everyone will perform such tasks in the same way (Rawls 1999:

[34] In Sect. 5.5.3.4, I discuss a broader form of labor law advocated by some authors: "workplace democracy."

374–375). Less stimulating jobs—such as night security work or cleaning services—have a diminished potential to integrate with an individual's life plan compared to more engaging roles like those in advertising or finance. When Marx wrote about the alienation of workers in the mid-nineteenth century, most employees were engaged in mechanical and repetitive labor, primarily factory tasks.

Both ethically and economically, it is a community's reasonable obligation to ensure that everyone has a fair opportunity to realize their potential and contribute to the cooperative system. We all aspire to live in a land of genuine opportunities—where, at twenty, we may have limited resources and take an uninspiring job, yet can reasonably expect that, through merit and effort, by the time we reach forty, we will enjoy a good standard of living and work that aligns with our life projects.

Diversity, in turn, appears to arise spontaneously in the market economies of liberal democracies. As Rawls has noted, a defining characteristic of these societies is their deep pluralism, with citizens developing and embracing conceptions of the good that can be vastly different from one another (Rawls 1993: 61). This pluralism becomes an advantage when individuals seek to integrate their life plans with their work. Because society is so diverse, modern life offers a wide range of occupations—from bakers to parachute instructors—and, moreover, the same profession can present different modalities, such as an accountant choosing between working in a large firm or providing independent services from home.

Furthermore, the market economy offers opportunities even to those who oppose its underlying philosophy. The commercial centers of a civilization often serve simultaneously as its cultural hubs. For example, someone seeking the most trenchant critique of market society is more likely to turn to the great libraries of London, New York, or Boston rather than those of Moscow, Pyongyang, or Havana. The market economy also generates its own critical intellectuals, who may develop their critiques through works studied and disseminated by students and professors across diverse academic institutions. The profound diversity of liberal democracies fosters a wide variety of occupations, thereby increasing the likelihood that individuals will find work that aligns with their life plan.

5.5.3.3 *The Role of Labor Unions*

As I mentioned earlier, labor law can be defined as a set of restrictions on contractual freedom within labor markets. On one hand, it includes protective regulations for workers concerning aspects such as working hours, health and safety, and related conditions. On the other hand, it encompasses redistributive provisions, such as minimum wage laws, severance pay, and similar safeguards.

I have also asserted that labor law gains its meaning in an oligopsonistic labor market, where employers hold significantly greater bargaining power than employees. A pertinent question, however, is how to ensure that these labor rights are effectively respected and, more generally, how to promote the interests of workers. The fundamental purpose of labor law is to address the greater bargaining power of employers; yet, it is precisely this power that enables some employers to pressure employees into relinquishing their labor rights (Anderson, E. 2017: 37–39). How, then, can such violations of the law be effectively prevented?

The mechanism that democracies have adopted is unionization. Labor unions are organized associations of workers that advocate for the protection and expansion of their rights through collective agreements. The rationale behind unionization is clear: an individual worker lacks the bargaining power to negotiate contract terms effectively with an employer, especially when other workers might undermine the effort by accepting conditions the first worker seeks to challenge. By uniting and acting collectively, workers can significantly enhance their negotiating power. This principle forms the basis of the third type of labor legislation: Farnam's so-called "permissive" laws, which facilitate the creation of institutions enabling joint worker action and collective bargaining.

The idea is that unions amplify workers' collective power relative to their employers, compelling the latter to negotiate contract terms with the unified *body* of employees. In this way, unions function as a form of "compensatory power," balancing the inherent disparities in bargaining strength (Galbraith 1952: 114–115). Unions can organize workers within a particular sector, across multiple sectors, or within a single workplace or company. Societies vary considerably in the extent to which their workers are unionized and in how their labor laws favor the formation and empowerment of unions. However, beyond these nuances, the underlying logic remains the same: in terms of FSC, unions are organizations engaged in *second-order* activities that rectify deficiencies in the cooperation scheme caused by a labor market that is not competitive on the demand side.

Unions represent a notable exception to the rule that second-order activities are the domain of the state. It is true that, when defining second-order cooperative activities, I mentioned the coercive aspect. However, to some extent, unions are authorized to resort to some form of coercion; for example, they can undertake certain measures of force, such as work stoppages or strikes. Union activities are probably the only type of second-order activity that is not carried out (at least not directly) by the state. In any case, for the purposes of this analysis, it will not be necessary to delve too deeply into the nature of these cooperative activities.

It is clear, then, that union cooperative activities center on uniting workers so that stronger organization and collective action translate into greater bargaining power. However, the effectiveness of these goals depends heavily on the internal structure of the union system. Like the state, the union system should operate internally as a cooperation scheme, with independent bodies ensuring the fulfillment of its functions. The system must be designed so that, while workers rely on the union framework as a whole, they do not depend on any single entity within it. This design ensures that the system can continue to function effectively even if a particular entity engages in anti-cooperative behavior.

In this regard, we can distinguish between two different union systems. The first is union monism. Under this system, the law recognizes a single federation that encompasses various unions, typically one for each profession, trade, or activity (or, on rare occasions, a single union covering all professions, trades, and activities). Although present in some liberal democracies, this system has been characteristic of authoritarian regimes such as Mussolini's Italy before World War II, Franco's Spain during the 1950s, and Salazar's Portugal in the 1960s (Kalamatiev and Ristovski 2012: 394).

The second is union pluralism. Under this system, the law permits the formation of multiple federations, allowing several unions per profession, trade, or activity. The principle of union pluralism is enshrined in Convention 87 of the International Labour Organization (ILO) as an extension of the right to freedom of association. It also serves to prevent dependence on a single federation, which might abuse its power or collude with the government to advance shared interests at the expense of workers' welfare.

As noted above, the union system engages in cooperative activities to address deficiencies inherent in an oligopsonistic labor market, while internally it should also reflect the logic of cooperation. The entire union system should be designed so that, while workers depend on it as a whole, they do not rely on any single union entity. This ensures that the system can continue to function even if an entity engages in anti-cooperative behaviors.

From the perspective of FSC, then, union monism is obviously problematic because it leaves workers at the mercy of a single federation (one union per sector or, even worse, one union covering all sectors). Potential anti-cooperative behaviors by that federation (e.g., collusion with employers or excessively high dues charged to members) could undermine the union system, preventing it from fulfilling its objectives in promoting workers' interests. This problem would persist whether the law mandates union membership or[35] leaves it to the worker's free choice. In the latter case, a worker in a specific sector would not be obliged to join, but with only one union option available, the worker would still be subject to the power of that single union entity as it remains the sole alternative to protect their labor rights from abuses by employers or other external parties.

One possible solution to this problem, without abandoning the union monism model, is for the federation itself to operate internally as a cooperative framework. This approach requires strict state regulations governing the internal affairs of the federation to democratize its functioning. The establishment of structures such as the separation of powers and checks and balances, along with active participation by all workers, could help realize this objective. By fostering cooperative activities within the federation itself, the union can be guided more effectively toward fulfilling its essential functions.

In any case, union pluralism appears to be more compatible with FSC. This model envisions multiple federations emerging, giving rise to several unions even within the same sector, allowing workers to choose the union they believe best represents their interests. Thus, while workers depend on the union system as a whole, they are not dependent on any particular entity. Indeed, this system is designed to withstand anti-cooperative behaviors by individual entities: if a union deviates from its functions, workers can disaffiliate and join another union under a different federation.

That said, it should be noted that this system could also have its drawbacks. The ILO itself, a defender of the principle of freedom of

[35] For example, Mark Reiff (2020) has argued that unionization should be universal and compulsory. According to him, unions are fundamental institutions in society, necessary to free workers from exploitation by employers.

association, has expressed concern about the abusive interpretation and application of this right (ILO 2010: 2). The organization highlights that, for example, in French-speaking African countries, the proliferation and fragmentation of union entities has generally weakened the labor movement, undermining its effectiveness and credibility. According to the ILO, the right to freedom of association must be exercised "with extreme caution as well as with an unwavering sense of loyalty and devotion to the cause of defending the rights and the interests of workers and trade union members, in the best possible manner" (ILO 2010: 11).

We can infer that when the ILO highlights the proliferation of union entities in French-speaking African countries as having weakened the effectiveness and credibility of the labor movement, it is indicating that workers' rights are not being adequately respected despite the presence of these organizations. Indeed, the protection of workers' rights is the fundamental purpose of unionism, making it the most appropriate criterion for assessing the performance of any union system.

However, it is not easy to determine whether the situation of workers in countries like Burkina Faso, Cameroon, Senegal, or the Democratic Republic of Congo is due to the proliferation of union associations (as the ILO claims), or rather to corrupt ruling classes and failed economic systems. In principle, these countries have experienced a significantly low degree of economic freedom, with governments that have suppressed independent business activity and hindered wealth creation.[36] Unions cannot perform miracles. When the political, social, and economic structures do not support them, unionism—whether unified or fragmented—has limited capacity to make a difference. To place responsibility for workers' conditions on union pluralism in such contexts seems overly simplistic.

In the case of Burkina Faso, for example, the ILO itself highlights that "poverty and unemployment have also contributed toward the problem of trade union proliferation" (ILO 2010: 44). It turned out that many union leaders, unable to raise substantial funds from membership dues due to low wages and high unemployment, created new entities to receive more state subsidies (as the government provided a small subsidy for each union entity). However, if high poverty and unemployment *contributed*

[36] See the Heritage Foundation's Index of Economic Freedom at https://www.heritage.org/index/pages/dataviz (last accessed: August 25, 2025). I have selected the 2010 edition, which is the year the ILO published its study.

to the proliferation of unions, it cannot be the case that this proliferation is *the cause* of poverty and unemployment. At most, it may exacerbate these problems, but there are other influencing variables.

On the other hand, the ILO mentions that the average wage in the Democratic Republic of Congo is less than one dollar and that the country is among the 10 poorest in the world (ILO 2010: 23). It seems evident that this cannot be attributed to the union system. For example, the country ranked 171st out of 180 countries evaluated in Transparency International's 2008 Corruption Perceptions Index (the ILO study is from 2010).[37] Similarly, the Heritage Foundation's 2010 Index of Economic Freedom asserts that inefficient customs administration, import restrictions and taxes, inadequate infrastructure, complex regulations, and extensive bureaucracy have increased the cost of trade[38] (which, quite plausibly, lowered wages for employees in these sectors). Once again, it is far from clear that we should focus on union pluralism when explaining the situation of workers in these countries.

Nevertheless, it should not be dismissed that union pluralism, when taken to the extreme of creating unions everywhere, can weaken the institution, making it difficult for unions to carry out their cooperative activities. This problem would not arise if several unions operated under the umbrella of a single entity, as the entity could organize them by sectors to prevent conflicts. However, when there is a wide proliferation of independent entities, each may lose strength. This is the thesis of the ILO in its analysis of African countries.

Although I will not elaborate on this issue here, one possible solution, without abandoning union pluralism, is to set a legally mandated maximum number of entities, thereby allowing for a controlled pluralism. Another option is to establish a mechanism for joint action and collective decision-making among the various entities. The law regulating union operations could, following negotiations between employers and unions, require these entities to make joint decisions. However, it would be necessary to evaluate whether such a system can genuinely qualify as *pluralistic*.

[37] https://www.transparency.org/en/cpi/2008 (last accessed: August 25, 2025).

[38] https://rai-see.org/wp-content/uploads/2016/01/Economic-Freedom-Index-2010.pdf (last accessed: August 25, 2025).

In short, FSC can offer a *general* theory of unionism and what should be expected from this practice: primarily, cooperative activities aimed at correcting deficiencies in a labor market that lacks strong competition on the demand side. It also cautiously provides a more specific theory on how the union system should function internally: ideally, through a system of union pluralism, while recognizing that this system is not without its challenges.

5.5.3.4 *Workplace Democracy?*

"Workplace democracy" refers to labor law systems that establish democratic forms of governance within companies, thereby granting employees greater power. These systems vary in scope, ranging from co-determination models—such as Germany's, which includes worker representatives on the boards of directors of large companies—to fully cooperative models, where companies are wholly owned by their workers (Frega, Herzog, and Neuhäuser 2019).

Robert Dahl argued that companies are similar, in a relevant sense, to political societies. Therefore, if democracy is justified in political societies, it is also justified within the internal life of companies (Dahl 1985: 111). This idea can serve as a starting point for analyzing whether, from the perspective of FSC, a more extensive labor law establishing workplace democracy is necessary.

In the previous chapter, I explained that, from the perspective of FSC, suffrage is one among the many institutions of the state. When people express their will as voters, they engage in an activity that is part of the broader processes within the state. The right to vote arises from the right to participate in the administration of the state. Ultimately, suffrage is a form of intra-state cooperation.

It is important to recall that, in FSC, intra-state activities are significant because the state holds the monopoly on coercion, making it an overly powerful agent that, if left unchecked, disturbs the equality that should underpin any cooperative scheme. Intra-state activities such as suffrage keep the state in check and compel it to properly fulfill its functions.

In other words, from the perspective of FSC, suffrage is not valuable because of the incentives it generates for public officials to act responsibly, nor because voting makes the citizen more autonomous, but because without suffrage the system would become more dependent on a ruling elite that holds the monopoly on coercion. This elite may be divided into different branches (separation of powers) and even spread across different territories with relatively autonomous local governments (federalism). Yet, the periodic renewal of offices adds another important criterion of decentralization by making the system even less dependent on particular individuals. Without suffrage, this form of decentralization is absent, and the dependence on certain individuals increases.

This same logic explains why, according to FSC, suffrage is not necessary in other associations, such as educational institutions or religious organizations. If suffrage is essentially an institution of the state, then it exists only where there is a state; and in turn, the state exists only where there is a monopoly on coercion.

Of course, stating that the state holds the monopoly on coercion does not imply that other associations lack forms of authority that might, in some sense, be considered coercive. For example, the Catholic Church enforces its own rules and may impose sanctions on members who disobey them. Similarly, universities can suspend students who violate certain codes of conduct. Beyond the degree of coercion, the fundamental difference is that members of such associations voluntarily choose to belong to them and can leave with relative ease.

Political society (and its authority, the state) is different because, as Rawls (1993: 222) asserts, it is not *voluntarily* accepted. People can emigrate, but the economic and emotional costs are usually high enough that it cannot be said that political societies are *genuinely* voluntary associations. This involuntary character is key to understanding the particular form of coercion exercised by the state and explains why the state is said to hold the "monopoly on coercion": the state exercises coercion within a non-voluntary association.

Dahl (1985: 115) argues that companies are more similar to political societies than to voluntary associations. The main reason is that employees generally cannot resign or be dismissed without suffering serious harm, at least until they find an equal or better job, if they find one at all. Consequently, a company is not a genuinely voluntary association, at least from the perspective of employees, who are *compelled* to obey the rules imposed by employers. In Dahl's argument, the non-voluntary nature of companies plays an important role in demonstrating that democracy is also required within companies.

Richard Arneson (1995: 138–143), on the other hand, maintains that the analogy between political societies and companies is implausible. Typically, in a market economy, there are multiple employment opportunities, which makes quitting a job relatively easy. In such cases, labor relations can be considered genuinely voluntary. This right to exit the employment relationship can, in turn, be reinforced by legal mechanisms such as unemployment insurance, a basic income, or other support systems required or promoted by the state.

Robert Mayer (2001: 235), for his part, focuses not on the possibility of exit but on the possibility of entry. As long as people have voluntarily consented to the employment relationship, democracy within that company will not be necessary, just as it is not necessary in a religious organization or any other association which we have voluntarily joined.[39]

It is also worth noting that, ironically, more extensive labor legislation could affect employees' freedom of choice. The aim of workplace democracy is to give employees a meaningful role in collective decision-making within that environment. However, with such legislation, employees might lose the ability to decide to enter into a more traditional employment relationship.

Many professionals who initially began working independently eventually choose to take on traditional employment. Various life circumstances can prompt this decision. Some prefer to give up the risks and stress associated with self-employment. While business ownership can yield significant rewards if successful, it also entails enormous costs if the venture fails. Being an employee allows one to avoid such responsibilities, enabling a clear separation between work and personal life: finishing the workday and disconnecting from work-related concerns. This frees up time to spend with family, friends, or hobbies, without the anxiety or pressure often experienced by those bearing greater decision-making responsibilities or business risks. Others may prefer employment to save time and energy otherwise spent on workplace politics, allowing them to focus on freelance or entrepreneurial projects (Bonin, Jones, and Putterman 1993).

[39] Other arguments in favor of workplace democracy, supposedly distinct from the analogy between the state and the company, have also been presented. For example, those based on the notion of non-domination argue that just as political participation is necessary to prevent domination between governments and citizens, it is also necessary to prevent domination between employers and employees (González-Ricoy 2014). Although I will not address this argument in detail, I suspect its plausibility also depends on the premise that labor relations are not genuinely voluntary for employees. As mentioned, this premise is questionable, especially if we assume that the state provides tools to empower employees, such as unemployment insurance or a basic income.

Part of the intuitive appeal of workplace democracy rests on the assumption that an employee starts and ends their working life necessarily employed by the same company. In a prosperous and diverse society, social mobility should be commonplace. A market economy that facilitates saving and private initiative, combined with economic stability, quality public services, and access to credit and other benefits, allows people to move fluidly between being employees, independent workers, or even employers, and back to employees if they wish. If such dynamism exists, then the debate about whether the state should *impose* forms of democracy within companies becomes less central.

5.5.3.5 Can the State "Stimulate" Employment?

Suppose it is our birthday, and we are hosting a big celebration at home. We invite family, friends, and their young children. Imagine that a friend's child accidentally breaks one of our window panes. Our friend immediately offers to pay for a new window. However, knowing it was an accident, we tell them it is not necessary and encourage them to enjoy the party without worry.

The bad news, then, is that we need to buy a new window. But as we say goodbye to our guests, a relative approaches and says: "Not all is bad news—after all, everyone must work to live. Accidents like these are necessary so people have jobs. What would glaziers live on if no windows were ever broken?".

The French economist Frédéric Bastiat (1850) explained why this type of reasoning is fallacious. His reflections were later popularized by the American journalist and public intellectual Henry Hazlitt (1952 [1946]), who named this reasoning "the broken window fallacy."

Bastiat argues that this fallacy consists of focusing on what is seen and overlooking what is not seen. What is seen is that the glazier has more work and therefore will earn more money. So, someone might think that the person who broke our window created jobs. But what is not seen is that, since we spend, say, eighty dollars on a new pane, we cannot spend that money on a different good, such as shoes or a book. What is not seen is that if we had not had to replace the glass, we could have benefited the shoemaker, the bookseller, or anyone else offering goods or services in the marketplace.

In other words, because someone broke our window, the glass industry experiences a boost. That is the visible effect. But if the accident had not occurred, some other industry could have been stimulated instead, and we would have preserved that opportunity. This is what remains unseen. The opportunity cost of buying a new pane lies in what we might have done with that money otherwise. Yet, opportunity cost, by referring to a counterfactual scenario—what could have been—is harder to grasp. The broken window fallacy thrives by exploiting this subtle complexity.

If we do not ignore this hidden cost, we can understand that the economy is not better off simply because someone broke a window. Let us compare two scenarios. In the first, where the accident occurred, we spend money to buy a new pane and end up with a window that is no better or worse than before. In the second, where the accident did not happen, we could use that same money, for example, to buy a pair of shoes—thus enjoying both an intact window and a new pair of shoes.

Bastiat explains that the broken window fallacy underlies many political arguments; for example, arguments in favor of raising taxes. Many people believe that raising tax rates can stimulate employment because the government can hire more workers—such as administrative personnel, senior officials, and public works professionals. These new jobs represent the visible benefits: what is seen. What is not seen, however, is that if those taxes did not exist, individuals could use that money to purchase goods and services in the private sector, thereby creating jobs there instead.

It should be clarified that Bastiat's argument is not a defense of anarchism. He does not propose abolishing all taxes or the state itself. He acknowledges that certain taxes are necessary to finance essential public services, such as security and street cleaning. His point is that justifications for taxation must appeal to arguments demonstrating why what will be financed with that money is important for society. In some cases, this is straightforward—security, for example, is clearly vital. Bastiat does not criticize these arguments; rather, he challenges the belief that taxes are good merely because they enable the government to hire more employees. The idea that government can stimulate employment by raising revenue and increasing spending ignores that citizens could have used their money for other purposes, creating jobs elsewhere. When evaluating the entire situation, it is incorrect to claim that employment has been stimulated: more people work in the public sector (what is seen), but fewer work in the private sector.

Some might object that Bastiat's argument overlooks that many people "freeze" their savings—that is, without certain taxes, people might not necessarily spend more in the private sector because their money forms part of savings that will not be immediately spent, thus failing to boost the economy.

However, this objection is based on a narrow notion of consumption. People with savings in banks are also, in a relevant sense, consuming. Banks rely on deposits to operate and provide services such as mortgages. Some people can buy houses because others have saved money in banks. Depositors benefit by receiving interest on their funds, while banks use these funds to offer loans that enable investments in the community. Raising tax rates could discourage these activities.

But what about those who have savings in foreign banks? That money is not useful for enriching the local economy. What might be the hidden cost of taxing these people more heavily? The hidden cost could be that, by having to use some of their foreign savings to pay taxes, they might replenish those savings with domestic money, potentially leading to layoffs, reduced hiring, or lower wages.

Ultimately, the rule is that the state cannot truly "stimulate employment" by increasing public spending. This illusion rests on our tendency to overlook opportunity costs.

5.6 The Economic System in Brief

In this chapter, I showed that FSC can explain the functioning of the economic system in a liberal democracy. First, I argued that private property solves some problems that would emerge in the primitive cooperation scenario. Basically, the institution of private property lowers monitoring costs and solves the problems of suboptimal production and excessive consumption. Then, I explained the foundation of money in this type of system: reducing transaction costs and facilitating trade. Moreover, after reflecting on the institution of criminal law as a way to protect the cooperation scheme, I analyzed, through the lens of FSC, the typical mechanisms of state financing: the tax system, public debt, and, in some cases, monetary issuance.

Furthermore, I argued that FSC explains the market as a dispersed cooperation scheme where people engage in first-order cooperative activities related to producing and providing goods and services; *in principle*, everyone's contribution is important, but no single contribution is indispensable. In this sense, the market economy differs from the centrally planned economy, which is incompatible with FSC because in such a system the economy's functioning depends on the correct performance of state bureaucracy (a performance that, for reasons given by Hayek, is destined to fail).

Likewise, I explained that skepticism toward the idea that the market is a cooperation scheme rests on two myths: that the market is a zero-sum game, and that only the best succeed in the market.

Finally, I argued that the state, through institutions such as antitrust legislation and labor laws—supported by non-state entities like unions—can undertake second-order activities aimed at addressing market failures that threaten the cooperation framework. These failures include monopolies, oligopolies, monopsonies, and oligopsonies.

CHAPTER 6

The State as a First-Order Cooperator

In the previous chapters, I showed that FSC can explain the economic and political institutions characteristic of liberal democracy. On one hand, FSC accounts for the typical forms of economic organization under liberal democracy—essentially, how the market institution operates, where agents engage in first-order activities related to producing and providing goods and services. On the other hand, FSC accounts for the organization and functioning of the state apparatus—both internally, with different agencies *cooperating* among themselves, and externally, through second-order activities aimed at safeguarding the overall cooperative scheme via coercion: from criminal law to labor and antitrust legislation.

This chapter aims to analyze another dimension of the state. In liberal democracies, the state performs functions that go beyond mere second-order cooperation. The state seeks not only to preserve the cooperative scheme but also to provide certain fundamental goods and services—such as sidewalks, streets, roads, transportation, healthcare, education, and subsistence resources, among others. These are first-order cooperative activities intended to ensure that the provision of goods and services

E. Spector, *Freedom as Social Cooperation*,
https://doi.org/10.1007/978-3-032-12217-9_6

essential for pursuing a life plan does not depend solely on market participants' performance.[1] In this way, state provisioning can be understood as reinforcing the cooperative scheme. Generally, provision occurs in two ways: directly, when the state itself delivers services (such as a public school), or indirectly, when the state encourages provision by contracting a company to carry out the project (such as infrastructure construction). Since FSC seeks to explain the dynamics of contemporary liberal democracies, it must also account for these state functions.

This chapter examines some of the main first-order activities undertaken by modern states: the provision of pathways (sidewalks, streets, and roads), transportation systems, healthcare, education, media, support for marginalized groups (which I call "integration tools"), and retirement savings mechanisms. Other first-order activities will be addressed only preliminarily; for example, when discussing infrastructure delivery systems for building sidewalks, streets, and roads, I will note that these models can also be applied to energy and hydraulic projects, although I will not delve into those here.

My aim is to analyze these state functions in light of FSC. This book began by defending a philosophical conception of freedom, but as the chapters have progressed, I have gradually lowered the level of abstraction to address institutional and increasingly concrete issues. As I have claimed, while FSC offers a philosophical account of freedom, its application to concrete political and economic institutions yields results that are familiar and consistent with established principles—such as the dispersion and decentralization of power and influence, as well as the symbiosis between the public sphere and private initiative. This chapter brings the discussion down to its most concrete level, with the aim of using those principles to clarify which systems of state provision of goods and services best align with FSC. However, I do not seek to reach definitive conclusions. This chapter should be understood as a reflective exercise meant to illustrate the *kind of reasoning* a supporter of FSC should follow when justifying state provision systems, rather than as a categorical defense of any particular modality. Even if I were mistaken, and the modalities I suggest were not the most suitable from the perspective of FSC, that

[1] The distinction between these two functions of the state is similar to the one James Buchanan (2000 [1975]: 93) makes between the "protective" state and the "productive" state: the former ensures and enforces the fundamental rules that safeguard individual rights, while the latter facilitates the provision of goods and services.

mistake would not invalidate the ideal of FSC, nor would it call into question the importance of reflecting on which institutional systems best align with that ideal.

One final clarification: in modern democracies, individuals have rights to these state-provided goods and services. Yet, from the FSC perspective, these rights should not be considered *positive* rights—or if they are, a crucial caveat must be made. A positive right entails a claim to receive something from someone else. Whenever a positive right exists, a correlating positive duty falls on another person or institution to provide what is owed. The concept of a positive right thus *suggests*—though it does not logically entail—a one-sided relationship between recipient and provider. To understand these rights from the point of view of FSC, it is essential to reject this view. The central idea of FSC is that everyone's freedom arises from the same cooperative scheme to which all contribute—freedom is a cooperative practice in which all individuals engage in mutual collaboration. Therefore, our right to state-provided goods and services is the right to benefit from a structure we help sustain. It is not merely a matter of one person holding a right and another bearing a duty; rather, it is a shared practice of mutual responsibility within a cooperative framework.

To be sure, this Hohfeldian[2] description can serve to capture the concrete situation of someone going to a public hospital and requesting medical care, for example. But on a deeper level, the relationship is not unilateral: we have the right because we are part of the system and contribute to maintaining it day by day.[3] The same reasoning applies here as in the previous chapters: the owner of the supermarket where the subway driver buys groceries is contributing to the public transportation industry. The trainer at the gym where the administrative staff of a state airline work out also contributes to the transportation sector by offering a place for them to relax and recharge before returning to work. FSC conceptualizes modern society as a cooperative scheme, where everyone depends on everyone else, without being at anyone's mercy.

[2] Wesley N. Hohfeld (1913) explained rights—more precisely, what he called "claim-rights"—in terms of their correlation with duties.

[3] This is the general rule. In Sect. 6.5, I analyze the case of individuals who are not integrated into the scheme. I will explain that the cooperative scheme itself includes tools to integrate those who are excluded, enabling them to begin making their contribution.

6.1 Circulation Infrastructure

We could not develop or carry out our life plan without moving from one place to another. Whether to get to work, school, the hospital, a restaurant, a museum, the cinema, a sports club, a social event, or any other destination, we rely on circulation infrastructure. Similarly, we depend on others coming to us to provide services—whether it is repairing a broken water pipe, fixing a car malfunction, or arranging pest control at home.

In this section, I offer a theory of circulation infrastructure that respects the ideal of FSC. We can distinguish between two types of circulation infrastructure: static and mobile. Static circulation infrastructure includes sidewalks, streets, and roads (and their lighting). Mobile circulation infrastructure refers to the various transportation modes that move people and goods from one place to another, such as buses, subways, and other transit systems.

6.1.1 Static Circulation Infrastructure

Static circulation infrastructure is made up of sidewalks, streets, roads (and their lighting). These goods are *public* benefits: they benefit everyone without excluding those who did not contribute to their financing. In the case of a gated community with its own sidewalks and streets, it is perfectly possible to exclude those who do not pay the fees. The situation is different when it comes to open neighborhoods, where people come and go constantly, making it unfeasible to charge for the use of streets and sidewalks (roads are an exception, since tolls could be charged). The state provides these goods and services under the understanding that their provision cannot depend on the market, since they are goods and services that people generally have no incentive to supply in such a context. Indeed, almost no one would be interested in producing a good or service that can be consumed without paying. On the one hand, the activity would not be profitable. On the other, it would be convenient to wait for someone else to produce it in order to benefit for free. As everyone reasons this way, the good or service goes unproduced (or at least not produced in sufficient quantities to meet demand). Faced with this situation, the state takes on the role of supplier.

6.1.1.1 *Infrastructure Delivery Systems: The Relationship between the State and the Private Sector*

Before analyzing static circulation infrastructure, it is important to distinguish between the different ways the state can lead these infrastructure projects. (1) Which infrastructure delivery system is more compatible with FSC: direct state provision or indirect state provision through a company? (2) Assuming the latter, what type of agreement between the state and the company best aligns with FSC?

Starting with the first question, two basic models can be identified. The first is a purely centralized model, where state-owned companies design, build, operate, and maintain infrastructure projects. This was the dominant model until the late 1980s: public infrastructure was built by governments, financed through taxes (or public debt), and managed by public agencies. The second model is decentralized, where private companies take on these responsibilities—or at least some of them, such as design and construction. This model assumes a prior, open, and competitive bidding process.

FSC generally advocates decentralizing authority to avoid making the system's stability overly dependent on the performance of any one participant. When a single entity is responsible for designing, constructing, operating, and maintaining infrastructure while also overseeing compliance, the system becomes too reliant on that entity. This occurs when state-owned companies handle all these tasks. While oversight bodies within the state may engage in intra-state cooperative activities by supervising the public entity, independence is better achieved if the supervisory institution is *entirely* separate from the one it oversees. Contracting private firms through competitive bidding appears more conducive to this ideal.

Note that, in this framework, the state fulfills both first- and second-order cooperative activities: first-order by providing goods and services through intermediaries, and second-order by controlling the firms responsible to ensure proper fulfillment of their duties.

Recent history demonstrates numerous benefits when the public sector opens traditional functions to the private sector, with many governments even welcoming foreign private investment. The private sector contributes expertise, discipline, and advanced technology that can significantly enhance efficiency. However, the FSC argument is not premised on private sector superiority in efficiency, but rather on the principle of separating the controlling authority from the entity being controlled.

Through an open and competitive bidding process, the selected firm is obligated to meet specific standards, with the state enforcing sanctions for any non-compliance.

Regarding the second question, the state has three primary ways to involve the private sector in infrastructure provision. The first entails the state contracting a firm through competitive bidding solely to design and build the project, fully financing it with tax revenues or public debt—including any unforeseen costs. Upon completion, the firm exits, and a government agency assumes responsibility for operation and maintenance. In this arrangement, the firm's role is limited, while the state bears the associated risks, such as budgeting errors, fluctuations in operational and maintenance costs, unexpected changes in revenue, technological obsolescence, and related uncertainties.

In the second modality, the company contracted by the state—also selected through a public tender—assumes nearly all responsibilities permanently: financing, designing, constructing, maintaining, and operating the project. This company bears all associated risks, including those arising from governmental actions such as changes in laws or regulations, as well as risks related to inflation, interest rates, exchange rates, and even the possibility of expropriation. In return, the company receives all the benefits generated by the project's success, primarily through its revenue (Engel et al. 2021: 17).

The third model represents a middle ground between the previous two. In this case, the state and the private company share both responsibility and risks—an arrangement commonly known as a Public–Private Partnership (PPP). According to the World Bank, PPPs are long-term contracts between a public institution and a private party for the provision of infrastructure or services, where the private party assumes a *portion* of the risks and management responsibilities, including securing much of the financing (Cangiano et al. 2006). The company typically finances, designs, and constructs the project, then operates and maintains it for a specified period—usually exceeding a decade—always adhering to governmental standards. In return, during the operational phase, the company receives revenue streams from user fees (such as tolls) or public funds that ideally cover and exceed its investment and costs. At the end of the concession, ownership of the assets reverts to the state (Engel et al. 2013: 84).

The major strength of this model lies in the optimal allocation of risks through the contract. Typical provisions in these agreements include detailed project descriptions and requirements; guarantees; maintenance obligations; performance monitoring; pricing and payment mechanisms; contract duration, extension, and termination clauses; methods for concession allocation; tax treatment; waivers of sovereign immunity; provisions for legal changes; and dispute resolution procedures. The core principle is that the contract identifies each specific risk and assigns responsibility to the party best positioned to manage or mitigate its impact (Wiss and Faria 2007: 191, 195).

The model most aligned with the ideal of FSC appears to be the third. The interaction between the state and private companies, with both assuming distinct responsibilities and risks, better honors the concept of social cooperation than models where only one party bears the burden. Assigning responsibility for each risk to the party best positioned to eliminate or at least minimize the associated costs strengthens the cooperation scheme because it disperses power and creates clear incentives for efficient management. Moreover, allocating certain risks—primarily those beyond the company's control—to the state encourages firms to offer their services by reducing the financial uncertainty they face, thereby enriching the cooperative framework. Conversely, assigning other risks to the company rather than the state motivates the government to initiate more projects of this kind, as it shifts some of the financial and operational burdens to the private partner.

The use of PPPs to substitute public infrastructure service provision is increasingly common. Many capital-intensive projects, such as highways, water, and sewage systems, are being developed through this mechanism. For example, the average annual value of €22.9 billion in PPP projects signed in Europe between 2002 and 2006 was three times the average annual value of the previous decade. Similarly, investment in PPPs in developing countries grew at an average annual rate of 28.3% between 1990 and 1997, followed by a slowdown after the East Asian crisis, and renewed growth starting in 2003, reaching $154.4 billion in 2008 (Engel et al. 2013: 83–84). Many Latin American countries have also employed this modality; for instance, Chile has developed numerous projects including roads, airports, and prisons, while Mexico has used this format for energy projects.

6.1.1.2 *Static Circulation Infrastructure and the Different Levels of Government*

Having explored the interactions between the state and private companies in financing, designing, constructing, operating, and maintaining infrastructure works, I now turn to analyzing which level of government should bear responsibility for these activities. I distinguish between two aspects of static circulation infrastructure: on one hand, its construction (including design), and on the other, its maintenance (and operation, where applicable). Regarding financing, it should generally be tied to the activity. For example, if local government is responsible for maintenance, it should also finance it (ideally contracting companies under a public–private scheme, as mentioned earlier). However, it should not be ruled out that, in some cases, the federal government may also contribute to local projects through subsidies, thereby complementing the scheme.

My analysis begins at the end of the story: assuming static circulation infrastructure is already built, I will first discuss its maintenance. Afterwards, I will evaluate its construction.

Maintenance

To honor the ideal of FSC, the maintenance system must be designed to minimize damage caused by anti-cooperative behaviors as well as to facilitate repair if such damage occurs. In this regard, we can distinguish among three models. I will set aside here the issue of whether governments perform these tasks through private companies and, if so, the contracting modality they adopt, focusing instead on the discussion of different levels of government.

The first model assigns responsibility to the federal government, which takes charge of maintaining static circulation infrastructure, including its lighting sources. The second model delegates this responsibility to smaller units: states, communities, or provinces (what we might call "the federal model"). The third model hands over responsibility to even smaller units, such as communes or municipalities.

My thesis is as follows: in principle, the smaller the unit to which responsibility for maintaining static circulation facilities is delegated, (1) the less damage anti-cooperative behaviors will cause, and (2) the easier the repair will be. (The phrase "in principle" is deliberate: as I will explain later, decentralization should not be undertaken without careful consideration of implementation issues).

The first point should by now be familiar: the more distributed a given responsibility, the greater the degree of cooperation and the less damage caused by non-compliance from any single responsible party. In the first, purely centralized model, state failures to fulfill responsibility jeopardize the maintenance of all streets, sidewalks, roads, and their lighting. This does not mean that a failed state necessarily refrains from all maintenance. It may focus on some provinces while neglecting others, or concentrate solely on certain cities. Alternatively, it could perform maintenance nationwide but poorly. The key point is that, whether due to inefficiency or corruption, a failed state jeopardizes at least a significant portion of the cooperative scheme.

Now suppose the scheme adopts the third model. In this case, various communes or municipalities with local authorities (ideally democratically elected) are responsible for maintaining and lighting sidewalks and streets (roads will be discussed later), with resources provided by local governments for these purposes. All these communes or municipalities form a system, but given their limited territorial jurisdictions (each local authority being in charge only of its corresponding part), anti-cooperative behavior by any single unit does not jeopardize the entire scheme, thereby approaching the FSC ideal.

It is true, however, that delegating responsibility to such small units might create coordination problems. For example, a broader authority might strategically plan road closures to repair one street or another, considering the impact on traffic. If that task is distributed among multiple municipalities or communes, disorganization could lead to excessive traffic congestion as vehicles attempt to move across jurisdictions. Of course, municipal or communal authorities could agree on a joint plan to prevent this. But if, for some reason, this proves unfeasible, the solution might be to adopt the second model, assigning responsibility to states, provinces, or communities. The key is to maintain a reasonably dispersed distribution of responsibilities to preserve the cooperative scheme.

Roads require a different analysis since they typically span unpopulated territories crossing multiple cities and municipalities, demanding greater investment of resources and time for maintenance. Assigning responsibility solely to municipalities—each handling only its portion of the road—would be impractical and too burdensome, diverting attention from local matters. In this case, it appears even clearer that the second model is appropriate, with states, provinces, or communities responsible for maintaining their respective sections. This is the case in the

United States, where states (sometimes with city collaboration) maintain all roads, including interstates, though the federal government, through the Federal Highway Administration, provides subsidies.[4] By contrast, in England, the main roads are maintained directly by a government-owned company.[5] As seen, the U.S. model fits better with the FSC ideal.

The second point is that decentralizing responsibility for maintaining static circulation infrastructure facilitates repairing damages caused by particular anti-cooperative behaviors. This is due to the proximity between maintenance authorities and users. Naturally, it is easier to hold a municipal authority accountable than the federal government. Municipal or communal authorities usually have closer contact with citizens because their jurisdictions are smaller. When it becomes necessary to assign responsibilities to broader units such as states, provinces, or communities—usually to reduce coordination costs or address other practical challenges—the connection to citizens becomes less direct but still remains closer than the relationship between ordinary citizens and the federal government.

Construction

The construction (and design) of static circulation infrastructure requires even greater logistical coordination than maintenance. It demands an urban planning scheme to determine the paths that sidewalks, streets, and roads will follow. This plan—which, as explained, is usually implemented by the state in collaboration with contracted companies—cannot be developed by uncoordinated units such as communes or municipalities. While these units could attempt a joint project, failure to reach agreement would likely necessitate coordination by a broader authority. For sidewalks and streets, state, provincial, or community governments could assume responsibility. Thus, the quantity and quality of these public services will be key factors that citizens will consider when "voting with their feet," that is, deciding where to live.

From the FSC perspective, the ideal scenario would be for state, provincial, or community governments to reach an agreement on the design and construction of roads that span multiple states (provinces or

[4] https://highways.dot.gov/highway-history/interstate-system/50th-anniversary/interstate-frequently-asked-questions#:~:text=Although%20the%20Federal%20Government%20provided,own%20and%20operate%20the%20roads (last accessed: August 27, 2025).

[5] https://nationalhighways.co.uk/our-roads/ (last accessed: August 27, 2025).

communities). They could jointly promote tenders, select the company to carry out the project, and share responsibilities and risks.

Such a scheme would also have the potential to withstand anti-cooperative behaviors. For example, anti-cooperative behavior might involve a state government choosing not to actively participate in the bidding process. In this scenario, the scheme could still function due to the collaboration of the remaining governments, which would proceed with the project. A more severe form of anti-cooperation could involve a state government refusing to allow a particular road to cross its territory—assuming no valid justification and acting solely out of a non-cooperative stance. In such a case, the federal government could undertake second-order cooperative actions aimed at preserving the scheme, such as sanctioning states that refuse to cooperate, thereby creating incentives for collaboration.

If a joint project proves unfeasible for any reason, the federal government should assume responsibility for the task. While this would not be ideal from the FSC perspective—since a critical circulation element would depend on the performance of a single actor—practical considerations might justify it. In such circumstances, the scheme should rely on internal federal oversight mechanisms (intra-state cooperative activities) as well as the delegation of powers between the state and contracted companies, as analyzed previously.

6.1.1.3 Horizontality and Verticality

In summary, the cooperation scheme supporting the provision of static circulation infrastructure can be understood as extending both horizontally and vertically: horizontally, from the state to the private companies it contracts; and vertically, from the top down through the various levels of government.

Regarding horizontality, I have argued that the Public–Private Partnership (PPP) system best embodies the FSC ideal. Concerning verticality, I have contended that responsibilities should be decentralized, though without overlooking coordination challenges and logistical constraints. In this context, I suggested that the optimal balance, generally for construction and maintenance, tends to lie in distributing responsibilities among provinces, states, or communities.

6.1.2 *Mobile Circulation Infrastructure*

Unlike the previously discussed goods and services, transport services are not, strictly speaking, public benefits. This means they can be targeted specifically to those who pay, excluding those who do not. For example, it is perfectly feasible to bar entry to a subway system for anyone who has not paid their fare. Generally, the state provides these goods and services because, although they could emerge through market mechanisms, their importance justifies public involvement to ensure provision does not solely depend on the private sector.

Much of what was said earlier about the distribution of responsibilities across different levels of government also applies to transport services. However, it is important to highlight a nuance. Regarding static infrastructure, decentralization appeared as the only cooperative alternative, without fully considering a mixed model in which both federal and local governments provide such infrastructure.

The idea behind a mixed model is that individuals could choose between benefits provided by the federal government and those offered by local governments. However, this alternative is often unfeasible for static infrastructure. If a person needs to travel a certain route across the country (from point A to point B), a mixed model would imply that drivers could choose between a federal route and a local route covering the same trajectory. While this duplication of routes is theoretically possible and could in some cases alleviate traffic congestion, it could also be highly inefficient, as it occupies valuable space that might be better utilized for other purposes. It is therefore reasonable to oppose the creation of redundant routes following identical paths.

By contrast, in the realm of mobile circulation infrastructure, cooperative work between federal and local governments is entirely feasible. Both levels of government can effectively provide transport services—such as trains, subways, buses, taxis, or airplanes—to their citizens.

Furthermore, distributing responsibilities between the different levels of government and private companies is key to enriching the cooperative framework. In general, the state provides transport services through private companies, though sometimes through state-owned entities. These services include trains, subways, buses, taxis, and sometimes airplanes. As in other sectors, the goal is to expand cooperation to broaden the range of options and reduce dependence on any single provider. As previously noted, markets function best when consumers have diverse alternatives. Yet, this system is strengthened when the state ensures the provision of essential goods and services, preventing reliance solely on market forces. Such first-order cooperative action by the state is vital for maintaining affordable services, especially in sectors where market concentration leads to price increases.

Nevertheless, the potential of the private sector to offer transportation services at reasonable prices should not be underestimated. By private sector, I refer to companies operating independently, not as state contractors—although they must comply with certain requirements, such as licensing. For example, even if the state, at any level, manages rail infrastructure and owns rail services, private companies may still provide train travel using their own trains, paying the state a fee for track access. Since 2018, Spain has been liberalizing its railway sector. The Rail Infrastructure Administration, a public entity, is responsible for building and managing railways. Renfe, a state-owned company, provides freight and passenger rail services. However, the system also welcomes private companies—and even state-owned companies from other countries, such as Ouigo—to participate. The only requirements are a railway operator license and a safety certificate. Although liberalization is recent and competition currently involves just three companies (Renfe, Ouigo, and Iryo), ticket prices have already fallen compared to the period before liberalization.

This reasoning applies equally to subways, buses, and even airplanes. Private initiative can greatly enrich the transport provision system and complement the state's offerings. Public and private transport can form a cooperative framework. Of course, "openness" does not mean "lack of coordination." The state can efficiently regulate routes, frequencies, and schedules. But there is no reason to exclude private participation; on the contrary, from the FSC perspective, openness is required.

To be sure, the line between coordination and anti-competitive closure is sometimes blurred. Governments may invoke coordination to create barriers that protect politically connected companies, often in exchange for campaign financing. Incumbents have strong incentives to lobby for restrictions that limit new entrants. These dynamics are found across various sectors, not just transportation. Barriers to entry can be direct or indirect. Direct barriers explicitly prohibit market entry, often citing market saturation when the real aim is incumbent protection. Indirect barriers formally allow entry but impose ambiguous and onerous bureaucratic requirements, enabling denials without appearing arbitrary.

Not only do the discriminated companies suffer from this dynamic, but public transportation users also bear the consequences, paying higher prices and enduring lower-quality services due to a concentrated market dominated by companies with little incentive to compete (Pincione 2015: 2457). As I pointed out in Sect. 5.5.2 of the previous chapter, under these circumstances, a state antitrust agency may be necessary to carry out second-order cooperative activities aimed at restoring the cooperative framework.

Often, market saturation is caused by the state itself. For example, in many countries, governments are responsible for opening and maintaining long-distance bus stations, either through a state agency or a specially contracted company. These stations naturally have limited capacity, with a maximum number of platforms and bays that can be built within a given space. This, in turn, limits the number of companies that can offer long-distance land transportation services, since by law buses generally must depart from and arrive at these stations. As a result, the market becomes "saturated." However, this need not be the case. Legislation could be relaxed to allow independent firms to open and maintain their own long-distance bus stations, charging bus companies a fee for using their platforms and bays. This approach would enable more bus companies to enter the market, bringing the associated benefits of lower prices and improved service quality.

Another example of how governments miss the opportunity to leverage the private sector's potential in transportation services is the strong restriction on competition in the taxi industry. For instance, Uber and other apps connecting drivers and passengers have made significant contributions by offering affordable services with safety standards that meet or even exceed those of state-run services. Yet, these apps are banned in many countries, typically because they do not comply with certain regulations. The key question is which of these regulations are genuinely appropriate and which unnecessarily hinder the operation of technologies that citizens demand and that often satisfy them.

Consider, lastly, the case of passenger air transport. Broadly speaking, states can adopt one of two policies for this sector: closed skies or open skies. A closed skies policy restricts which airlines may take off or land within the country's territory. In contrast, an open skies policy imposes no such restrictions, instead regulating only routes, schedules, and frequencies. Additionally, these policies can differ between national and international air transport; a state might apply an open skies policy internationally but maintain closed skies domestically, or vice versa.

It is important to note that between these extremes lies a spectrum of intermediate policies, with markets varying in openness. Regarding international transport, countries rarely liberalize markets unilaterally, typically doing so through reciprocal agreements. For instance, in the 1990s, European Union countries, led by the EU, adopted an open skies policy that increased the number of airlines and lowered prices. Consequently, air travel between European countries has become markedly cheaper. Similarly, in 2007, the EU and the United States concluded an open skies agreement permitting airlines from both regions to operate routes between European and North American cities.

Importantly, markets for different modes of transport are not always isolated from one another. Changes in one mode—such as subways, buses, taxis, railways, or airplanes—affect that sector and can ripple across others. For example, as discussed in Sect. 5.5.2 of the previous chapter, when a high-speed train began operating between Madrid and Seville, the modal split shifted dramatically from 33% rail and 67% air to 82% rail and 18% air. Clearly, many travelers view air and rail as alternative means for domestic travel, with competition spanning all airlines and railway lines connecting those cities (Sowell 2015: 167).

In short, the state, at its various levels, and even through private companies contracted for this purpose, can make a significant contribution by providing transportation services. Moreover, the potential of the private sector to enrich this system should not be underestimated. Both public and private transportation services can form a diverse and integrated structure, where users rely on the overall system rather than depending on any single component.

6.2 Healthcare

6.2.1 Healthcare and FSC

In this section, I analyze healthcare from the perspective of FSC. The World Health Organization (WHO) defines health as "a state of complete physical, mental and social well-being and not merely the absence of disease or infirmity."[6]

The positive aspect of this definition is that it understands health in a broad sense. Today, many physically healthy people suffer from severely incapacitating mental conditions, such as anxiety disorders or panic attacks. Even individuals who are physically and mentally healthy may face social circumstances that can eventually harm them physically and mentally, such as bullying. Therefore, the idea of defining health in terms of physical, mental, and social elements is apt.

The downside, however, is that *complete* physical, mental, and social well-being is impossible to achieve. Everyone is affected by some condition, even if it is only stress. The problem with such a demanding definition is that, if health is considered a right, it can never be fully respected and will always be violated. Defining a right in a way that makes it impossible to uphold seems to be problematic.

In any case, this problem can be resolved if we conceive the WHO's definition as a regulative ideal. Assuming it is unattainable, this ideal can nonetheless give rise to various duties aimed at bringing us as close to it as possible. In this way, the concept of health would serve as a sort of beacon indicating which path to take—an impossible goal, yet worthy of our best efforts.

In FSC, social cooperation is the very essence of freedom. More precisely, freedom is understood as a cooperative practice through which individuals develop and carry out their life plans within a stable framework—one that relies on the collaboration of all members collectively, yet on no one in particular. In this sense, the health of the participants in the framework is essential not only for each individual but also for the entire scheme. In other words, a participant's health not only strengthens their own potential to formulate and execute their life plan but also enhances the potential of all participants. This is so for two reasons.

[6] https://www.who.int/about/governance/constitution (last accessed: August 30, 2025).

The first concerns the quality of each participant's contribution: healthier individuals can contribute more effectively to the cooperative scheme. The second concerns the stability of the framework: if only an elite group has access to healthcare, then only they—and possibly a few fortunate individuals who have yet to require care—will have the full capacity to contribute. In this scenario, the scheme's functioning depends narrowly on these people, conflicting with the egalitarian requirement central to FSC. Universal healthcare, therefore, supports the stability of the cooperative framework.

Ultimately, if a social cooperation scheme is a context in which people help one another elaborate and realize their life plans, then ensuring everyone's access to healthcare strengthens this scheme, enhancing the freedom of all participants.

6.2.2 *Health Service as a Scheme of Cooperation*

If the health system is to uphold the ideal of FSC, it should rely on all its agents collectively rather than on any individual agent alone. This ensures that access to healthcare is not subject to the discretion of specific individuals or particular actors. Like other sectors, achieving this requires decentralization. Below, I analyze three decentralization criteria essential for designing a health system compatible with FSC: (1) the balance between public and private healthcare, (2) the distribution of responsibilities between national and regional levels, and (3) the integration of preventive and curative medicine.

6.2.2.1 Public Health and Private Health

The state's role as a first-order cooperator stems from the necessity to ensure the provision of certain goods and services does not rely solely on market forces. Health is a paradigmatic example of this, given its crucial importance for personal development and individuals' ability to contribute effectively to the cooperative scheme. A public health system that offers free or at least affordable services is essential to guarantee that access to healthcare does not rest entirely in private hands.

As Kenneth Arrow argued, the medical market has peculiar characteristics that distinguish it from other markets, such as those for food or clothing, and may distort its functioning. In the medical market, demand tends to be irregular and unpredictable, the expected behavior of medical professionals is more based on solidarity than self-interest, and the quality of medical services cannot be easily evaluated, among other factors (Arrow 1963: 948–954). These peculiarities provide additional reasons supporting the need for a public system.

The state health system can take two forms: institutions and insurance. Public health institutions typically include hospitals, clinics, and rehabilitation centers, which provide health services to the public, often free of charge or at subsidized rates.

Insurance systems distribute risk among individuals. Those exposed to certain risks pay a premium, and the collected funds are allocated to those who actually suffer the contingency. It functions as a reverse lottery: the winner is not the fortunate one, but the person who suffers the contingency, while all contributors are protected against that risk.

State insurance systems, in particular, have two fundamental characteristics. First, the package of benefits to which insured individuals must have access is established by law. Second, the cost of benefits provided to each person is independent of their purchasing power, so that everyone contributes according to their means and receives according to their needs (Tobar 2010: 110–111).

Nevertheless, while the medical market is indeed different from other markets, a private health system can still play a valuable role within a broader framework that includes the public system. The private system is important to ensure that the overall structure does not rely solely on public provision.

Private healthcare is often viewed as an alternative—and sometimes as a threat—to public health. The perception is that there is a zero-sum game between the public and private sectors: the more the private system expands, the more limited the public system becomes, potentially harming those with fewer resources. However, this view is far from accurate. In many cases, a private healthcare system, despite its flaws, can prevent the public system from collapsing. The reason is simple: the private sector absorbs part of the demand, relieving pressure on the public system. This allows the public system to deliver higher-quality services to its users. It is not that the private system weakens the public one; rather, it becomes essential precisely when the public system is struggling. The COVID-19 pandemic clearly illustrated this point. Most public health systems around the world became overwhelmed—not due to intrinsic weakness, but because of a sudden and massive increase in demand. The joint efforts of both public and private sectors were crucial in managing the crisis.

Let us consider another example: the Cuban healthcare system is entirely state-run. It is difficult to ascertain its current condition due to government restrictions on access to information. However, several doctors who have gone into exile from Cuba have sought to demystify the system by highlighting its precarious state, pointing to shortages of equipment, medications, and other critical issues.[7] From the perspective of FSC, the problem with relying solely on a single system is that everyone becomes vulnerable to its performance. A private healthcare system, driven by entrepreneurial initiative and operating within a framework that allows the importation of medical supplies, could help alleviate the burden on the public system by absorbing some of the demand and providing room for improvement. As noted earlier, a private system is not incompatible with a public one; rather, it can serve as a motivator for improvements in the public system.

In any case, the complementarity between public and private healthcare systems remains important even if the public system were ideal and fully capable of meeting demand. From the FSC perspective, the most relevant question is not whether the state system functions well, but whether access to healthcare depends solely on a single system. To be sure, the virtues of social cooperation become especially vivid when some participants act non-cooperatively, yet the system as a whole continues to function because it does not rely on any single actor. But FSC is less concerned with whether any particular system works well and more focused on whether we depend exclusively on a single system.[8]

[7] See, for example, the comments of doctors Alexander Pupo and Johan Pérez: https://diariodecuba.com/cuba/1614329360_29130.html (last accessed: August 30, 2025).

[8] It may be argued that the question of whether a particular system works is not less relevant. For example, even a defender of FSC should agree that having one system that succeeds is preferable to having several systems that fail. However, it is not clear why, or under what circumstances, we would be forced to choose between many failed systems or one successful system within a society. A more realistic concern is the following: once we have a system that works, should we accept it as it is or introduce additional systems to provide alternatives in case the first system eventually fails? From the FSC perspective, the answer is clear.

The original dilemma becomes somewhat more realistic at the global level, though it still demands considerable imagination. Suppose we must decide where to migrate, choosing between societies with one successful system and those with many failing systems. Which choice best respects FSC? As I will suggest in the next chapter, when applying FSC to the international context, it does not determine which choice is correct. Rather, it prescribes a global cooperation scheme of autonomous societies, none of which is

It is a concept of freedom where people are truly free only when their participation in a system does not leave them reliant on any specific component. The collaborative functioning of public and private healthcare systems helps realize this ideal by ensuring pluralistic access and reducing dependency on one sole provider.

Private healthcare can also take the form of institutions such as hospitals, clinics, and rehabilitation centers, as well as insurance providers. On the one hand, private institutions typically charge fees for their services. On the other hand, unlike public insurance, private insurers can offer customized benefit packages that vary in price depending on the coverage provided. This means that access to different plans depends on individuals' ability to pay. A competitive market for private insurance has the potential to offer affordable options across social classes, which is particularly important when the public system is insufficient.

Interestingly, insurance systems—both public and private—can be seen as cooperative arrangements in themselves: their effectiveness relies on the collective contributions of all members rather than the participation of any single individual. This means the system can continue functioning even if some participants behave non-cooperatively; the problem arises if such behavior becomes widespread. Consider two such behaviors. The first is failing to pay premiums. Those who fail to pay lose their insurance benefits, but the system itself is not severely affected. Moreover, because it is relatively easy to exclude such members, this behavior is unlikely to become common.

The second form of uncooperative behavior requires deeper analysis. It is known as "moral hazard." In these cases, the insured, either consciously or unconsciously, seeks to take full advantage of their insurance coverage. One way this occurs is by increasing the likelihood of the insured event happening—for example, driving more recklessly when having car insurance. In the context of health insurance, policyholders sometimes exploit the system differently: they increase their use of covered services by repeatedly attending medical consultations or undergoing tests even when unnecessary. The insured often perceive that their benefits are substantial since the costs are shared among all contributors. In fact, this behavior is

indispensable, allowing people to choose alternatives if some act anti-cooperatively by establishing dictatorial or authoritarian systems. This is how FSC can account for the principles of sovereignty, self-determination, and refugee rights in international law.

sometimes encouraged by healthcare professionals who, aiming to maximize their income or satisfy patients, perform or recommend procedures that are not cost-effective (Tobar 2010: 112).

If this behavior becomes widespread, the system may lose stability and eventually collapse. Governments and private companies have adopted various strategies to discourage overconsumption incentives. One such approach is the copayment system, where the insurer and the insured share the cost of medical services. This system is widely used in Europe and the United States.

The copayment system has proven effective in reducing the consumption of medical resources. However, the goal should not be to do so at any cost. People might avoid using medical resources they do not need, but in an effort to save money, they could also forego necessary care. Evidence shows that low-income families are the most likely to reduce their use of medical resources under a copayment system (Beck 1974). This is particularly harmful for high-risk patients (Mas et al. 2011).

One possible solution is a progressive copayment system, where the percentage paid increases with the client's economic status. Another approach is to exempt vulnerable groups, as is done in Germany, France, Italy, and Portugal. A separate issue is whether such social measures should apply only to public insurance or if private insurers should also be legally required to adopt them.

6.2.2.2 Healthcare at Different Levels of Government

Previously, I analyzed the cooperative dynamics between the state and the private sector regarding the provision of health services. However, in this context, the state should also function internally as a cooperative framework. The public health system should not be entirely dependent on the federal government, as this places the responsibility for public health provision in the hands of a single participant within the system.

Of course, this does not mean that the federal government should refrain from providing health services. But local governments should *also* play a role in their provision, thereby expanding public health alternatives. In some countries, such as the United States, public health is primarily the responsibility of state governments. In others, like Argentina, responsibility is shared: there are public hospitals administered by the federal government alongside those run by provincial authorities. What runs counter to the principles of FSC is for the public system to rest solely on the federal government.

Regarding healthcare, there are reasons to believe that decentralization of responsibilities should not extend to municipalities or communes for certain services. High-complexity equipment, such as advanced CT scanners or MRI machines, is extremely costly. It is generally unrealistic to expect municipalities to have the necessary funds for such equipment. Therefore, it may be more practical for national or state-level hospitals—large enough to serve patients from multiple jurisdictions—to assume responsibility for acquiring and maintaining these resources.

That said, municipal clinics can still manage simpler healthcare needs by providing urgent care for minor injuries or mild infections. Some of these services, such as vaccinations, are already offered through pharmacies, helping to reduce hospital congestion. Centralizing the practice of medicine among physicians is important when dealing with symptoms or conditions that have not responded to initial treatment. However, the first stage of care can be effectively handled by nurses, trained pharmacists, or other healthcare professionals. This approach would not differ significantly from the near-automatic protocols physicians follow in emergency services when assessing patients who initially present with symptoms that do not *appear* serious.

For example, patients presenting with a sore throat may have anything from mild laryngitis to laryngeal cancer. Generally, doctors begin by assuming the less severe possibilities, based on statistical likelihood. They commonly prescribe medication to treat bacterial or viral infections and advise the patient to return if symptoms do not improve within a reasonable time. While these initial consults are typically handled by physicians, my point is that this task could also be carried out by other healthcare professionals (of course, if the patient returns without having been cured, they would then be referred to doctors). This modality decentralizes the structure and makes it less dependent on a single profession. This is especially vital in congested health systems.

6.2.2.3 Preventive Medicine and Curative Medicine

So far, I have argued that if the healthcare system is to honor the ideal of FSC, it should rely on all its participants but on no one in particular. This can be achieved by decentralizing responsibilities to minimize the harmful effects of uncooperative individual behaviors. In this regard, I have explored two criteria for such decentralization. The first is the distinction between public and private healthcare providers. The second focuses on how public healthcare can be delivered through different levels of government. Now, I intend to analyze a third criterion that might serve the purpose of decentralization: the distinction between preventive medicine and curative medicine.

Medicine should not be viewed merely as a tool for curing diseases. Over recent decades, awareness of the importance of prevention—and the consequent development of preventive methods and practices—has advanced significantly. We can distinguish two forms of preventive medicine: one that requires the assistance of a healthcare professional (or some form of medical intervention), and another that depends solely on the patient's own commitment. Examples of the former include vaccinations, blood tests, breast cancer screenings, dermatological exams, and colonoscopies. Examples of the latter are using condoms to prevent sexually transmitted infections; avoiding smoking to reduce the risk of lung, throat, or tongue cancer; and maintaining a healthy diet and regular exercise to prevent hypertension, high cholesterol, and some autoimmune diseases such as type 2 diabetes.

Both forms of preventive medicine strengthen the cooperative framework by further decentralizing the responsibility for health provision. Not only do we have public and private systems, and various public systems operating at different government levels, but the individual also becomes a provider of their own health by taking the initiative to undergo preventive check-ups or committing to a healthy lifestyle. Thanks to this alternative source of health—namely, the individual—the system's dependence on particular agents is reduced, as prevention decreases the likelihood of severe illness.

Of course, the probability of falling ill can never be reduced to zero. Some serious diseases may occur even when an individual has adopted the healthiest habits, as certain conditions are not influenced by lifestyle choices—for example, some forms of childhood cancer. Nonetheless, lowering the likelihood of contracting serious illnesses through preventive screenings and healthy behaviors remains crucial. This approach adds another source of health—one derived from the individual's own behavior—making them more self-sufficient and, consequently, less dependent.

A society committed to FSC should implement strategies to raise awareness about disease prevention. Most countries have conducted public campaigns emphasizing the importance of screenings for breast, prostate, colon, skin, and other cancers that can be prevented or more effectively treated when detected early. Since the 1990s, governments worldwide have promoted condom use to prevent sexually transmitted infections. Additionally, some countries—such as Chile and Argentina—have enacted front-labeling laws requiring warning labels on products high in saturated fats, sugars, calories, or sodium.

Furthermore, evidence shows that vaccines represent one of the most important advances in medicine. They have enabled the prevention of diseases such as smallpox, tetanus, measles, hepatitis, and some forms of meningitis, among many others. In this regard, all countries have enacted laws establishing mandatory vaccination schedules, although the specific vaccines included vary by country. These regulations constitute a significant step toward realizing FSC ideals, as they enhance the self-sufficiency of individuals within the cooperative healthcare framework.

Finally, it should be noted that preventive medicine not only reduces individual dependence but also benefits the entire system. First, it helps prevent the spread of contagious diseases. Second, it alleviates pressure on healthcare systems by freeing resources for patients with diseases that cannot be prevented, often due to primarily genetic causes or conditions yet to be fully understood, such as lupus or certain forms of sclerosis.

6.2.2.4 Health: "A Responsibility for All"

In summary, a health system aligned with FSC is a broadly diversified framework in which individuals, although relying on the system as a whole, do not depend on any single component in particular. This can be achieved through cooperation between public and private healthcare providers, as well as collaboration between the federal government and local governments in providing public health services. Crucially, this should not detract from the individual's own responsibility to take preventive measures, thereby becoming less dependent and simultaneously helping to alleviate the strain on a system that is often overwhelmed.

6.3 Education

6.3.1 The Education of the Participants in the Scheme

From the perspective of FSC, education serves as the primary means through which young people integrate into the cooperative scheme and begin contributing. Through education, young individuals acquire the essential tools to become cooperative members of society.

FSC defines freedom as a cooperative practice aimed at the development and realization of life plans. This cooperative practice occurs within a system whose stability depends on everyone, yet not on any individual in particular. The same reasoning applied to health also holds true for education. Training future participants in the cooperative scheme is vital not only for each individual but for the scheme as a whole. In other words, educating an individual enhances their ability to design and pursue a life plan while simultaneously strengthening the collective potential of all participants. Firstly, educated participants have more tools at their disposal and can make more meaningful contributions. Secondly, if only an elite few receive education and possess the specific skills needed for certain tasks, the entire cooperative scheme becomes dependent on them for those tasks, which diverges from the ideal of FSC. Universal education is therefore fundamental to the stability and resilience of a cooperative scheme.

Ultimately, if a social cooperation scheme is a context in which individuals help each other develop and realize their life plans, then the education of each participant reinforces this scheme and thereby advances the freedom of all.

6.3.2 The Educational System as a Cooperation Scheme

According to FSC, education can be regarded as the means through which young people enter the cooperation scheme. However, this should not be taken to imply that the educational system exists *apart from* the cooperation scheme. To put it metaphorically, if the scheme were a building, the educational system would be the entrance hall—the way to *access* the building, but still an integral part of it. Through education, individuals become integrated into the scheme, yet the educational system is not an external structure; it is part of the scheme itself. The conclusion, then, is that since the educational system is part of the cooperation scheme, it should operate according to the scheme's own principles.

In Sect. 5.5.2 of the previous chapter, I explained why the concept of monopoly is, in principle, incompatible with FSC. When there is a monopoly in the production of a good or service, the participants in the scheme who wish to consume it find themselves at the mercy of that single provider. In the case of the state's coercive monopoly, the solution has been to divide power among various branches. For monopolies, monopsonies, oligopolies, and oligopsonies in the provision of goods and services, solutions have included labor regulations and antitrust laws. In any case, a cooperation scheme should first aim to prevent such practices and, if prevention is not possible, to regulate them effectively.

The case of education requires a similar analysis. The greater the educational supply—including both public and private schools—the less power any single provider holds, and the more vibrant and resilient the cooperation scheme becomes. As a result, families depend on having an educational system with a *variety* of institutions offering diverse options but are not dependent on any one institution in particular. In this way, public and private education complement each other, enriching the overall cooperative framework.

Educational supply has two dimensions: quantity and variety. Quantity refers to the number of education providers in society, whether within the private or public sector. In the private realm, quantity denotes the number of education entrepreneurs engaged in creating and managing educational institutions—where "entrepreneurs" broadly includes both businesspeople and philanthropists. In the public sector, the most basic model has a single provider: the state. However, as we will see, the state may opt for a decentralized model where administrators of educational institutions enjoy considerable autonomy.

Variety, on the other hand, refers to the *diversity* of educational offerings. In this respect, both public and private systems may be more or less diverse, depending on how many educational models adapted to different types of students exist.

6.3.2.1 Quantity

The number of public and private institutions primarily depends on demand. However, demand in this market tends to exhibit some rigidity because elementary and secondary education are generally compulsory in modern societies. Demand for education can fluctuate, but it exhibits less elasticity compared to the demand for other goods, such as hamburgers or automobiles, which are purely discretionary and driven solely by individual preferences. Due to the mandatory nature of elementary and secondary education, individuals may express preferences regarding the choice of educational institution, but not with respect to whether to participate in education at all.

In the private system, greater demand will encourage education entrepreneurs to open more institutions because they will see this increased demand as an opportunity for professional and economic advancement. In the public system, greater demand will also compel the state to build more institutions; however, its motivation will not be personal gain but the necessity to ensure the educational system covers all students.

Generally, since a single educational institution can accommodate hundreds of students, an increase in demand does not immediately necessitate the establishment of new schools. Instead, it is often decided to expand existing facilities or, more controversially, to increase the number of students per class. The criteria and processes guiding such decisions ideally differ depending on whether the decision-maker is a public authority or a private education provider.

Suppose an education entrepreneur concludes that having 40 students per class is more economically profitable than maintaining smaller classes of, say, 20 students. Smaller class sizes require greater investment in human resources and infrastructure, leading to higher costs. Consequently, the entrepreneur may choose to open a school with classes of 40 students, even if there is evidence suggesting that smaller class sizes yield better learning outcomes.[9] However, the entrepreneur might reach a different conclusion—for instance, if competitors are opening schools with smaller class sizes and more personalized attention that attract a larger number of students. Ultimately, the decision will be contingent upon and shaped by the specific dynamics of the relevant market.

The public education system, in contrast, does not operate according to commercial logic but is guided primarily by academic and pedagogical principles. Here, the issue of student enrollment intersects with the imperative of maintaining educational quality. As a counterbalance to the private sector, the public system's role should be to provide superior alternatives that set higher educational standards—both in terms of class size and across all other aspects of educational service. By offering a high-quality public education, the state establishes a minimum standard below which private institutions would find it difficult to compete, as most students would prefer public schools. While private schools are generally required

[9] This issue is extensively debated in education research. For example, a study conducted by Finn and Achilles (1999) found that students in smaller classes demonstrated superior academic performance compared to those in larger classes, with particularly significant benefits for students from disadvantaged neighborhoods. Although this study has faced some methodological criticism, it sparked further research employing more sophisticated statistical techniques (see Finn et al. 2005; Wössmann and West 2006).

by law to meet certain standards, enforcing compliance across all institutions is challenging in practice. Consequently, a robust public education system that influences the incentives of private education providers serves as a vital complement to the overall educational landscape.

In turn, the private education system can serve as an important complement to the public system, especially when inefficiencies within the state hinder the provision of quality public education. In such contexts, a competitive private sector can offer alternative options tailored to the diverse needs of students, including those from low-income families. This is achievable if the private education market remains competitive enough to keep tuition affordable while providing schools with reputational incentives to attract talented students through partial or full scholarships (Tooley and Dixon 2006).

In fact, when faced with a flawed public education system, the state might seek to integrate low-income families into the private education sector. One way to achieve this is by providing vouchers to families, which function like money but are strictly designated for purchasing educational services. Under such a voucher system, families would have the freedom to choose between public and private institutions. Each voucher represents funds that the institution receives from the state for every enrolled student.

The evidence on the effectiveness of voucher systems is mixed. Since 1992, Sweden has operated a similar model that appears to function effectively. However, research conducted in U.S. states, as well as in countries like India and Chile, indicates that the voucher system has not significantly improved academic performance in private schools (Carnoy 2017). Still, the positive impact of school vouchers might lie not in private schools themselves but rather in incentivizing public schools to become more engaging and attractive, given that students can always opt for private alternatives. This question remains fundamentally empirical, and I do not delve into related studies here. But I want to emphasize that supporting multiple educational options aligns with the ideal of FSC, and an educational system that embraces such multiplicity should be viewed favorably from this perspective.

6.3.2.2 Variety

In addition to quantity, educational offerings encompass a dimension of variety, which can be understood in terms of methods and orientations. Methods refer to the distinct approaches used to deliver content—for example, traditional lectures where the teacher primarily conveys information, versus collaborative group work that encourages students to actively seek knowledge themselves. Orientations, by contrast, denote the curricular focus or emphasis, such as programs centered on science or on the arts.

The need for diversity in education stems from a fundamental reality: each young person possesses unique talents, skills, interests, and concerns. Consequently, it is improbable that a single educational model can adequately serve the millions of young individuals within any given society. Educational offerings must therefore be sufficiently diverse to accommodate the wide range of individual differences, ensuring that the education system can effectively adapt to each student's distinct needs.

However, diversity alone—although necessary—is insufficient for educational offerings to genuinely reflect the varied differences among youth. While the state may acknowledge the need for diversity and attempt to provide multiple educational models within the public system or mandate private institutions to do so, it faces a fundamental challenge. A *centralized* authority is scarcely equipped to accurately assess the needs of millions of young people in any given society. Educational diversity must align with the unique talents, skills, interests, and concerns of individuals within a given society. Such nuanced knowledge is unlikely to be systematized in a central database; rather, it is knowledge that principals and teachers acquire through daily interaction with students, observing their personalities and how they evolve over time.

Therefore, diversity in educational offerings should emerge from institutions endowed with considerable autonomy to adopt the methods and orientations that best meet the needs of their students. It is the principals and teachers who are best positioned to discern which models are most effective for their student bodies.

When considering educational diversity, private institutions often come to mind, as it is commonly assumed that diversity can only be achieved through market mechanisms. However, public institutions can also enjoy autonomy and offer diverse educational alternatives. Two examples will help to illustrate this point.

The first example refers to the education system in Finland, where virtually the entire system is public, yet it consistently ranks among the best in the world. The Finnish education system has attracted extensive research due to its significant progress between 1970 and 2000.

A defining characteristic of this system is that schools enjoy considerable autonomy in decisions related to educational methods and content. While the national government sets basic regulations—such as guaranteeing free education and limiting instructional hours—the municipalities have the freedom to tailor educational programs to meet the needs of their students. Furthermore, individual schools possess autonomy in interpreting and implementing these programs. Notably, Finland does not employ rigorous school inspections or standardized testing for students and teachers. Instead, the system relies heavily on trust in teachers' professionalism and on local self-evaluation to ensure quality and innovation (Sahlberg 2013: 128, 133).

The second example refers to charter schools in the United States, which are a distinctive type of public school. Like traditional public schools, they receive state funding and must adhere to baseline standards applicable to all public schools. However, charter schools enjoy greater autonomy in managing their budgets and in how they meet those standards. They design their own educational programs and have more flexibility in hiring and dismissing staff. Additionally, teachers in charter schools are not necessarily required to have formal education degrees; instead, demonstrating expertise in the subject they teach may suffice. For example, a chemist with subject matter expertise might teach chemistry without formal training as a professional educator (Schmidtz and Brighouse 2020: 20). Studies have suggested that students from vulnerable groups, such as Black and Hispanic students, perform better academically in charter schools. These schools serve all kinds of students but represent a particularly promising alternative for disadvantaged groups (CREDO 2015: 36, Schmidtz and Brighouse 2020: 34–35).

As can be seen, autonomy and diversity are not exclusively characteristic of the private system but can also exist within the public system, provided there is political will in that direction.

More broadly, educational diversity today takes forms that would have been unimaginable decades ago. Alongside the traditional method (in its various versions), alternative methods are now available, such as the Montessori or Waldorf systems, in which the student essentially has the freedom to direct their own activities and acquire knowledge independently, *guided* but not *directed* by the teacher. In some countries, such as Canada and Denmark, parents have the option to educate their children at home through homeschooling, often supported by private tutors. Additionally, many high schools offer students the possibility to choose among different academic tracks—such as humanities, arts, and technology—allowing for greater alignment with students' interests and concerns. Nonetheless, it is important to reiterate the earlier point: more valuable than abstract diversity is diversity attuned to the particularities of the millions of young people in a given society. This goal is best achieved not from a central office, but by granting substantial autonomy to the staff of individual educational institutions.

In summary, a broad educational offering—in both quantity and variety—across private and public sectors appears necessary for the education system as a whole to operate cooperatively in the sense of FSC, where individuals depend on the collective system without depending on any one institution in particular.

6.3.3 *Compulsory Schooling?*

Should education be compulsory? Is an educational institution the only place where people can be educated? Some authors distinguish between education and schooling. Education is the acquisition of skills necessary to function effectively in adult life. Schooling, also called "formal education," refers to attendance at an institution recognized by the state and fulfilling the goals established by that institution. John Stuart Mill, for example, supported compulsory education but expressed reservations about mandatory schooling (West 1994: 20). According to this line of thought, the state could set certain educational standards for individuals to meet and verify compliance through exams or other methods, without imposing a specific way to achieve them (see, for instance, the previous reference to homeschooling).

While schooling is one way for someone to acquire an education, it does not seem to be the only way: family, religious institutions, newspapers, television, radio, and especially the Internet are also sources of knowledge. In fact, many lessons in subjects like the hard sciences that were once only learned in face-to-face meetings with a teacher can now be learned through YouTube videos (such as those found on Khan Academy).

I do not delve deeply into whether schooling should be compulsory. The answer depends on whether people can acquire the same tools through other means. However, it is worth clarifying that, if this were possible, then a state committed to FSC should abandon the mandatory nature of formal education. All other educational avenues that individuals might take would strengthen the cooperation scheme. Indeed, by broadening their range of options, people would become less dependent on any one institution in particular.

6.3.4 *Religion in Schools?*

In Chapter 3, I emphasized that FSC is neutral in its content. The cooperation scheme that FSC identifies as constituting freedom does not presuppose any particular religious, moral, or philosophical conception of the good life. Within this scheme, participants are free to live according to their own worldview, with the sole requirement that their life plans be compatible with social cooperation—for example, harming others, refusing to pay taxes, or stealing would violate the conditions of social cooperation.

On the one hand, first-order cooperation refers to activities typically associated with the market, though some are also carried out by the state. On the other hand, second-order cooperation involves the state's role in protecting and maintaining the environment in which first-order cooperative activities occur, through laws designed to prevent and sanction behaviors that undermine social cooperation.

I have also stated that, from the perspective of FSC, education is the primary means by which young people integrate into the cooperation scheme and thereby contribute to the freedom of all. Young people join this scheme by acquiring certain tools through the educational process.

In this regard, I distinguish between two types of knowledge. The first type is essential for integrating into and actively contributing to the cooperation scheme within which individuals develop and realize their life plans. Since those possessing this knowledge will contribute more effectively to the shared scheme in which all participate—for example, through better-constructed buildings, improved medical treatments, higher-quality computers, or better-drafted laws—it is in everyone's interest that each individual acquires such knowledge during their education. This includes communication skills (such as speech and writing), knowledge across various fields (including the sciences, the social sciences, arts, and computing), the development of argumentative skills (such as informal logic), social skills, efficient management of time and material resources, and an understanding of the importance of social cooperation for life planning (a form of civic education based on FSC), among others.

The second type of knowledge does not contribute directly to the cooperation scheme but forms part of an individual's personal life plan. For example, religious instruction may not enhance one's contribution to the shared cooperation scheme; rather, it reflects the desires of certain parents who wish for their children to internalize particular religious doctrines. Because receiving such instruction does not necessarily improve one's ability to contribute to the cooperation scheme, it is not in everyone's interest that all acquire this knowledge, but only in the interest of certain individuals regarding their children.

This distinction clarifies why public institutions are compatible with FSC as long as they restrict themselves to imparting the first type of knowledge—the kind that positively impacts the cooperation scheme shared by all. Public institutions cease to be compatible with FSC if they begin to teach the second type of knowledge. As noted earlier, FSC involves reciprocity: everyone contributes to the scheme that constitutes the freedom of all. This reciprocity is undermined if public institutions start imparting a religious doctrine, as this would compel all taxpayers to subsidize the life plan of some individuals. However, religious instruction provided by private institutions poses no such tension with FSC; rather, it represents one among many personal life plans that can coexist within the broader cooperation scheme.

One may wonder whether a pluralistic model of religious education in the public sphere could be compatible with FSC. Rather than completely excluding religion, public schools could accommodate different religious and non-religious perspectives on an equal footing, providing space to teach various confessions either separately or jointly, as well as agnostic or atheistic views. If such a proposal proves feasible, then it aligns with FSC; precisely because it respects the principle of neutrality that is inherent to this conception of freedom.

However, I suspect that, in pluralistic societies, neutrality is best expressed through omissions rather than affirmative actions. Given the vast diversity of religious beliefs and doctrines, it may be practically impossible for public institutions to design policies or curricula that simultaneously satisfy all religious perspectives. Any attempt to actively endorse or integrate multiple religions would probably privilege some viewpoints over others, potentially generating conflicts and undermining neutrality. In short, I think that the most feasible approach for a state committed to FSC is to maintain impartiality by refraining from endorsing or promoting particular religious doctrines within public education.

6.4 Media

6.4.1 *Freedom of Expression as a Cooperative Practice*

Article 19 of the Universal Declaration of Human Rights defines "freedom of expression" as the right of every person "not to be disturbed because of their opinions, the right to seek, receive, and impart information and ideas through any media and regardless of frontiers."

As a conception of freedom rooted in cooperation, FSC holds a particular view on freedom of expression. According to this view, seeking, imparting, and receiving information are themselves collaborative efforts that sustain and enrich the social fabric. The constant flow of different types of information through the cooperation scheme contributes in various ways to the development and realization of life plans by all participants. Seeking, imparting, and receiving information are activities that are part of the cooperative environment within which people create and carry out their projects. In short, FSC views freedom of expression as a kind of cooperative practice.

To honor the ideal of FSC, the flow of information should depend on all participants collectively, yet not be reliant on any one individual or group in particular. We can conceive of a cooperation scheme with thousands or even millions of participants, each contributing diverse types and sources of information. The greater the diversity of these information sources, the less the scheme depends on any single participant or group, resulting in greater decentralization, resilience, and inclusiveness in the cooperative process. The opposite scenario involves information concentrated solely in particular participants of the scheme, whether the state or an economic group. This concentration contradicts FSC principles because the provision and flow of information no longer depend on the cooperative scheme as a whole but rather on specific participants, thus making the scheme vulnerable to the behaviors and interests of individuals or groups.

In this context, the state contributes to the scheme in at least two ways. First, the state performs first-order cooperative activities, complementing the private sector in disseminating relevant information. Second, the state carries out second-order cooperative activities by providing tools to citizens to report false information that might harm the scheme. Although the primary focus of this chapter is to explore the role of the state as a first-order cooperator, in this section I also refer to the second-order activities the state undertakes to protect the information scheme from falsehoods that could degrade it.

6.4.2 *Different Types of Information*

As noted in the previous section, the constant flow of information integrates the cooperation scheme within which people develop and carry out their life plans. We can distinguish between three types of information: practical information, journalistic information, and scientific information. Another form of expression is cultural or artistic content, which I will address at the end of this section.

6.4.2.1 Practical Information

Practical information refers to the kind of knowledge people use to navigate everyday life. For instance, individuals seek weather updates to decide whether to hold outdoor events, check traffic conditions to estimate travel times, and learn which areas of a city are more dangerous to avoid them. They also look up cultural or sports events to attend during their leisure time, such as art exhibitions, plays, movie premieres, and football matches.

Similarly, commercial activity would be impossible without a constant flow of information (the role of the price system in transferring information was elaborated in the previous chapter). People continuously seek data about available products and their quality. Thanks to technological advances, more information is readily accessible, providing greater opportunities for commerce by enabling better-informed decisions and more efficient markets.

Today, consumers have tools to identify the best products available. They read reviews about sellers on Amazon or Mercado Libre, or Tripadvisor reviews to select a restaurant, or Airbnb ratings to decide whether renting a particular house or apartment is worthwhile. There are also WhatsApp groups on all kinds of topics; nowadays, parents can almost instantly learn if a teacher behaves inappropriately at their children's school. Even those searching for a partner can use free apps to connect with people in similar situations whom they would never have met otherwise.

Moreover, people can now obtain information that was completely inaccessible to an ordinary citizen just a few decades ago. For example, within a day of receiving a worrying diagnosis, patients can use the

Internet to learn much of what specialist doctors know about treatment options and prognosis.

Theoretically, practical information can come from both private and state sources, which complement each other to enrich the cooperation scheme and reduce dependence on particular sources. Generally, state-provided practical information is limited to services it offers, such as how to access social assistance, buy government bonds, pay taxes via a mobile app, or understand which vaccines children should receive. However, states sometimes provide other practical data through public media, including weather forecasts, traffic updates, theater premieres, and announcements about new shopping centers.

Today, the sources of practical information are so diverse, and the number of contributors to this continuous flow is so large, that we can say it forms a cooperative system in which everyone depends on everyone else, but not on any one participant in particular.

Finally, regarding practical information related to commercial activities, the state undertakes an important second-order cooperative activity by giving consumers the ability to report false information or fraudulent advertising by companies. State consumer protection agencies receive complaints from citizens and often represent them legally to obtain compensation from companies. Consumer protection is a second-order activity because it seeks to protect, from fraudulent practices, the environment in which goods and services are offered (first-order cooperation).

6.4.2.2 Journalistic Information

Journalistic information can be divided into two types. On the one hand, there is information about current events involving private individuals (for example, news about worker strikes, disputes among youths outside a nightclub, security incidents, and so forth). On the other hand, there is information about current events involving political figures (internal government conflicts, creation of a new political party, approval of a new bill, corruption scandals, etc.). While there is also journalistic information about events that do not involve any persons—such as natural disasters—I will leave that type of information aside for the purposes of this discussion.

In modern democracies, there are usually various private media outlets, such as TV and radio channels, newspapers, magazines, and increasingly, internet-based platforms like YouTube channels, Spotify podcasts, and digital news websites. However, the state often reserves the right to maintain some public media outlets to complement private media.

From the perspective of FSC, this complementarity between public and private media could strengthen the cooperation scheme, making people less dependent on particular media outlets. In this respect, a purely public or purely private media system would have shortcomings.

According to Milton Friedman, political rights, including freedom of expression and, in particular, the right to criticize the government, would be at risk if the government controlled the media (today, we could add internet access) (Friedman, M. 1962: 7–17). In this sense, private media, being independent from the state, act as a vital counterbalance that helps ensure freedom of expression does not depend solely on the state system. In a free media market, private outlets offer a variety of products, perspectives, and editorial approaches, thus guaranteeing pluralism. This diversity allows citizens to access multiple viewpoints on political, social, and cultural matters, preventing monopolization of information. Let me explain this point further.

In a free market, the primary goal of media sellers is to maximize profits, not to reward or punish consumers based on their political opinions. Private media ownership provides owners with *economic*, rather than *ideological*, incentives to disseminate ideas. Those media outlets that apply ideological criteria to allocate airtime or editorial space risk losing market share to competitors focused solely on reaching and attracting the broadest possible audience. Consequently, the economic imperative encourages private media to offer diverse and engaging content that appeals to a wide range of consumers, promoting pluralism through market competition.

A government controlling the media can disregard the costs of spreading ideas contrary to public demand with impunity, since unlike a private business, the government can use coercion, such as taxation, to obtain the necessary resources. This ability enables the state to maintain media outlets even when their content is unpopular or contested. Conversely, in an unregulated media market, the likelihood that diverse ideas will be disseminated is higher, as private entrepreneurs seek to maximize profits by responding to a wide range of consumer demands. This competition encourages pluralism and greater diversity in the marketplace of ideas, as media outlets strive to attract different audiences with varying viewpoints.

The logic of this process is analogous to why, in a free market, there exists a greater variety of colors, fabrics, and patterns of ties compared to a regime where a bureaucrat dictates which types of ties will be produced.

Similarly, if the private media market is competitive, we can expect it to be sufficiently pluralistic to reflect a substantial portion of citizens' preferences. Competition incentivizes media outlets to differentiate their content offerings to capture diverse audiences, much like how manufacturers respond to consumer tastes by producing a wider array of products (Pincione 2015: 2417–2418; Hazlett 1998).

However, while a private media market increases the likelihood that all voices will be represented, this outcome is not guaranteed. Some voices may be overlooked, especially those of very small minorities, though the Internet has somewhat reduced this risk. Returning to the previous example, a free market for ties will typically offer enough variety for most consumers, but it is unlikely that any manufacturer would produce ties exclusively in fuchsia for just four or five people who prefer this color. Similarly, the media market may lack sufficient incentives to give voice to marginalized groups, such as small indigenous communities or followers of lesser-known religions. This highlights a limitation of relying solely on market mechanisms to ensure comprehensive pluralism.

Given this situation, public state media begin to make sense. From the perspective of FSC, the foundation of public media is to complement the private media system so that individuals' ability to express themselves—especially the most unpopular or marginalized voices—is not left solely to the mercy of market forces. Public media thus serve as a necessary counterbalance by ensuring diverse perspectives are included, particularly those unlikely to be economically viable in a purely competitive media market.

Thus, different public and private media can complement each other to form a cooperation scheme where people's ability to make their voices heard depends on the entire media system but not on any particular outlet.[10] This is a form of "polycentrism," where multiple sources exist from which people can obtain information—and, we might add, through which they can also express themselves (Sartori 2014: 82). The more sources there are, the less indispensable each one becomes.

At the same time, the state usually performs second-order cooperative activities by providing citizens with legal tools to report false news. In

[10] On the importance of a media system including both public and private media, see Nino (2013: 265–267).

particular, civil law—and sometimes criminal law—in modern democracies treats defamation, which includes slander and libel, as a wrongful act that may give rise to a duty for the wrongdoer to compensate the victim.

On the one hand, it seems clear that participants in the cooperation scheme should be legally protected against these behaviors. For example, falsely accusing another of wrongdoing introduces anti-cooperative elements into the scheme. Cooperation requires some degree of certainty and stability. Slandering or libeling a participant is itself an anti-cooperative act that undermines the victim's capacity to engage. The victim suffers psychological harm and must devote time and energy to defending themselves, distracting from cooperative activities. Moreover, these acts subtly harm the cooperative atmosphere: other participants who believe the false accusations will be less inclined to engage in business or professional dealings with the accused.

On the other hand, it is evident that the legal system cannot impose overly strict standards in protecting participants. When journalists and individuals publish information—even after multiple checks—they accept there is a margin of error. Imposing sanctions for false information when the publisher has reasonably verified sources could discourage people from expressing themselves, thereby disrupting the flow of information. It is crucial for citizens to be informed about issues such as corruption or other matters of public interest so they can act accordingly, for example, by deciding not to support a political party. This constitutes a form of cooperation toward the public good. However, if communicators fear lawsuits and stop expressing themselves, that form of cooperation halts.

The outcome is that a middle ground is needed between total flexibility and absolute rigidity. The system should protect citizens from slander and libel but not discourage information contributions.

In this regard, it is reasonable to assert that not all journalistic information deserves the same level of protection. A particularly important distinction exists between information involving "ordinary citizens" (for example, one citizen defrauding another) and information concerning those with greater power within the cooperation scheme—typically high-ranking public officials (such as corruption scandals). Discouraging contributions regarding the latter type of information is especially dangerous, as these matters can significantly impact the entire cooperation scheme.

A reasonable solution is provided by the U.S. Supreme Court in New York Times v. Sullivan (376 U.S. 254, 1964). To interpret the First

Amendment, which enshrines freedom of expression, the Court created the "actual malice" doctrine. Under this doctrine, those providing information about public officials are exempt from liability for defamation—even if the information later proves to be false—if two conditions are met. First, the communicator did not publish the information knowing it was false. Second, the communicator had a reasonable belief in the truth of the information after verifying sources diligently. This doctrine balances protecting individuals' reputations with avoiding discouragement of information contributions on matters of public interest. However, if the communicator knowingly published false information or acted with reckless disregard for the truth, they may be held legally responsible.

As noted, "actual malice" applies to public officials, not citizens. Information about citizens typically does not pertain to issues that threaten the entire scheme.[11] Therefore, it may be appropriate to raise the standard for communicators who publish information affecting individual reputations—for instance, by requiring more than reasonable source verification and demanding greater certainty about the facts. While the legal system must specify these details, it seems plausible that a higher standard is warranted when it comes to protecting citizens.

6.4.2.3 Scientific Information

Scientific information can be categorized into two types. First, there are statistics that depict a country's condition, such as poverty rates, unemployment, and inflation. Second, there are theories developed by experts across various fields—for example, studies on the long-term effects of sugary drink consumption, the link between reduced working hours and higher employment rates, or the impact of smaller class sizes in schools. In modern democracies, both the state and private organizations undertake first-order cooperative activities to provide these two types of information.

Regarding the first category, statistics published by the state and private organizations may differ methodologically but generally yield comparable results. The state sector comprises diverse entities capable of conducting

[11] Of course, exceptions are possible. Some anti-cooperative behaviors by citizens can threaten the scheme, while some anti-cooperative behaviors by officials may be relatively harmless. For example, an individual might plan to carry out a terrorist act that will kill thousands of people. Or an official might use the official checkbook to pay for a private dinner. The legal system in question could either explicitly address these exceptions or maintain ambiguity so that judges resolve them on a case-by-case basis.

these measurements. While there may be a dedicated official statistics institute, state universities, public research centers, and even legislative commissions can also perform this work. In the private sector, various foundations, universities, research institutes, and similar bodies often contribute. Considering the entire system, encompassing both public and private sectors, no single institution is indispensable, reflecting the ideal of FSC.

People generally place greater trust in the official statistics institute specifically established to conduct these measurements (such as France's National Institute of Statistics and Economic Studies, Ecuador's National Institute of Statistics and Census, and the U.S. Census Bureau). However, the system must remain resilient to anti-cooperative behavior, even from such an institute. The diversity of agencies involved in conducting these measurements strengthens the system's robustness in this regard.

When such diversity exists, each public or private agency faces significant reputational costs for fabricating studies, as conflicting trustworthy research would quickly expose any deceit. Even if an agency were to disregard these costs and engage in anti-cooperative behavior, the system could continue functioning through other reliable sources of information. A well-known example occurred in Argentina between 2008 and 2015, when the National Institute of Statistics and Census (INDEC) employed questionable methodologies to measure poverty and inflation. The official statistics differed significantly from more rigorous studies conducted by Congress and private institutions such as the Catholic University of Argentina. As a result, the credibility of the official data was compromised. Crucially, however, the public did not rely solely on INDEC for trustworthy information, turning instead to alternative sources.

The second category of scientific information pertains exclusively to academia. It appears in articles and books where specialists—such as physicists, economists, and sociologists—develop theories. Providers of this information are typically smaller entities: individual researchers or small teams working within public or private organizations. When publishing their results, these researchers declare their organizational affiliations but are recognized as the authors of their work.

Since these investigations are carried out by smaller entities, diversity within academia is even greater than among the public or private bodies responsible for official statistics. The academic debate in modern democracies is vibrant, with frequent seminars, congresses, symposia, and other events facilitating the exchange of ideas. Cooperation among academics both within countries and internationally continues to grow steadily. Ironically, this cooperation strengthened after the COVID-19 pandemic. Before the pandemic, virtual events were rare; during the pandemic, they became the norm. Today, academics blend the best of both worlds—while in-person events remain common, virtual participation is embraced when cost or logistics make it necessary.

Should the state protect society from the threat posed by fraudulent studies, both in public statistics and academic research?

First, it is important to distinguish between *fraudulent* and *incorrect* studies. Scientific research inherently involves errors, and knowledge is always subject to improvement. In this context, a free marketplace of ideas is essential. Rather than harm, the clash of true and false theses enriches debate. For example, Mill (2009 [1859]) argues that both true and false ideas contribute to the debate: true ideas advance knowledge but must be continually challenged, while false ideas help keep true ideas alive by opposing them, preventing them from becoming dead dogmas.

Fraudulent studies go beyond simple errors: in these cases, researchers intentionally manipulate the methodology to produce desired results. Should the state implement measures to prevent or sanction such anti-cooperative behaviors?

Regarding public statistics, the private market for sources capable of providing this information is sufficiently diverse that the state need not sanction private entities involved in fabricating studies. As mentioned earlier, a diverse structure exists to resist particular anti-cooperative actions. The contrast provided by rigorous studies from other organizations is enough to diminish the credibility of flawed statistics. Moreover, it should not be overlooked that the purpose of these statistics is to capture the reality in which people live. People tend to notice when certain studies produce absurd results that fail to reflect their lived experiences, and they have tools to expose such deceptions—for example, social media.

The case differs for public organizations. These bodies are funded by taxes contributed by all participants in the system, particularly to provide reliable information. In a fundamental sense, these organizations belong to all participants, so cooperative behavior can legitimately be expected of them. The state should engage in intra-state cooperative activities by auditing these organizations through designated oversight entities and by sanctioning them in cases of anti-cooperative behavior.

The conclusions are similar regarding studies conducted in the academic context. A researcher working in a public research center who fabricates studies should be sanctioned by that institution on behalf of all participants who contribute funding through taxes to support such research.

Of course, in practice, it may not be clear when studies are fabricated. It is important to note that serious academics may disagree on the best methodology for a given scientific study. Disagreements can be even more pronounced in social sciences. The fact that a researcher has used a different or novel methodology does not imply that the study lacks academic rigor. It is essential that the legal norms regulating professional ethics in scientific research capture this diversity. Sanctions should be reserved for clear cases of misconduct, allowing a wide margin for reasonable disagreement, and penalties should be withheld when there is any doubt.

In the private sphere, state sanctions are inappropriate because public funds are not involved. The loss of reputation for researchers who fabricate studies, as well as for the private organizations that continue to support them, constitutes a sufficient sanction. The marketplace of ideas itself punishes such anti-cooperative behavior.

6.4.2.4 Artistic Expressions

Artistic or cultural expressions do not qualify as information because they cannot be true or false. Rather, they are creations. Literature, painting, music, dance, and acting, among other forms, do not primarily aim to describe the world; rather, they seek to depict the imagined or, at most, to offer a personal, expressive interpretation of reality without claiming objective truth.

In modern democracies, the state often funds artistic or cultural projects of all kinds (generally through a ministry or secretariat of culture). However, the compatibility of such projects with FSC is questionable.

FSC is a conception of freedom that seeks to explain how modern democracies function. In other words, FSC is not only a theory of freedom but also a theory of liberal democracy, presenting a vision of the *raison d'être* of its political and economic institutions. However, this does not mean that FSC must justify every institution that exists within current liberal democracies. As a theory of liberal democracy, FSC serves both to justify many of these institutions and to critique those that, despite their presence, divert the system from the ideal of FSC. State agencies whose purpose is to promote a particular form of culture or art are examples of institutions that may fall under such critique.

As explained in Chapter 3, FSC is a conception of freedom that, unlike positive notions such as those proposed by Marx and Hegel, remains neutral with respect to different life plans. From the perspective of FSC, neutrality is not merely an incidental feature of the cooperation scheme defining freedom; rather, it is intrinsic to that scheme. The cooperation scheme embodied by FSC is not a separate entity detached from individuals—it is constituted by the people themselves cooperating. In this view, social cooperation constitutes the context within which individuals develop and realize their respective life plans. Therefore, any scheme that privileges certain plans over others is incompatible with genuine social cooperation and consequently with FSC.

So far, I have referred to neutrality in terms of life plans. However, the same reasoning can be applied to artistic and cultural expressions. An artistic or cultural expression is not itself a life plan but often forms part of one. As such, it embodies a conception of what is valuable—such as a sense of beauty, sophistication, evocative or unsettling qualities, or a personal appreciation of reality. In FSC, social cooperation is the environment in which individuals design and carry out their life plans, which may include artistic or cultural conceptions. Therefore, using the cooperation scheme to introduce or impose particular conceptions violates the very idea of social cooperation embedded in FSC. The cooperation scheme provides the context within which individuals elaborate and realize their conceptions of the good, but this differs fundamentally from using that scheme to promote or impose any specific conception.

The distinction between, on the one hand, elaborating and pursuing a conception of the good through the cooperation scheme, and on the other, *using* the scheme to disseminate or promote it, is essential for understanding why, from the perspective of FSC, artistic and cultural expressions should be confined to the private sphere without state promotion. In the first case, individuals are simply developing and pursuing a conception of the good, perhaps peacefully sharing it. In the second case, however, the state apparatus is used to promote a particular conception of the good; even if it does not compel others to accept it, it does require them to finance it through taxation. This is what occurs when the ministry or secretariat of culture funds certain artistic or cultural projects. Inevitably, these projects embody a particular conception of what is valuable, yet they are financed by all participants in the scheme, including those who do not identify with that conception. Such state sponsorship is incompatible with the notion of social cooperation central to FSC.

Now, it is commonly argued that the state should promote art and culture so that all citizens—not only the wealthiest—can access and experience them. However, my thesis is that this position presupposes what should instead be questioned: namely, the assumption that the forms of art and culture prevalent in wealthier social sectors are inherently superior.

When we do not assume that a certain artistic or cultural expression is superior to another, and we seriously adhere to the idea of neutrality, we should conclude that people do not need state resources to participate in artistic or cultural expressions. Art and culture do not need protection by the state for the same reason that human thought does not need state protection. As long as human existence persists, they are indestructible because they are manifestations of personality, and anyone can express them regardless of socioeconomic status. They can be found among refined people playing classical music, but also among youths in working-class neighborhoods composing rap music. They exist among those who paint works exhibited in prestigious museums and those who paint graffiti as protest against injustice. They were already present tens of thousands of years ago when individuals designed pictograms on cave walls. All these artistic and cultural expressions deserve equal respect, for the same reason all people deserve equal respect: their artistic or cultural expressions are forms of manifesting joy, fears, lacks, concerns, sadness, etc. If all deserve equal respect, then we have no reason to believe that the state should coerce some to abandon their culture and adopt another.

Finally, it should be clarified that this critique does not imply that poorer sectors should be neglected by the state. Much has been and will be said in this chapter about the state's crucial role in performing first-order cooperative activities and providing basic goods and services accessible to all. However, these cooperative activities—such as health, education, and social protection—should enable all individuals to design and realize their life plans, which may include their preferred forms of art and culture. This role differs fundamentally from state actions *aimed at* encouraging or prescribing certain forms of art or culture while discouraging others.

6.5 Integration Tools

6.5.1 *Integration for Cooperation*

According to FSC, freedom is a cooperative practice for the development and fulfillment of life plans. In other words, freedom is constituted by social cooperation: individuals cooperate with one another and assist each other in designing and realizing their projects.

A timely question is what happens to those who are not fully integrated into the cooperative framework and therefore cannot fully develop and realize their projects. This question should not be dismissed even in the most advanced democracies. It seems clear that the market economy has created wealth and improved general living conditions. However, it is entirely possible that it does not fully integrate every citizen. There are people who suffer poverty and other incapacitating conditions. These individuals typically are unable to contribute to the cooperative scheme and are thus *partially* excluded.

To be sure, it would be inaccurate to say that these people are *entirely* excluded from the cooperative framework. Even in the extreme case where they lack access to housing or other basic resources, they can still move through public spaces, access the public health system, and are (or at least should be) protected by security forces if threatened by others.

Now, if these individuals do not yet contribute to the cooperative framework, why then do they receive these benefits? The answer is that these benefits, along with other essential goods and services the state should provide (which will be discussed in this section), are precisely the tools individuals need to begin contributing to the cooperative framework. Through this participation, they can access its *full* benefits, become integrated members of society, and ultimately develop and realize their life plans.

As explained in Chapter 3, FSC is a normative conception of freedom. In particular, it encompasses an idea of equality and human dignity.

It implies a form of equality because those who cooperate contribute to the scheme from which they benefit (i.e., all benefit from everyone's cooperation), but no single contribution is indispensable for the scheme to continue functioning. Participants in a cooperative scheme are equal in the sense that each depends on others to realize their life plan (i.e., depends on the whole scheme), but not on anyone in particular. FSC draws inspiration from cooperative games that have allowed individuals to design and carry out their life plans within a context of equality—that is, within a scheme structured so that no one holds enough power to cause its collapse.

It also entails a form of dignity. According to FSC, everyone depends on everyone else to be free because freedom can only be realized within a cooperative framework. On the other hand, although everyone *depends on* everyone else, no one is *at the mercy of* another, because no single participant is indispensable for the scheme's continuation. This means no participant can control others' lives by threatening to withdraw cooperation. While we depend on others, each of us retains the right to say "no" to any particular person. This power to refuse is, if not the entirety, at least a significant part of what constitutes our dignity as independent individuals.

Ultimately, FSC is not only a new way to define freedom but also carries a normative dimension: by incorporating notions of equality and dignity, it provides a justification for why people *should* enjoy FSC. Consequently, it becomes necessary to explain how to integrate those who are not yet fully part of the cooperative framework.

As mentioned above, it cannot be said that these people are completely excluded from the scheme since they can use freely public spaces and resources and must be protected by security forces like anyone else. Still, it is clear that this is only a small part of what the cooperative framework can offer. Since these individuals cannot contribute to the scheme, they do not receive many of its benefits. They cannot earn money because they do not have a good or service to offer, or if they do, it is not profitable for some reason. They cannot acquire basic goods and services (not even housing) because they lack sufficient funds. They cannot access loans because they are not integrated into the banking system. From the perspective of FSC, having one foot outside the cooperative scheme means these people cannot fully develop and realize their projects.

Given this situation, the state should engage in first-order cooperative activities, providing these individuals with certain tools. However, it is important to emphasize that, from the FSC perspective, these public policies should be designed solely to integrate individuals into the cooperative framework so they can begin contributing. Only these redistributive measures follow from FSC.

It is reasonable to assert that, generally, these people genuinely wish to integrate: to have a home, a job, hobbies, a social circle, medium and long-term projects, and so on. Of course, it is always possible that some individuals may be content to keep one foot outside the scheme, even if this means not receiving state resources, satisfied with living on the streets and begging. However, if such cases exist, they are likely isolated and practically unidentifiable by the state—in other words, it is impossible for the state to distinguish these individuals from those who genuinely wish to integrate when deciding whom to deny benefits. But let us imagine a caricatured scenario in which these individuals voluntarily approach the government and declare that they do not wish to contribute to the scheme, even if it means renouncing all state benefits reserved for those who want to integrate. Should the scheme then deny these few people *all* kinds of benefits simply because they have expressed a refusal to contribute?

In practice, this alternative would be unfeasible. Denying all benefits would mean expelling them from the territory, so they cannot even circulate in public spaces. Additionally, there are humanitarian reasons not to do this, unrelated to social cooperation.[12] There is no need to elaborate on this issue here, as these cases, if they exist, are too isolated to require deep analysis.[13]

6.5.2 *Participants in the Redistribution Scheme*

The redistribution scheme has two types of participants: those who contribute and those who receive contributions. Those who contribute are already integrated into the scheme. Those who receive contributions,

[12] These humanitarian reasons would also justify providing attention—indeed, even greater attention—to those who, despite their desire, are currently incapable of making a contribution (even a small one) and will *certainly* never be able to do so. Such cases are rare but exist. All normative conceptions of freedom must recognize their limitations. For example, Sen's capabilities approach implies that citizens should receive certain resources to become *capable* of achieving their goals. But what about those who are permanently unable to exercise their capabilities? Sen's approach should draw on humanitarian ethics to justify why the state must care for these individuals. Similarly, FSC does not claim to be the *unique* value, though it does claim *central* importance.

[13] A different situation arises when those who do not want to be included engage in subversive behavior and attack the scheme. Since FSC is a normative (moralized) conception of freedom, those people are not permitted to act against the scheme, as they would be threatening something morally valuable. Therefore, if they do so, they must accept the consequences, since the scheme has full right to defend itself. Technically, the response would not constitute punishment, because punishment by definition is directed only at members of the community. That subversive behavior would be akin to a declaration of war, which justifies a response from the scheme; in such cases, the logic of war, rather than that of punishment, would be the appropriate framework.

as noted above, are partially excluded from the scheme. The former extend a helping hand to the latter to enable their full integration into the cooperative framework.

As explained, the moral force of FSC—grounded in its notions of equality and dignity—is sufficient to justify the need to integrate the excluded. That said, ideally, the redistribution scheme should adopt a cooperative logic that fosters collaboration between those already integrated and those who need to integrate. The goal is for the excluded to join the cooperative framework through an activity that is itself cooperative and that strengthens the freedom of those already inside as well.[14] Fortunately, this cooperative logic in redistribution is possible. Let me explain why.

6.5.2.1 *The Contributors*

When I refer to these participants, I mean the taxpayers who pay their taxes to extend a helping hand to those not yet fully incorporated into the scheme. My thesis is that these contributors have a *reason* to allocate a small portion of their earnings to finance a redistributive system that integrates new participants. Indeed, redistribution ultimately strengthens the cooperative framework, enhancing the freedom of all. In other words, by making contributions, these individuals are not merely helping the excluded to become free; they are enriching the cooperative scheme and, consequently, reinforcing their own freedom.

First, marginality dissolves the communal bonds among people. Few people enjoy being rich in misery. People generally prefer to live, grow, and raise their children in prosperous environments. This preference is not only because marginality breeds insecurity (an important factor), but also because people value building communal ties with their fellow citizens. Such ties become more challenging when individuals inhabit vastly different realities—some fully integrated into the scheme, others partially excluded. Of course, among those integrated, social differences exist, which give rise to various social groups. Yet, they are united by the bond of "rowing in the same boat": a minimal communal bond that constitutes the cooperative framework.[15]

[14] I think that showing the *rational* basis of fulfilling that *moral* demand further strengthens FSC's case for redistribution.

[15] This argument, which rests on a principle of community, is inspired by Cohen (2011: 30–31).

As an example, in recent decades, affluent sectors in structurally poor countries have chosen to move to gated communities, attempting to live their lives within that microclimate where they feel more comfortable and, ironically, freer. When this bubble is so closed off, it practically becomes a different society—a cooperative scheme independent in most of its aspects. From the perspective of FSC, freedom is not only about having resources but about inhabiting a prosperous environment where one can establish economic and social ties with fellow citizens. In such micro-societies, people find the appropriate ground to develop and pursue their life plans—something they cannot find in the broader society, where they cannot build this minimal communal bond because many fellow citizens are not integrated.

Second, when more people integrate into the scheme, the resources and opportunities available increase, power becomes more dispersed, and dependence on particular participants decreases. In other words, as the number of independent units within the scheme increases, reliance on each individual unit diminishes. This dynamic, by definition, strengthens the cooperative framework and, from the perspective of FSC, ultimately enhances the freedom of all participants.

Now, if including new participants benefits those already integrated, why then do these contributors not voluntarily allocate part of their wealth to eradicate poverty? Why is it necessary to impose taxes?

To be sure, many people voluntarily contribute (a topic that will be addressed later). However, it is evident that these voluntary contributions are insufficient. Taxes are necessary because, for those already integrated into the scheme, the inclusion of the excluded constitutes a "public benefit." As explained in the previous chapter, public benefits are those goods or services that, once provided, benefit all individuals without excluding those who did not contribute to their financing. From an individual standpoint, one knows that poverty will not be eradicated by the small contribution one can make. It requires contributions from others. But once others make these contributions, individual input is no longer necessary: one can enjoy the benefit without contributing. Given this incentive structure, which leads each person to expect others to contribute, redistributive taxes become necessary.

To be genuinely cooperative, the redistributive system should be designed so that it does not depend on any particular contributor or small group of contributors. The same logic outlined in the previous chapter regarding taxes in general should apply here: the idea is that everyone contributes a relatively small portion, varying in size according to the contributor, but always sufficiently small so as not to become indispensable. In this way, contributors can be confident that the system will not depend on any single contributor, ensuring its continuity even if, for example, a contributor decides to cease participation or switch to another scheme. The redistributive system will be able to include new people (with the benefits this entails *even for contributors*) without relying on any particular contribution. Thus, the redistributive system is also guided by the idea of cooperation among contributors.

6.5.2.2 *The Recipients*

These individuals are those who are *partially* excluded from the cooperative framework and will be incorporated through the integration tools provided by the redistributive system. Since this system is guided, as claimed, by the idea of cooperation, we can say that the excluded will integrate into the cooperative scheme through an activity that is itself cooperative. In other words, the excluded depend on the redistributive system to integrate, but since each contributor provides a relatively small portion, the excluded do not depend on any particular contributor.

As mentioned, the foundation of redistribution is the importance of *integrating* the excluded into the cooperative scheme. Therefore, if this is the foundation, the resources transferred cannot be just any resources but must be those—and only those—that the excluded need to integrate and, in turn, begin to contribute. A redistributive system based on FSC is not guided by the notion of material equality, but by the idea of social cooperation: it does not seek to use state coercion to ensure everyone has the same, but to integrate everyone into the cooperative scheme to which they can contribute and within which they can develop and pursue their life plans.

6.5.3 *Integration Tools*

The tools that the state should provide to individuals are divided into tangible (which can be monetary or non-monetary) and intangible.

6.5.3.1 *Intangible Tools*

Intangible tools mainly consist of formal rights. When discussing "vulnerable sectors," we often imagine stereotypical images such as beggars sleeping on the street with no income other than alms. While such individuals certainly exist, this description does not represent a large portion of the poor population.

The reason many people remain poor is not that they lack the skills or resources to start their own ventures, but that government policies render these ventures illegal, transforming resources into dead capital. For example, a person who could potentially launch a chain of Mexican restaurants in Arizona, USA, instead channels their energy into selling homemade food by the roadside in a rural area in Mexico. Their business lacks public registration and legal documentation; as far as the government is concerned, it does not exist. Without legal ownership, they cannot sell shares or franchises, thereby preventing them from raising investment capital. Consequently, they are unlikely to accumulate sufficient funds to open their own restaurant (Johnson et al. 2019: 75).

Sometimes people build houses in informal settlements, but because these dwellings lack legal recognition, they cannot be used as collateral for mortgages or other types of credit to start productive activities. Moreover, these properties are constantly at risk; lacking formal ownership makes them vulnerable to theft and dispossession.

Marx argued that, in capitalist society, the poor have formal rights but lack real property—what use is legal protection of property when one owns none? Yet in many cases, the reverse is true: the poor possess significant real assets but lack formal recognition by the state.

The economist Hernando de Soto (2000: ch. 2) has conducted various studies on this topic. For example, he noted that a clothing workshop on the outskirts of Lima could be ready to operate within days, but formalizing it with the government requires many procedures. Registering the business could take six hours a day for 289 days. Moreover, even if the workshop is designed for a single worker, legal registration costs could amount to 31 times the monthly minimum wage in Peru.

In the Philippines, individuals who have built homes in urban settlements on state or private land must form associations with their neighbors to qualify for state-financed housing programs. According to reports, this process involves 168 steps across 53 public and private offices and can take between 13 and 25 years.

In Egypt, those wishing to acquire and register a desert land plot owned by the state must navigate at least 77 bureaucratic procedures involving 31 public and private offices, a process that can take between

5 and 14 years. Furthermore, constructing a legal house on former agricultural land can take 6–11 years.

In Haiti, an individual can legally settle on state land only after renting it for five years and subsequently purchasing it. The renting process involves 65 bureaucratic steps and takes over two years, while the purchase requires navigating an additional 111 bureaucratic hurdles and can take up to 12 more years. In total, becoming legal landowners may take as long as 19 years.

As can be seen, often all people need to fully integrate into the cooperative framework is for the government to allow them to do so. Reducing regulations and bureaucratic barriers constitutes an intangible form of assistance, but often it is all that people need to make progress.

Once their formal rights are recognized, individuals can join the financial system. This is important because they can apply for loans to expand their businesses. Many countries (such as the United States, Brazil, and Bangladesh) have community development banks that operate with the goal of promoting economic development in low-income areas, sometimes providing low-interest loans without requiring formal documents. However, with fully recognized formal rights, people can even join the traditional banking system like any other citizen.

6.5.3.2 *Tangible Tools*

Some excluded individuals cannot integrate into the scheme on their own by relying solely on intangible tools. Sometimes, people need greater support—tangible tools that facilitate their transition and integration process into the scheme.

The foundation of these social measures remains the same: to enable those who are still partially excluded from the scheme to become fully integrated. Therefore, intangible and tangible tools should be regarded as complements, not substitutes. Intangible tools clear the path for integration by removing obstacles, while tangible tools provide the necessary support for individuals to navigate this path when they cannot do so unaided.

Tangible tools can be categorized into two types. First, tangible tools of a monetary nature, such as money. Second, tangible tools of a nonmonetary nature, such as food, housing, medicine, and similar resources.

Among monetary tangible tools, one that has gained prominence in recent years is "universal basic income" (UBI). Essentially, citizens receive a fixed amount of money monthly or annually, regardless of whether they work or intend to work.

Presented this way, it is not immediately clear that universal basic income is compatible with FSC. Recall that in the FSC framework, redistribution is grounded in fully incorporating excluded individuals into the cooperative scheme. Universal basic income could conflict with this principle for two reasons. First, it provides subsidies to those who are already working—that is, those already integrated into the scheme. Second, it subsidizes everyone who is not working, *including those who are uninterested in working*; thus, the program's underlying message is that whether a person integrates into the scheme or not is irrelevant. This undermines the program's potential to serve as a genuine *integration* tool.

It has been argued that because universal basic income is unconditional, it grants individuals greater bargaining power when accepting or rejecting job offers, and thus can serve as a complement to labor rights (Van Parijs 1992; Casassas 2020: 19).

However, strengthening individuals' bargaining power does not require a *fully* unconditional program like universal basic income. Instead, it could be a program *conditioned* on the person not working. This means the program would be unconditional with respect to the reasons for not working—that is, anyone not working, regardless of the reason, would receive it. However, it would be conditional on the fact that the person is *actually* not working: if the person is working (and, we might add, earning more than the amount they would receive through the basic income), then they would not receive this state benefit. In this way, the individual's bargaining power would be preserved.

Unlike the previous version, in this iteration of the program, a person stops receiving the payment once they start working. This addresses the first issue: the government no longer subsidizes individuals who are already integrated into the scheme. Thus, at least in this respect, the program can be considered an *integration* tool.

Nevertheless, it does not resolve the second issue: by subsidizing all people who are not working, regardless of the reason, the government benefits not only those who want to work but lack opportunities, but also those who are simply not interested in working.[16] This sends the message

[16] In Sect. 6.5.1, I assumed that, generally, people want to integrate into the scheme, and that those who prefer not to work and live by begging are isolated cases, if they exist at all. Here, I assume that some people may indeed prefer not to work because, thanks

that it does not matter whether a person integrates into the scheme and contributes or chooses to remain outside it. Consequently, it becomes difficult to view the program as a genuine *integration* tool.

That said, in practice it is challenging to distinguish between those who lack job opportunities and those who have opportunities but choose not to take them. Nevertheless, the characteristics of the cooperative scheme can offer some guidance. If political and economic institutions function properly, the government can reasonably assume that, in general, people will have access to job opportunities—jobs that, it can be added, provide incomes surpassing the basic income. Of course, opportunities may not arise immediately, and for this reason—as I discussed in the previous chapter—unemployment insurance can play an important role.

Additionally, the job opportunities available may not always align with our life plans when we first enter the workforce. However, as argued in the previous chapter, developed market economies tend to offer flexibility and pathways for individuals to adjust and improve their situation over time. Given a supportive context, the prevailing expectation will be that individuals can integrate into the labor system and make use of their talents and abilities.

If this is the case, then the exceptions—those who cannot integrate—will be individuals facing genuinely difficult circumstances, such as addiction or other serious limitations, as well as those who suffer discrimination due to criminal records, social background, and similar barriers. The conclusion, from the perspective of FSC, is that monetary integration tools should be targeted specifically at these groups, which are not difficult to identify; indeed, because these measures are focused, they could provide a higher level of support to those who truly need it to join the scheme.

On the other hand, non-monetary tangible tools can take various forms. For example, governments in Chile and Argentina have implemented programs that provided school supplies and netbooks to public school students, helping to support education and digital inclusion. The European Union runs a program that distributes fruits, vegetables, and milk in schools to promote healthy eating habits. The United States operates the Supplemental Nutrition Assistance Program (SNAP), which offers "food stamps" to low-income or no-income individuals.

to the basic income, the alternative is no longer poverty but having their basic needs met without working.

Housing is another non-monetary tool that governments often provide in different ways. It is one of the most desired assets for people and, in fact, one of their main forms of wealth. Governments could invite citizens to apply for housing, land plots, or housing subsidies (such as mortgage assistance) and then evaluate each case individually to select those who truly need support and have no other options. Governments in Uruguay and Colombia, for example, have run programs of this kind.[17]

From the perspective of FSC, policies aimed at providing non-monetary tangible tools should also be targeted toward excluded sectors, just like monetary tools. As stated, within FSC, the foundation of redistribution is to integrate people into the cooperative scheme.

The advantage of non-monetary tools over monetary ones is that the state can ensure individuals receive exactly what will help them join the scheme. Money, however, can be exchanged for a wide variety of goods, some of which may not contribute to integration (for example, gambling). The downside is that non-monetary tools are typically intended for immediate consumption and therefore are less useful for creating new wealth—housing being a notable exception, as it can be mortgaged. In contrast, a person receiving a monthly cash benefit could save a small portion each month and eventually start their own business in the medium term.

In any case, these tools are not mutually exclusive; they can perfectly complement each other. Would this represent an excessive expense for the government? Not necessarily. According to FSC, these tools should be directed at vulnerable groups, since redistribution in this theory of freedom is grounded in integration. With fewer beneficiaries compared to universal programs, the state can provide greater support at a lower overall cost.

6.5.4 *Coordination Between Different Levels of Government*

As I explained earlier, it would not be accurate to say that the recipients of integration tools are completely excluded from the scheme. Even in extreme cases where they lack access to housing or other resources,

[17] https://www.gub.uy/ministerio-vivienda-ordenamiento-territorial/politicas-y-gestion/compra-vivienda-promovida and https://mintransporte.gov.co/publicaciones/9950/programa-mi-casa-ya/#:~:text=Es%20el%20programa%20implementado%20por,que%20se%20agoten%20los%20cupos (last accessed: September 2, 2025).

they still circulate through the streets and other public spaces, have access to the public health system, and are—or at least should be—protected by security forces if their rights are threatened. We can say, then, that they *partially* benefit from the cooperative logic. They move toward *full* integration when they begin to contribute. This is precisely the goal of the integration tools that fall under the redistributive system. Furthermore, as argued, since the redistributive system adopts a cooperative logic between contributors and recipients, we can say that the excluded integrate into the cooperative scheme through an activity that is itself cooperative. According to FSC, this is the ideal way to integrate.

So far, I have referred broadly to the state as the provider of integration tools. However, we can refine this observation by acknowledging that both the federal government and local governments can carry out this provision. From the perspective of FSC, as with other resources provided by the state, proper integration of those not yet fully incorporated requires coordinated work among different levels of government. For example, the federal government could provide monetary integration tools, while local governments could offer non-monetary integration tools. This division of responsibilities makes sense since local governments are better acquainted with the specific needs of their populations and are therefore in a better position to decide which non-monetary resources to provide. Clearly, transferring money does not require detailed knowledge of a specific population since the money is the same for everyone.

The advantage of distributing responsibilities among different governments is clear from the standpoint of FSC: if one government alone were responsible for distributing all integration tools, recipients would become entirely dependent on that single government. In contrast, if responsibility is shared between the federal government and local governments, dependence on each individual entity is reduced.

That said, it is important to distinguish between two ways local governments can assume this responsibility. The first is by acting as intermediaries between the federal government and citizens. In this arrangement, the federal government performs two roles: on the one hand, it distributes integration tools *directly* to those who need them; on the other hand, it transfers funds to local governments so they can convert these into non-monetary integration tools.

The second way local governments can take on this responsibility is by using a portion of the revenue collected from local taxes to directly create and provide integration tools for those in need. In this scenario, the federal government continues to supply some integration tools directly but delegates to local governments the responsibility of *raising* funds and redistributing them.

As can be seen, only the second model is compatible with FSC. The first model represents a form of quasi-decentralization. In reality, the dependency on the federal government remains, as it is ultimately behind all allocations; local governments merely act as intermediaries.

More generally, intermediary roles in wealth redistribution prove inadequate. This form of pseudo-decentralization simply increases the number of intermediaries handling the funds before they reach the intended recipients. Consequently, it raises the risk that resources may not fully—or at all—reach their targets, amplifying opportunities for corruption and other malpractices. For instance, in Argentina, various social movements have acted as intermediaries between the state and benefit recipients. Reports have revealed cases where these movements charged vulnerable groups commissions in exchange for granting access to state-originated benefits.[18]

6.5.5 *Cooperation of Non-state Entities*

So far, I have referred to the state, at its various levels of government, as the primary provider of integration tools. However, while the state remains the main provider, it is not the only one. In modern democracies, private foundations funded by donations also play a significant role in assisting vulnerable populations. These organizations typically offer tangible resources such as food, clothing, and school supplies, among other essentials. Additionally, they may provide intangible support like vocational training to help beneficiaries later enter the labor market.

One might think that the existence of such foundations signals a failure of the state to properly fulfill its responsibilities. After all, if the state were effectively performing its duties, there would be no need for private foundations to undertake functions that ostensibly belong to the government.

However, this inference is premature. Foundations of this kind operate in countries across the development spectrum, from the poorest to the wealthiest. In less-developed countries, foundations often compensate for

[18] https://www.iprofesional.com/politica/364666-escandalo-por-planes-sociales-plata-que-se-queda-en-el-camino (last accessed: September 2, 2025).

governmental shortcomings by performing roles that failed states cannot fulfill. In contrast, in wealthier nations, these foundations complement government efforts and enhance the state's capacity to achieve its social objectives.

From the perspective of FSC, it is essential that the provision of integration tools not rely on a single entity. Even when a single entity encompasses multiple sub-entities—such as federal and local governments—the cooperative scheme benefits when non-state organizations contribute to these efforts. While the state remains the principal actor responsible for providing integration tools, the participation of diverse foundations helps mitigate the potential negative effects of any anti-cooperative behavior by the state.

Indeed, the state itself could take steps to increase the number of integration tools providers. For example, it could offer tax exemptions to companies that donate part of their wealth. The U.S. system is well-known for applying such incentives.

In any case, the potential of individuals to organize for social purposes should not be underestimated. In many countries, organizations known as "mutual aid societies" have flourished. These operated as insurance providers that, in exchange for a small premium, offered various services in times of need (such as health issues or the need for food or clothing). Records show these societies existed as early as the beginning of the twentieth century in countries like the United States, England, and Argentina.

In the specific case of the United States, the abundance of mutual aid societies created a competitive environment that benefited clients by offering quality services at affordable prices. For example, in 1919, over 93% of African American families in Chicago had at least one member insured by such societies. That same year, 98% of African American families in Philadelphia had at least one insured member (Beito 1990: 718–719).

In England, by 1911, at least 9 out of the 12 million people covered by the state health insurance system were already members of mutual aid societies that provided medical services (Green, D. 1985: 95).

In Argentina, between 1858 and 1918, mutual aid societies played a particularly important role in providing basic services to immigrants. In fact, people of Italian origin joined these associations in far greater numbers than any other institution. Moreover, these societies also served as social circles where immigrants could meet and share the customs of their home countries (Baily 1982: 486).

In short, the state is not the only entity—and from the perspective of FSC, it is preferable that it not be the only one—responsible for supplying integration tools to individuals who are not yet fully incorporated into the cooperative scheme.

6.6 Retirement Mechanisms

6.6.1 Pension Systems

According to FSC, freedom is a cooperative practice through which individuals develop and carry out life plans *over time*. This means that the cooperative scheme provides the environment in which people create and pursue their short-, medium-, and long-term life plans. In this regard, another fundamental cooperative activity typically performed by the state is the provision of custody and investment services for a portion of each participant's capital, with the purpose of returning it to them during old age (or returning an equivalent amount that correlates in some way with their contributions).

In a broad sense, pension systems date back to 13 BC when the Roman Empire granted soldiers who had served at least 25 years a sum equivalent to 13 years of salary. However, it was in Germany where the first modern pension system was created by Otto von Bismarck in 1881.

Generally, people cannot opt out of these services; they are required to contribute a portion of their earnings to the pension system, which provides them with income in old age. Underlying this obligation is a paternalistic idea that participants need protection from their own tendency to prioritize immediate preferences over future ones (Thaler and Shefrin 1981). Without this assumption, the primary justification for requiring them to contribute part of their money would vanish, since they could manage these funds independently.

The legal retirement age is determined by the state as the minimum age at which a person can begin receiving their pension. This age typically ranges from 57 to 67 years, depending on the country. Upon reaching the legal retirement age, retirement becomes a right, though in some cases, it may also be mandatory—for example, in Spain, retirement is generally voluntary after reaching the legal age, except in certain situations such as for government employees.

Retirement systems can be distinguished based on three criteria. First, they can be either non-contributory or contributory. A non-contributory system does not require prior contributions to receive a pension. This system has a strong redistributive component and indeed does not fully fit the earlier definition of a "retirement system," because the pension is not a *return* of capital—at least not for those who did not contribute. Instead, it serves to ensure minimum living conditions for all elderly citizens, regardless of their life circumstances.

In contrast, in a contributory system, access to pensions requires prior contributions made during a person's working life.

Second, the system may be either pay-as-you-go or funded through individual capitalization. The pay-as-you-go system relies on intergenerational "solidarity," where the working population contributes money that the state uses to finance monthly pensions for retirees.

In recent years, this system has faced criticism due to its growing unsustainability. This is because life expectancy has increased substantially while fertility rates have declined (GBD 2019 Demographics Collaborators [study published in 2020]). In simple terms, the number of retirees now exceeds the working population, creating a dilemma for the model: whether to provide very low pensions or dignified pensions funded by some form of debt.

The individual capitalization system is one in which active workers accumulate their own capital through monthly contributions, entrusting these funds to private or state-managed investment companies. The accumulated capital, including investment returns, is then paid out to the individual upon retirement. While this system tends to be more robust than the pay-as-you-go system, it faces criticism for its vulnerability to financial market cycles and fluctuations in both domestic and international markets.

An intermediate model between pay-as-you-go and individual capitalization is the "notional capitalization" system. In this model, each worker contributes to a notional (or fictional) account that is adjusted based on various economic indicators, such as GDP. This hypothetical capital tracks the individual's contributions over time. Although the state distributes funds via a pay-as-you-go method, the system aims to maintain a *strict* correspondence between what was contributed and what is received upon retirement.

Third, the system can be administered either publicly or privately. In the former case, a government agency manages the system; in the latter, private companies administer it under state regulation.

In theory, these three criteria can combine to form various models. For example, a system may be contributory, pay-as-you-go, and publicly administered; or contributory, individually capitalized, and privately administered. It is also conceivable to have a contributory, individually capitalized system managed by the state, or a contributory pay-as-you-go system run entirely by a private company. However, by its nature, a pay-as-you-go system requires centralized authority, so if privately administered, it would likely involve a single private company under strict government regulation.

6.6.2 FSC and Mixed Systems

A pension model guided by the principles of FSC should be a complex structure comprising different systems that enable individuals to develop and carry out their life plans. Essentially, it is a scheme where people do not become dependent on any single system. This ensures that the ability to create and fulfill life plans is not jeopardized by the failure or anti-cooperative tendencies of any particular system.

In fact, modern democratic pension frameworks tend to move in this direction. Various organizations, including the World Bank and the OECD, have highlighted Switzerland as a pioneer in this approach. The idea of a pension arrangement based on three pillars (three different schemes) was established in the Swiss Constitution in 1972 and took its definitive form with a federal law in 1982 (Leimgruber 2008: 2–3).

The first pillar is a pay-as-you-go system funded by mandatory worker contributions deducted from salaries. This fund is administered by the state and finances pensions designed to cover retirees' basic needs.

The second pillar is an individual capitalization system. It consists of occupational plans funded by both workers and their employers and is also mandatory. These funds are administered by foundations, which may be created by companies for their employees, by insurance companies, or by trade unions. The purpose of this pillar is to help people maintain a standard of living similar to that of their active working years.

The third pillar is a voluntary savings plan that complements the first two pillars and is managed by private companies. This pillar allows individuals to accumulate additional retirement savings.

Today, mixed pension systems operate in several democracies, each with its own nuances. For example, in New Zealand, the government oversees three distinct systems. First, it provides a basic non-contributory state pension for those who have earned little or no income.

Second, there is a voluntary individual capitalization scheme known as "KiwiSaver."[19] In this system, employees can choose to contribute 3%, 4%, 6%, 8%, or 10% of their income, while employers are required to contribute at least 3% of that income to the employee's account. Contributions are made to Inland Revenue, New Zealand's tax authority, which forwards the funds to the private company selected by the employee to manage their savings. Only private companies authorized by the state can serve as KiwiSaver providers.

Finally, to complement these contributions, there are private occupational pension plans that are voluntary and sponsored by employers.

Another example is Sweden, which offers a guaranteed minimum pension (non-contributory), and for those with substantial earnings, it has a state-managed notional capitalization system, where employees contribute 6% of their income and employers contribute 10%. Additionally, the law mandates an individual capitalization scheme where individuals must allocate 2% of their income, choosing between private and public fund managers.

FSC is a conception of freedom grounded in social cooperation and, in particular, inspired by how people organize themselves to develop and realize life plans collaboratively. Specifically, regarding pensions, my thesis is that a system inspired by FSC should adopt a mixed model. Such a system can combine non-contributory and contributory elements, incorporate both pay-as-you-go and capitalization methods, and involve public as well as private administration.

6.6.2.1 *First Dimension: "Contributory / Non-Contributory"*

FSC perfectly accounts for the contributory dimension of a pension system, particularly in pay-as-you-go systems that rely on intergenerational solidarity. The fundamental characteristic of a cooperative scheme is that participants benefit from the very system to which they contribute. In a contributory system, those who receive benefits are the same individuals who make contributions, thereby fulfilling this essential condition.

[19] https://www.ird.govt.nz/kiwisaver/kiwisaver-individuals/how-kiwisaver-works (last accessed: September 2, 2025).

The non-contributory dimension, however, presents greater challenges. In such a system, the recipients of benefits are not *necessarily* the contributors.

In the previous section, I examined various integration tools designed to include those not yet fully incorporated into the system. I argued that FSC is not only a new way of defining freedom but also carries a normative dimension: by incorporating notions of equality and dignity, it shows why people *should* enjoy FSC. Therefore, it becomes necessary to explain how individuals who are not yet fully part of the cooperative scheme can be integrated.

I also argued that participants in the scheme should be willing to allocate a portion of their income to finance the integration of those not yet included. On one hand, people enjoy building community bonds with their fellow citizens, and marginalization weakens these ties. Such bonds are more difficult to establish when individuals live in vastly different circumstances—some fully integrated into the scheme, while others remain practically excluded.

On the other hand, as more people join the scheme, resources and opportunities increase, power becomes more widely distributed, and reliance on individual participants diminishes. By definition, this strengthens the cooperative scheme, which, from the perspective of FSC, ultimately enhances the freedom of all participants.

Now, if the state were able to integrate all individuals into the scheme—thus honoring the equality and dignity central to FSC—there would be no need for a non-contributory dimension within the pension system, as everyone would have the ability to contribute. From the FSC standpoint, therefore, the non-contributory aspect of the pension system derives from the state's imperfect performance—whether due to incompetence, corruption, or circumstances beyond its control. In such cases, the state must at least provide excluded individuals with basic tools to ensure they can live their old age in healthy conditions. If the state's performance is reasonably good (even if not perfect), the number of people requiring this benefit should be small enough to be financed through general taxation, similar to how the state funds integration tools and other social benefits.

Of course, this is not an ideal scenario. Under FSC, cooperation is the context in which individuals fully develop themselves. Hence, timely integration of all people into the scheme is crucial. However, if this fails, the scheme's responsibility takes a different form: to assist those who could not be included.

Moreover, participants in the scheme have reasons to accept that a small portion of their income goes toward financing a basic income for these few individuals. This justification rests on one of the arguments previously used to support integration tools. People prefer to live in prosperous environments, and marginalization deteriorates these environments. Community bonds with fellow citizens enrich people's lives, which is why people tend to prefer neighborhoods where they feel at ease with their neighbors and often decide where to go based on the company they expect to find. These bonds are harder to maintain between those integrated into the system and those practically excluded. Marginalization weakens the social ties everyone values, providing a collective interest in combating it within society.

6.6.2.2 *Second Dimension: "Pay-as-You-Go / Capitalization"*

The non-contributory system should coexist with the contributory system so that individuals do not become dependent on any single system. Within the contributory system, there are two modalities: pay-as-you-go and capitalization.

As I explained earlier, the pay-as-you-go system faces challenges from declining fertility rates and increasing life expectancy. It is currently a highly sensitive model. Nonetheless, as illustrated by the previous examples, it can function effectively as part of a broader pension structure and thus alleviate some of the pressure. The structure can operate as follows.

First, contributions from the active workforce may finance a relatively modest pension—higher than the non-contributory basic pension—exclusively for those who have contributed for a specified number of years. Depending on the system's design, there may be greater or lesser correspondence between contributions and benefits. Whether resources are distributed through notional capitalization, as in the Swedish system, also depends on design choices.

Second, a portion of the active population's income may be directed toward a mandatory individual capitalization system, where authorized companies manage and invest contributions, returning the accumulated funds to individuals upon retirement. Ideally, individuals should have a broad range of choices, with companies offering different saving and investment options. As mentioned earlier, individual capitalization carries the disadvantage of being highly dependent on financial market stability and fluctuations. However, when combined with a pay-as-you-go system, risks are better diversified.

Finally, individuals may choose to allocate part of their income to private savings plans, whether occupational or non-occupational, managed by banks, insurers, or other entities. These plans can be encouraged by the state through tax incentives, for example.

In short, there is no perfect individual system, but two or more imperfect systems can reinforce each other, each serving as insurance against the failure of the others. Success is not guaranteed, but by having multiple systems operating simultaneously, participants become less dependent on any single one.

6.6.2.3 Third Dimension: "Public Administration / Private Administration"

A complex pension structure thus consists of the interaction between a non-contributory and a contributory arrangement, and within the contributory arrangement, an interaction between pay-as-you-go and individual capitalization modalities. Furthermore, both public and private entities can be responsible for managing and investing individuals' funds within the individual capitalization system. As with other first-order cooperative activities carried out by the state, the collaboration between the public and private sectors can enrich the overall scheme.

Of course, this enrichment will only occur if private options are genuinely private in a meaningful sense. The advantage of public companies providing these services is that the state can publicly express its vision regarding where, when, and how pension funds should be invested, ensuring that individuals are not confined to the perspectives of private companies alone. At the same time, the state should not dictate to private companies where, when, or how to invest funds. If different private companies have the freedom to offer their services, a diversity of perspectives is likely to emerge, further decentralizing the scheme. If the state regulated investments of both public and private companies, a significant state-level mistake could devastate the entire pension system.

Clearly, this does not mean that private companies should be exempt from all regulation. For example, the law must enshrine the right to switch from one system to another. That is, someone dissatisfied with their private (or public) provider should be able to transfer their funds to another provider, whether private or public. Thus, the diversity of options offered by a pension arrangement plays a crucial role not only at the initial choice but throughout an individual's working life, as they retain the right to choose alternatives.

These and other regulations, such as transparency and accountability requirements, are reasonable and should be mandatory for all companies, whether public or private. However, regarding investment modalities, private companies should have considerable freedom to offer their own services; otherwise, their existence would make no real difference and fail to enrich the overall scheme.

Ultimately, following the logic of FSC, the goal is for individuals to have multiple options within a rich, complex arrangement without becoming dependent on any single component.

6.6.3 The Structure in Brief

The previously proposed pension scheme, inspired by modern arrangements in some countries, is a complex structure with interacting systems that ensure life planning and fulfillment in old age do not depend on any single system.

In this structure, the non-contributory system interacts with the contributory system, so individuals do not need to have contributed to receive a pension. Within the contributory system, pay-as-you-go interacts with individual capitalization, minimizing the impact of flaws in any single mechanism by providing mutual support. Within the capitalization modality, various public and private providers offer individuals a range of saving and investment options, which they can select and even change throughout their working lives.

Of course, FSC does not prescribe a unique structure. Many variations are possible while still being compatible with the FSC ideal. For example, individual capitalization could be mandatory in one society and voluntary in another; one society might have more private providers than public, or vice versa. These details are matters of specific institutional design. The key is that the structure be a complex scheme with diverse systems serving individuals, making the overall scheme resilient to failures in any single component.

6.7 Conclusion

This chapter discussed the role of the state as a first-order cooperator that provides certain goods and services necessary for individuals to realize their life plans, in such a way that this provision does not solely depend on the performance of market participants. Thus, the state's provision can be understood as a strengthening of the cooperative scheme.

Specifically, I examined in detail some of the key activities carried out by the state: the provision of pathways (sidewalks, streets, and roads), transportation systems, healthcare, education, media, support for marginalized groups (which I called "integration tools"), and retirement savings mechanisms. Besides exploring the state's role in performing these activities, I discussed how it can complement the market without underestimating the latter as an important source of provision.

In modern democracies, people have a right to state-provided goods and services. However, from the FSC perspective, these rights should not be understood as positive rights; or if they are interpreted as such, it must be clarified that the unilateral relationship typically associated with positive rights does not apply. The notion of a positive right suggests (though it does not logically imply) a one-sided relationship between a recipient and a provider. To properly understand these rights within the FSC framework, this unilateral vision must be discarded.

The general idea of FSC is that freedom arises from a shared social scheme to which everyone contributes, making freedom a cooperative practice: all collaborate with all to be free. Similarly, our right to state-provided goods and services is the right to benefit from a collective structure to which we contribute. This right does not simply entail that we hold a claim while others bear a duty; rather, it arises because we are integral members of the system and actively participate in maintaining it every day (or will do so eventually, in the case of individuals undergoing integration).

CHAPTER 7

Conclusions

Forty thousand years ago, humans discovered the main key to progress: cooperation. They became the wisest of primates when they learned to make agreements among themselves. Collaborating so that everyone could develop and realize their life plans is a distinctly human form of organization. Had humans been solitary creatures, no matter how intelligent or strong, none could have achieved a fraction of what an average person accomplishes within a cooperative framework. We live our lives focused on short-, medium-, and long-term projects, striving to achieve them, yet often overlook that our success depends on the contributions of millions of people we will never meet. Collaboration is central to the design and realization of life plans; so central, in fact, that an adequate conception of freedom as applying to the social world should include the dimension of cooperation.

This book pursued two goals. The first goal was to develop a conception of freedom that gives social cooperation a central role: "freedom as social cooperation" (FSC). From the FSC perspective, freedom is neither a mere abstention by others (negative freedom), nor a particular mental or material condition (positive freedom), nor a form of independence (republican freedom). *Freedom is a cooperative practice among people*: an environment where individuals mutually collaborate over time so all can develop and carry out their life plans. Thus, FSC understands social cooperation not as a means to freedom but as *constitutive* of freedom itself.

E. Spector, *Freedom as Social Cooperation*,
https://doi.org/10.1007/978-3-032-12217-9_7

I have also argued that FSC is not incompatible with previous conceptions of freedom; on the contrary, it retains the elements that made them appealing while highlighting the significance of social cooperation in crafting and realizing life plans.

FSC does not seek to embody an abstract ideal, nor to capture the true essence of a term, but rather to recover the best version of human social practices—the ways people have ingeniously created cooperative environments in which to develop and realize life plans. These social practices have taken many forms, ranging from simpler cooperative arrangements among primitive tribes to the sophisticated political and economic institutions of modern liberal democracies.

Therefore, FSC is a conception of freedom that aims to capture how people create and realize life plans *in society*. It is no surprise, then, that FSC includes the idea of social cooperation. Indeed, social cooperation lies at the core of societies where people have been able to develop and carry out their projects, particularly liberal democracy, the highest degree humanity has achieved in this regard.

FSC defines freedom as a cooperative practice for developing and realizing life plans. However, not every collaborative endeavor forms the right context for crafting and realizing life plans. FSC alludes to a particular form of cooperation: one in which individuals contribute to a scheme such that no single contribution is indispensable on its own for the scheme's functioning, even though the entire set of contributions is collectively essential. When FSC refers to cooperation schemes, it means schemes independent of individuals; that is, schemes whose operation does not rely on the behavior of any particular person. In other words, these schemes are resilient to individual actions. Otherwise, if individual behaviors could dismantle the scheme, it would not provide a suitable setting for formulating and realizing life plans.

As can be seen, FSC's conception of cooperation implies a form of equality among people: full cooperation occurs only when each person contributes to the scheme, yet no individual contribution is essential by itself for the scheme to continue functioning. This notion assumes that participants are equal in this respect: each depends on others to realize their life plan—that is, on the scheme as a whole—but not on any particular individual. On this view, full cooperation necessarily occurs among people who need each other to be free, yet no single participant is indispensable for the scheme's operation. This does not imply that all participants contribute equally, only that no single contribution is so critical that the entire scheme depends solely on it.

Furthermore, this notion of cooperation involves a concept of dignity. This concept is non-metaphysical and does not rely on any claim about an intrinsic human essence, but instead arises from the equal status individuals hold within that scheme. According to FSC, everyone depends on everyone else to be free because people can be free only within a cooperative scheme. Yet, although everyone depends on everyone, no one is at anyone's mercy, because no participant is essential for the scheme to function. The consequence of this equality is that no participant may attempt to control others' lives by threatening to withdraw cooperation. Although we depend on everyone, we retain the right to say "no" to any individual. The right to say "no" constitutes, if not everything, then a significant part of our dignity as independent persons.

In short, FSC is a normative conception of freedom. That is, it seeks not only to provide a theory of how to understand freedom but also to show that freedom, thus understood, is a *valuable* ideal.

The "primitive cooperation" model served to illustrate the ideal of FSC and, in particular, to distinguish between two forms of cooperation: (1) first-order cooperation, aimed at producing the goods and services everyone needs to realize their life plan; and (2) second-order cooperation, directed at protecting—even through coercive means—the environment in which first-order cooperation takes place. This example also served as a starting point for achieving the second goal of this book: using FSC to develop a theory of liberal democracy.

To this end, I narrated a story about how the primitive cooperation society evolves into what we now understand as liberal democracy, without *fundamentally* changing—that is, maintaining the same social cooperation structure. Since that primitive society is hypothetical, the account of its evolution toward liberal democracy is fictional. Nevertheless, the story aimed to show that the liberal democratic system can be understood as a more sophisticated cooperation scheme, yet a cooperation scheme nonetheless—simply a more evolved form of FSC.

The first part of the story focused on political institutions, showing that they can be understood as refinements of some aspects of "primitive cooperation." I explained the emergence of the state in this context. With the marked increase in participants, second-order cooperative activities—primarily the exercise of coercion to preserve the cooperation scheme—become inefficient. Facing this problem, participants adopt two strategies: specialization and centralization. On one hand, participants note that it is far more efficient if those engaged in production (first-order cooperation) are different from those responsible for preserving the cooperation scheme (second-order cooperation). On the other hand, they observe that a centralized coercive system greatly reduces organizational costs. For these reasons, they forge a sort of social contract that leads to the creation of the state.

Once operational, the state becomes another participant in the cooperation scheme—an entity seeking to cooperate by performing second-order activities related to maintaining the scheme.

I also argued that, for compatibility with FSC, the existence of the state must not imply centralizing power in a way that makes the scheme dependent on particular individuals. How can this be avoided? First, participants ensure that the social contract, besides establishing the monopoly on coercion, clearly defines the functions of this monopoly and recognizes them both as duties and as powers. As duties, these functions are mandatory and the state is obliged to fulfill them; as powers, they are limited and the state cannot overstep them.

In turn, to explain the state's functions in such detail, the social contract must include a description of the cooperation scheme, its foundations, and its basic principles. After all, the purpose of coercion is to protect the scheme—ensuring a predictable environment where participants know what to expect from one another, an environment in which they can fully develop themselves and express that fullness through their contributions to the scheme. Clearly stating the scheme's foundations and basic principles enables the state to better understand its functions, while enshrining them as both duties and powers reflects the special responsibility resting on this monopoly. In this way, the social contract becomes what we today call a "constitution."

Second, participants seek that the state, while participating in the cooperation scheme by performing protective tasks (second-order cooperation), itself functions as a cooperation scheme—meaning that it internally operates through cooperation among independent institutions (intra-state cooperative activities) that collectively push the state toward the proper fulfillment of its functions.

To this end, people introduce clauses into the social contract that decentralize power. The first clause divides the state's monopoly into three separate monopolies assigned distinct tasks—commonly known as the "separation of powers." The second clause grants each branch the tools to check the others and, if necessary, prevent actions that would undermine the cooperation scheme ("checks and balances"). In this way, the state as a whole remains a participant in the scheme with significant powers but is also itself a cooperation scheme, with internal institutions oriented to preserving the state's structure and preventing deviations from its functions.

The third clause establishes the institution of suffrage. This institution—comprising all people who vote—is also part of the state. The right to vote arises from citizens' right to participate in state administration.

Suffrage also performs intra-state cooperative activities aimed at further decentralizing power, making the state even less vulnerable to particular interests. By ensuring periodicity in office and promoting alternation in power, suffrage helps to prevent the state from deviating from its proper functions. Additionally, suffrage itself functions internally as a cooperation scheme, depending on all voters but on none individually.

However, no state institution functions without limits, and suffrage is no exception. The judiciary, characterized by counter-majoritarian power, controls majorities by invalidating measures that, although voted on, violate the terms of social cooperation by harming minorities. This intra-state form of cooperation is known as "judicial review."

The fourth clause incorporates federalism. The federal system can be conceptualized as a cooperation scheme in which distinct states, provinces, or communities participate. Each local state—where "state" refers not only to the government but also to its citizens—functions cooperatively both internally and externally.

Internally, through mechanisms such as the separation of powers and checks and balances, alongside other political institutions like suffrage, and employing coercion to preserve the local cooperation scheme (second-order cooperation), preventing and sanctioning conduct that could harm the cooperative environment, among other activities.

Externally, the federal system drives the nation's economy through first-order cooperative activities, such as developing local industries and contributing goods and services beneficial to society as a whole. Since each state enjoys relative autonomy, the functioning of the nation depends on the collective efforts of all states rather than on any single state individually. Thus, the operation of the general cooperation scheme is conditioned not by the performance of any particular state but by the aggregate of all their contributions.

The second part of the story focused on the economic system. First, I argued that private property solves certain problems that would arise in "primitive cooperation." Essentially, the institution of private property reduces monitoring costs and addresses issues of suboptimal production and overconsumption. Then, I explained the foundation of money in such a system: reducing transaction costs and facilitating trade. After reflecting on criminal law as a means to protect the cooperation scheme, I examined, through the lens of FSC, typical state financing mechanisms: taxation, public debt, and, in some cases, money issuance.

Second, I argued that FSC accounts for the market institution (the environment where people engage in first-order cooperation related to the production and provision of goods and services), since the market can be seen as a deeply dispersed cooperation scheme where everyone's contribution is essential but each individual contribution is, *in principle*, dispensable. In this sense, the market economy differs from centrally planned economies, which are incompatible with FSC because their functioning depends on correct bureaucratic performance—an outcome that Hayek argued is likely to fail.

Furthermore, I argued that skepticism toward the idea of the market as a cooperation scheme rests on two myths: the belief that the market is a zero-sum game and the notion that only the best succeed in the market.

Lastly, I argued that the state, through institutions such as antitrust legislation and labor law (with the support of non-state entities like unions), could engage in second-order cooperative activities aimed at correcting market failures that threaten the cooperation scheme: monopolies, oligopolies, monopsonies, and oligopsonies.

The last part of the story focused on the role of the state as a first-order cooperator in providing certain goods and services necessary to realize life plans, ensuring that these activities do not depend solely on the performance of market participants. In this way, state provision can be understood as strengthening the overall cooperation scheme.

Specifically, I examined some of the main goods and services offered by modern states. I started with circulation infrastructure, which I divided into "static" (such as sidewalks, streets, and roads) and "mobile" (such as subways, trains, and airplanes). I then continued with health services, the education system, the media, support for vulnerable groups (which I called "integration tools"), and pension systems. Besides exploring the state's role in these activities, I discussed how it can complement the market, without underestimating the latter as an important source of provision.

Finally, I clarified that although people in modern democracies have rights to these state goods and services, from the FSC perspective, these rights should not be considered positive rights, or at least it must be clarified that the unilateral relationship typically associated with positive rights does not apply.

The idea of positive rights suggests (though it does not logically imply) a unilateral relationship: the receiver and the provider. To understand the nature of these rights in FSC, this vision must be discarded. The general idea of FSC is that everyone's freedom arises from the same cooperative scheme to which all contribute. On this view, freedom is a cooperative practice whereby individuals mutually collaborate with one another. Likewise, our right to goods and services provided by the state is the right to benefit from a structure we help to sustain. It is not simply that one person holds a right and another bears a duty; rather, this right emerges because we are all integral parts of a shared system that we maintain day by day—or will do so eventually, in the case of individuals undergoing integration.

Although in this book I have applied the idea of FSC to various institutions of liberal democracy, some topics remain unaddressed. In particular, two especially interesting subjects will be reserved for future work.

The first is the institution of the family. I do not develop a theory of family law based on FSC here. Nevertheless, I suspect that this conception of freedom offers significant insights for the norms governing family life. It is not implausible to suggest that the family could replicate the logic of cooperation internally. In such a case, family law should aim to divide power equally between spouses so that the marital relationship exhibits the kind of equality that, according to FSC, should characterize all *political* institutions.

Mill (1996 [1869]: 158–159) argued that marriage, as structured then, reinforced male domination over women. For example, until the nineteenth century, English and American law followed the doctrine of coverture, under which a wife's rights were subsumed under her husband's. Women were denied property ownership, the right to earn income, and more. The Spanish Civil Code of 1889 is another example: upon marriage, a woman was legally diminished, as her legal capacity was revoked in many respects; for instance, a married woman's capacity to consent to contracts was equated with that of "minors, the mentally ill, and illiterate deaf-mutes." Latin America was no exception. Argentina's Civil Code of 1869 granted married women the same legal status as minors, with legal representation vested in the husband (Spector, E. 2018: 245–246).

Such a form of family organization is profoundly incompatible with FSC, because family life—especially the woman's life—becomes subject to the husband's will. From the perspective of FSC, family law should afford no privileges to men; property ownership and contractual rights must be equally held by both spouses.

However, the absence of privileges, though necessary, is not sufficient. Given the evident historical inequality endured by women, family law should also include rules actively protecting them, advancing the equality that FSC holds as characteristic of cooperative relations. For example, although more women are participating in the workforce outside the home, they still bear the greater share of domestic work, including childrearing. This imbalance affects women's competitiveness in the labor market, leading to economic dependence. Consequently, women become more vulnerable, lacking resources to separate or pursue independent projects if abuse arises or the marriage fails. The community property regime, wherein earnings acquired by either spouse during marriage are combined and divided equally after divorce, disperses power, thereby producing the equality central to FSC cooperative relations.

Moreover, from the perspective of FSC, dividing power equitably between spouses has the advantage that proper childrearing will not depend solely on the performance of one spouse—a reasoning analogous to that which justifies the separation of powers in governance. When all rights lie with one spouse, the family scheme depends on that individual's good conduct. Decentralizing power thus renders the family scheme less vulnerable to uncooperative or negligent behavior by either parent. An open question remains: what is the nature of cooperative activities within the family? This warrants deeper analysis since the family can be seen as a kind of internal society where parents provide goods and services to children and occasionally employ coercive measures to enforce rules.

The second pending topic is the global community. According to FSC, freedom is a cooperative practice for designing and realizing life plans. I argued that FSC can account for the institutions of liberal democracy, as these societies can be seen as environments where individuals formulate and pursue their projects. These schemes aim to function as arenas where people collaborate mutually in their life projects, each depending on the collective support of all, rather than relying on any single person in particular. In this light, it is interesting to ask which elements of FSC the global community embodies.

On the one hand, certain principles of international law, such as those enshrined in the Charter of the United Nations and in instruments like the International Covenant on Civil and Political Rights, can be understood in terms of FSC. For example, the principle of sovereignty—that each state is sovereign within its own territory—and the principle of self-determination—that peoples should have the right to decide their own fate—both support the idea that the international community should function as a system not dependent on any single organization or entity. Conversely, if an international body—such as the United Nations—were to function as a "world state," the global community would inherently come into conflict with FSC. However, it remains to be seen whether such conflict could be mitigated through the separation of powers and checks and balances within that state, similar to those found in liberal democracies.

On the other hand, the ongoing flow of people across countries—international migration—is familiar to FSC. The possibility of moving to better-functioning cooperation schemes that allow individuals to flourish reduces dependence on *particular societies*. People depend on a global network of societies, but not on any single one: if a government acts against its population, citizens can leave and choose another scheme. Though migration costs are often high, FSC highlights the importance of the freedom to move and even provides a basis for specific norms, such as refugee rights. More broadly, FSC sheds light on what kind of immigration policies a liberal democracy should adopt if it wishes to belong to an international community respecting FSC ideals.

In sum, this book has sought to develop a novel conception of freedom firmly rooted in social cooperation. While FSC offers a philosophical conception of freedom, its application to concrete political and economic institutions yields results that are familiar and consistent with established principles such as the dispersion and decentralization of power and influence, as well as the collaborative interaction between state governance and market forces. At a philosophical level, FSC presents a general conception of freedom, but in practice, it is embodied in political and economic institutions that decentralize and disperse power while maintaining complementary roles. With this framework, we have a new theory of liberal democracy.

Bibliography

ABENDROTH, W., 1972: *Short History of the European Working Class*. Trans. N. Jacobs and B. Trench. London: New Left Books.

ANDERSON, E., 2017: *Private Government: How Employers Rule Our Lives (and Why We Don't Talk About It)*. Princeton: Princeton University Press.

ANDERSON, J., HONNETH, A., 2005: "Autonomy, Vulnerability, Recognition and Justice", in J. Christman and J. Anderson (eds.): *Autonomy and the Challenges to Liberalism*. Cambridge: Cambridge University Press: 127–149.

APPIAH, K. A., 2003: *Thinking it Through*. New York: Oxford University Press.

ARENDT, H., 1961: "What is Freedom?", in *Between Past and Future: Eight Exercises in Political Thought*. New York: The Viking Press: 143–171.

ARENDT, H., 1963: *On Revolution*. New York: Viking Press.

ARISTOTLE, 1999 [350 BC]: *Politics* (trans. B. Jowett). Kitchener: Batoche Books.

ARNESON, R., 1995: "Democratic Rights at the National and Workplace Levels", in D. Copp, J. Hampton and J. Roemer (eds.): *The Idea of Democracy*. New York: Cambridge University Press: 118–148.

ARROW, K., 1963: "Uncertainty and the Welfare Economics of Medical Care", *The American Economic Review*, 53 (5): 941–973.

ATIENZA, M., 1982: *Marx y los derechos humanos*. Madrid: Mezquita.

AXELROD, R., 1980: "Effective Choice in the Prisoner's Dilemma", *Journal of Conflict Resolution*, 24 (1): 3–25.

AXELROD, R., 1982: "The Emergence of Cooperation Among Egoists", *The American Political Science Review*, 75 (2): 306–318.

E. Spector, *Freedom as Social Cooperation*,
https://doi.org/10.1007/978-3-032-12217-9

BADER, R. M., 2018: "Moralized Conceptions of Liberty", in D. Schmidtz and C. Pabel (eds.): *The Oxford Handbook of Freedom*. New York: Oxford University Press: 59–75.

BAILY, S. L., 1982: "Las sociedades de ayuda mutua y el desarrollo de una comunidad italiana en Buenos Aires, 1858-1918", *Desarrollo Económico*, 21 (84): 485–514.

BASTIAT, F., 1850: "What is Seen and What is not Seen", available at https://oll.libertyfund.org/page/wswns#toc (last accessed: September 3, 2025).

BECK, R. G., 1974: "The Effects of Co-Payment on the Poor", *The Journal of Human Resources*, 9 (1): 129–142.

BEITO, D., 1990: "Mutual Aid for Social Welfare: The Case of American Fraternal Societies", *Critical Review*, 4 (4): 709–736.

BENTHAM, J., 1843: "Anarchical Fallacies", in J. Bowring (ed.): *The Works of Jeremy Bentham*, vol. 2. Edinburgh: Tait; London: Simpkin, Marshall: 489–534.

BERLIN, I., 2002 [1958]: "Two Concepts of Liberty", in H. Hardy (ed.): *Liberty*. New York: Oxford University Press: 166–217.

BERNHARD, M., NORDSTROM, T., REENOCK, C., 2001: "Economic Performance, Institutional Intermediation, and Democratic Survival", *Journal of Politics*, 63 (3): 775–803.

BONIN, J., JONES, D., PUTTERMAN, L., 1993: "Theoretical and Empirical Studies of Producer Cooperatives: Will Ever the Twain Meet?", *Journal of Economic Literature*, 31 (3): 1290–1320.

BOWLES, S., GINTIS, H., 2011: *Cooperative Species: Human Reciprocity and its Evolution*. New Jersey: Princeton University Press.

BUCHANAN, J., 2000 [1975]: *The Limits of Liberty: Between Anarchy and Leviathan*. Indianapolis: Liberty Fund.

CANGIANO, M., ALIER, M., ANDERSON, B., HEMMING, R., PETRIE, M., 2006: "Public-Private Partnerships, Government Guarantees, and Fiscal Risk", *International Monetary Fund*, available at https://www.elibrary.imf.org/display/book/9781589064935/9781589064935.xml (last accessed: September 3, 2025).

CARNOY, M., 2017: "School Vouchers Are Not a Proven Strategy for Improving Student Achievement", Economic Policy Institute, available at http://www.epi.org/files/pdf/121635.pdf (last accessed: September 3, 2025).

CASASSAS, D., 2020: "Poder de negociación y distribución social de capacidades para la nacionalización de la vida económica: ¿por qué la renta básica es un proyecto democratizador?", *Daimon. Revista Internacional de Filosofía*, 81: 215–229.

CENTER FOR RESEARCH ON EDUCATION OUTCOMES (CREDO), 2015: "Urban Charter School Study: Report on 41 Regions 2015".

CHEIBUB, J. A., 2007: *Presidentialism, Parliamentarism, and Democracy*. New York: Cambridge University Press.

CHRISTIANO, T., 1996: *The Rule of Many*. Boulder, CO: Westview Press.

CHRISTMAN, J., 2009: *The Politics of Persons. Individual Autonomy and Socio-historical Selves*. Cambridge: Cambridge University Press.

CHRISTMAN, J., 2013a: "Can Positive Freedom Be Saved?", in S. Cahn and R. Talisse (eds.): *Political Philosophy in the Twenty-first Century. Essential Essays*. Boulder CO: Westview Press: 155–168.

CHRISTMAN, J., 2013b: "Freedom, Autonomy, and Social Selves", in B. Baum and R. Nichols (eds.): *Isaiah Berlin and the Politics of Freedom: "Two Concepts of Liberty" 50 Years Later*. New York: Routledge: 87–101.

CICERO, M. T. 1998 [around 54-51 BCE]: *The Republic and the Laws*. Oxford: Oxford University Press.

COHEN, G., 1988: *History, Labour, and Freedom: Themes from Marx*. Oxford: Clarendon Press.

COHEN, G., 2001: "Freedom and Money", Revista Argentina de Teoría Jurídica, 2 (2): 1–27.

COHEN, G., 2009: *Why Not Socialism?* Princeton: Princeton University Press.

CONSTANT, B., 1819: "The Liberty of Ancients Compared with that of Moderns", *Online Library of Liberty*, available at https://oll.libertyfund.org/titles/constant-the-liberty-of-ancients-compared-with-that-of-moderns-1819 (last accessed: September 3, 2025).

COSTA, V., 2016: "Republican Liberty and Border Controls", *Critical Review of International Social and Political Philosophy*, 19 (4): 400–415.

COTTINGHAM, J., 1979: "Varieties of Retribution", *Philosophical Quarterly*, 29 (116): 238–246.

CROCKER, L., 1980: *Positive Liberty: An Essay in Normative Political Philosophy* (Melbourne International Philosophy Series v 7). La Haya: Martinus Nijhoff.

DAGGER, R., 1997: *Civic Virtues: Rights, Citizenship, and Republican Liberalism*. Oxford: Oxford University Press.

DAHL, R., 1956: *A Preface to Democratic Theory*. Chicago: University of Chicago Press.

DAHL, R., 1985: *A Preface to Economic Democracy*. Berkeley, CA: University of California Press.

DARWALL, S., 1999: "Sympathetic Liberalism: Recent Work on Adam Smith", *Philosophy & Public Affairs*, 28 (2): 139–164.

DE SOTO, H., 2000: *The Mystery of Capital: Why Capitalism Triumphs in the West and Fails Everywhere Else*. New York: Basic Books.

DE TOCQUEVILLE, A., 1838 [1835]: *Democracy in American* (Vol. I) (trans. Henry Reeve). London: Saunders and Otley.

DEWEY, J., 1998 [1928]: "Philosophies of Freedom", in L. Hickman and T. Alexander (eds.): *The Essential Dewey. Volume 2: Ethics, Logic, Psychology*. Bloomington/Indianapolis: Indiana University Press: 302–314.

DICEY, A. V., 1982 [1885]: *Introduction to the Study of the Law of the Constitution*. Indianapolis: Liberty Classics.

DWORKIN, R., 2011: *Justice for Hedgehogs*. Cambridge, Mass.: Harvard University Press.

ELSTER, J. (ed.), 1998: *Deliberative Democracy*. Cambridge: Cambridge University Press.

ENGEL, E., FISCHER, R., GALETOVIC, A., 2013: "The Basic Public Finance of Public-Private Partnerships", *Journal of the European Economic Association*, 11 (1): 83–111.

ENGEL, E., FISCHER, R., GALETOVIC, A., 2021: *Economía de las asociaciones público-privadas: Una guía básica*. México: Fondo de Cultura Económica.

ENGELS, F., 2010 [1884]: *The Origin of the Family, Private Property and the State*. London: Penguin Books.

FARRAND, M., 1937: *The Records of the Federal Convention of 1787*. New Haven: Yale University Press.

FESTENSTEIN, M., 2010: "Pragmatism, Inquiry, and Political Liberalism", *Contemporary Political Theory*, 9 (1): 25–44.

FESTENSTEIN, M., 2022: "Pragmatism and Autonomy", in B. Colburn (ed.): *The Routledge Handbook of Autonomy*. London: Routledge: 85–95.

FINE, K., 2012: "Guide to Ground", in F. Correia and B. Schnieder (eds.): *Metaphysical Grounding: Understanding the Structure of Reality*. New York: Cambridge University Press: 37–80.

FINN, J., ACHILLES, C., 1999: "Tennessee's Class Size Study: Findings, Implication, Misconceptions", *Educational Evaluation and Policy Analysis*, 21 (2): 97–109.

FINN, J., GERBER, S., BOYD-ZAHARIAS J., 2005: "Small Classes in the Early Grades, Academic Achievement, and Graduating from High School", *Journal of Educational Psychology*, 97 (2): 214–223.

FOWERAKER, J., LANDMAN, T., 2002: "Constitutional Design and Democratic Performance", *Democratization*, 9 (2): 43–66.

FRACCAROLI, N., SOWERBUTTS, R., WHITWORTH, A., 2020: "Does Regulatory and Supervisory Independence Affect Financial Stability?", *Bank of England*, working paper 893, available at https://www.bankofengland.co.uk/working-paper/2020/does-regulatory-and-supervisory-independence-affect-financial-stability (last accessed: September 3, 2025).

FREGA, R., HERZOG, L., NEUHÄUSER, C., 2019: "Workplace Democracy—The Recent Debate", *Philosophy Compass*, 14 (4): e12574.

FRIEDMAN, D., 2000: *Law's Order: What Economics Has to Do with Law and Why It Matters*. Princeton, NJ: Princeton University Press.

FRIEDMAN, M., 1962: *Capitalism and Freedom*. Chicago: University of Chicago Press.

FULLER, L., 1958: "Positivism and Fidelity to Law: A Reply to Hart", *Harvard Law Review*, 71 (4): 630–672.

GAHVARI, F., 1989: "The Nature of Government Expenditures and the Shape of the Laffer Curve", *Journal of Public Economics*, 40 (2): 251–260.

GALBRAITH, J. K., 1952: *American Capitalism: The Concept of Countervailing Power*. Boston: Houghton Mifflin Co.

GARNETT, M., 2021: "Unity and Disunity in the Positive Tradition", in J. Christman (ed.): *Positive Freedom: Past, Present, and Future*. Cambridge: Cambridge University Press: 8–27.

GBD 2019 DEMOGRAPHICS COLLABORATORS, 2020: "Global Age-Sex-Specific Fertility, Mortality, Healthy Life Expectancy (HALE), and Population Estimates in 204 Countries and Territories, 1950–2019: A Comprehensive Demographic Analysis for the Global Burden of Disease Study 2019", *The Lancet*, 369 (10258): 1160–1203.

GONZÁLEZ-RICOY, I., 2014: "The Republican Case for Workplace Democracy", *Social Theory and Practice*, 40 (2): 232–254.

GONZÁLEZ-RICOY, I., GOSSERIES, A. (eds.), 2016: *Institutions for Future Generations*. New York: Oxford University Press.

GOODHART, C., 1988: *The Evolution of Central Banks*. Cambridge, MA: MIT University Press.

GORTON, G., 1985: "Clearinghouses and the Origin of Central Banking in the United States", *The Journal of Economic History*, 45 (2): 277–283.

GREEN, D., 1985: *Working Class Patients and the Medical Establishment: Self-help in Britain from the Mid-nineteenth Century to 1948*. Aldershot: Gower.

GREEN, T. H., 1986 [1879]: "On the Different Senses of "Freedom" as Applied to Will and to the Moral Progress of Man", in P. Harris and J. Morrow (eds.): *Lectures on the Principles of Political Obligation and Other Writings*. Cambridge: Cambridge University Press: 228–249.

GREEN, T. H., 1986 [1881]: "Lecture on "Liberal Legislation and Freedom of Contract"", in P. Harris and J. Morrow (eds.): *Lectures on the Principles of Political Obligation and Other Writings*. Cambridge: Cambridge University Press: 194–212.

GREEN, T. H., 1986 [1895]: "Lectures on the Principles of Political Obligation", in P. Harris and J. Morrow (eds.): *Lectures on the Principles of Political Obligation and Other Writings*. Cambridge: Cambridge University Press: 13–193.

GREEN, T. H., 2003 [1883]: *Prolegomena to Ethics*, D. Brink (ed.). New York: Oxford University Press.

GUTMANN, A., & THOMPSON, D., 1996: *Democracy and Disagreement*. Cambridge: Harvard University Press.

HABERMAS, J., 1998: *Between Facts and Norms: Contributions to a Discourse Theory of Law and Democracy* (trans. William Rehg). Cambridge: MIT Press.

HAMILTON, E. J., 2000: *El tesoro americano y la revolución de los precios en España, 1501–1650* (trans. Ángel Abad). Barcelona: Crítica.

HAMILTON, W., MAY, S., 1923: *The Control of Wages*. New York: George H. Doran.

HAYEK, F., 1944: *The Road to Serfdom*. Chicago: University of Chicago Press.

HAYEK, F., 1945: "The Use of Knowledge in Society", *The American Economic Review*, 35 (4): 519–530.

HAYEK, F., 1960: *The Constitution of Liberty*. Chicago: The University of Chicago Press.

HAYEK, F., 1978: *The De-Nationalization of Money*. 2nd edition. London: Institute of Economic Affairs.

HAZLETT, T. W., 1998: "The Dual Role of Property Rights in Protecting Broadcast Speech", *Social Philosophy and Policy*, 15 (2): 176–208.

HAZLITT, H., 1952 [1946]: *Economics in One Lesson*. New York: Harper & Brothers.

HEGEL, G. W. F., 1969 [1812]: *Science of Logic* (trans. A. V. Miller). London: George Allen & Unwin.

HOBBES, T., 1998 [1651]: *Leviathan*. J. C. A. Gaskin (ed.). New York: Oxford University Press.

HOHFELD, W. N., 1913: "Some Fundamental Legal Conceptions as Applied in Judicial Reasoning", *The Yale Law Journal*, 23 (1): 16–59.

HORAN, R., BULTE, E., SHOGREN, J., 2005: "How Trade Saved Humanity from Biological Exclusion: An Economic Theory of Neanderthal Extinction", *Journal of Economic Behavior and Organization*, 58 (1): 1–29.

HUME, D., 2000 [1739]: *Treatise of Human Nature*. Oxford: Oxford University Press.

HUSSAIN, W., 2023: *Living with the Invisible Hand: Markets, Corporations, and Human Freedom*. A. Ripstein and N. Vrousalis (eds.). New York: Oxford University Press.

INTERNATIONAL LABOUR OFFICE, 2010: "Trade Union Pluralism and Proliferation in French-Speaking Africa", available at https://www.ilo.org/wcmsp5/groups/public/---ed_dialogue/---actrav/documents/publication/wcms_143551.pdf (last accessed: August 25, 2025).

JOHNSON, C., LUSCH, R., SCHMIDTZ, D., 2019: *Commercial Society: A Primer on Ethics and Economics*. London/New York: Rowman & Littlefield.

KALAMATIEV, T., RISTOVSKI, A., 2012: "Trade Union Pluralism – Progression or Regression in the Protection of Workers' Rights in the Republic of

Macedonia?", *SEER: Journal for Labour and Social Affairs in Eastern Europe*, 15 (3): 391–399.

KANT, I., 1991 [1797]: *The Metaphysics of Morals*. (trans. M. Gregor). Cambridge: Cambridge University Press.

KELLY, E., 2018: *The Limits of Blame*. Cambridge, Mass.: Harvard University Press.

KELSEN, H., 1942 [1835]: "Judicial Review of Legislation: A Comparative Study of the Austrian and the American Constitution", *The Journal of Politics*, 4 (2): 183–200.

KRAMER, S., 1981: *History Begins at Sumer*. Philadelphia: University of Pennsylvania Press.

KRAMER, M., 2003: *The Quality of Freedom*. Oxford: Oxford University Press.

KUHN, S., 2019: "Prisoner's Dilemma", available at https://plato.stanford.edu/entries/prisoner-dilemma/ (last accessed: September 3, 2025).

LABORDE, C., 2010: "Republicanism and Global Justice: A Sketch", *European Journal of Political Theory*, 9 (1): 48–69.

LACEY, N., PICKARD, H., 2021: "Why Standing to Blame May Be Lost But Authority to Hold Accountable Retained: Criminal Laws as a Regulative Public Institution", *The Monist*, 104 (2): 265–280.

LEIMGRUBER, M., 2008: *Solidarity without the State?* New York: Cambridge University Press.

LEONARD, J. N., 1994: *Orígenes del hombre: La Revolución del Neolítico (I)*. Barcelona: Folio.

LEVINE, S., 2020: "The Identity of Self and Act: Pluralism, Growth, and Our Social Interest", in R. Frega and S. Levine (eds.): *John Dewey's Ethical Theory: the 1932 Ethics*. New York: Routledge: 134–155.

LEWIS, D. 1969: *Convention*. Cambridge, Mass.: Harvard University Press.

LIJPHART, A., 1999: *Patterns of Democracy: Government Forms and Performance in Thirty-six Countries*. New Haven, CT: Yale University Press.

LINZ, J., 1994: "Presidential or Parliamentary Democracy: Does It Make a Difference?", in J. Linz and A. Valenzuela (eds.): *The Failure of Presidential Democracy: The Case of Latin America*. Baltimore: Johns Hopkins University Press: 3–87.

LIST, C., VALENTINI, L., 2016: "Freedom as Independence", *Ethics*, 126 (4): 1043–1074.

LOCKE, J., 2003 [1689]: *Two Treatises of Government*. 14th reprint. P. Laslett (ed.). Cambridge: Cambridge University Press.

LOMASKY, L., 1987: *Persons, Rights, and the Moral Community*. Oxford: Oxford University Press.

MACCALLUM, G., 1967: "Negative and Positive Freedom", *Philosophical Review*, 76 (3): 312–334.

MACGILVRAY, E., 2004: *Reconstructing Public Reason*. Cambridge: Harvard University Press.

MACHIAVELLI, N., 1997 [1531]: *Discourses on Livy*. Oxford: Oxford University Press.

MACKENZIE, C. & STOLJAR, N., 2000: *Relational Autonomy: Feminist Perspectives on Autonomy, Agency, and the Social Self*. New York: Oxford University Press.

MADISON, J., 1787a: *The Federalist no. 10*, available at https://guides.loc.gov/federalist-papers/text-1-10 (last accessed: September 3, 2025).

MADISON, J., 1787b: "Letter to Thomas Jefferson", available at https://www.consource.org/document/james-madison-to-thomas-jefferson-1787-10-24/ (last accessed: September 3, 2025).

MADISON, J., 1788: *The Federalist no. 51*, available at https://guides.loc.gov/federalist-papers/text-51-60 (last accessed: September 3, 2025).

MAINWARING, S., SCULLY, T. R., 1995: "Introduction: Party Systems in Latin America", in S. Mainwaring and T. R. Scully (eds.): *Building Democratic Institutions: Party Systems in Latin America*. Stanford, CA: Stanford University Press: 1–34.

MARX, K., 1975 [1844]: "On the Jewish Question", in Q. Hare (ed.): *Early Writings*. London: Penguin Books: 211–242.

MARX, K., 1977 [1867]: *Capital*. Vol. 1. New York: International Publishers.

MARX, K., 2005 [1844]: "Economic and Philosophic Manuscripts of 1844", in P. Gasper (ed.): *The Communist Manifesto: A Road Map to History's Most Important Political Document*. Chicago: Haymarket Books: 149–155.

MARX, K., 2018 [1844]: "Economic and Philosophical Manuscripts of 1844", in A. Bailey, S. Brennan, W. Kymlicka, J. Levy, A. Sager and C. Wolf (eds.): *The Broadview Anthology of Social and Political Thought: From Machiavelli to Nietzsche*. Peterborough, CA: Broadview Press: 596–608.

MAS, N., CIRERA, L., VIÑOLAS, G., 2011: "Los sistemas de copago en Europa, Estados Unidos y Canadá: Implicaciones para el caso español", IESE, working paper D/939.

MAYER, R., 2001: "Robert Dahl and the Right to Workplace Democracy", *The Review of Politics*, 63 (2): 221–247.

MAYNOR, J., 2003: *Republicanism in the Modern World*. Cambridge: Polity Press.

MCCURDY, C. W., 1998: "The "Liberty of Contract" Regime in American Law", in H. N. Scheiber (ed.): *The State and Freedom of Contract*. Stanford, CA: Stanford University Press: 161–197.

MILL, J. S., 1996 [1869]: *On Liberty and the Subjection of Women*. Hertfordshire: Wordsworth Editions.

MILL, J. S., 2009 [1859]: *On* Liberty. Auckland: The Floating Press.

MONTESQUIEU, 2015 [1748]: *The Spirit of the Laws.* 20th edition. A. Cohler, C. Miller, and H. Stone (eds.). Cambridge: Cambridge University Press.

MOYES, P., 1988: "A Note on Minimally Progressive Taxation and Absolute Income Inequality", *Social Choice and Welfare*, 5 (2–3): 227–234.

MUSGRAVE, R., 1959: *A Theory of Public Finance.* New York, NY: McGraw-Hill.

NEUMARK, D., WASCHER, W., 2006: "Minimum Wages and Employment: A Review of Evidence from the New Minimum Wage Research", *NBER*, working paper 12663, available at https://www.nber.org/papers/w12663 (last accessed: September 3, 2025).

NINO, C. S., 1996: *The Constitution of Deliberative Democracy.* New Haven & London: Yale University Press.

NINO, C., 2013: *Fundamentos de derecho constitucional: Análisis filosófico, jurídico y politológico.* 4ta reimpresión. Buenos Aires – Bogotá: Astrea.

NOZICK, R., 1974: *Anarchy, State, and Utopia.* New York: Basic Books.

NUSSBAUM, M., 1988: "Nature, Function, and Capability: Aristotle on Political Distribution", *Oxford Studies in Ancient Philosophy*, Supplementary Volume: 145–184.

NUSSBAUM, M., 1997: "Capabilities and Human Rights", *Fordham Law Review*, 66 (2): 273–300.

NUSSBAUM, M., 2000: *Women and Human Development: The Capabilities Approach.* Cambridge, Cambridge University Press.

NUSSBAUM, M., 2011: *Creating Capabilities: The Human Development Approach.* Cambridge, Mass.: Harvard University Press.

OISHI, S., SCHIMMACK, U., DIENER, E., 2012: "Progressive Taxation and the Subjective Well-Being of Nations", *Psychological Science*, 23 (1): 86–92.

OSHANA, M., 2006: *Personal Autonomy in Society.* Hampshire, UK: Ashgate.

OSSA, F., 1992: "Dinero y sistemas monetarios alternativos", *Cuadernos de Economía*, 86: 1–33.

PATTEN, A., 1999: *Hegel's Idea of Freedom.* New York: Oxford University Press.

PETTIT, P., 1997: *Republicanism: A Theory of Freedom and Government.* Oxford: Oxford University Press.

PETTIT, P., 2001: *A Theory of Freedom.* Cambridge: Polity Press.

PETTIT, P., 2008: "Republican Political Theory", in M. Fleurbaey, M. Salles, and J. Weymarc (eds.): *Justice, Political Liberalism, and Utilitarianism: Essays from Harsanyi and Rawls.* Cambridge: Cambridge University Press: 389–410.

PETTIT, P., 2012: *On the People's Terms.* Cambridge: Cambridge University Press.

PETTIT, P., 2023: *The State.* New Jersey: Princeton University Press.

PICKETT, K., WILKINSON, R., 2011: *The Spirit Level: Why Greater Equality Makes Societies Stronger.* New York: Bloomsbury Press.

PIKETTY, T., SAEZ, E., 2003: "Income Inequality in the United States, 1913–1998", *Quarterly Journal of Economics*, 118 (1): 1–39.

PINCIONE, G., 2011: "The Constitution of Nondomination", *Social Philosophy and Policy*, 28 (1): 261–289.

PINCIONE, G., 2015: "Filosofía de la Propiedad", in J. Fabra and E. Spector (eds.): *Enciclopedia de Filosofía y Teoría del Derecho*, vol. 3. México: UNAM: 2405–2469.

POCOCK, J., 1981: "Virtues, Rights, and Manners: A Model for Historians of Political Thought", *Political Theory*, 9 (3): 353–368.

POLYBIUS, 2011 [around 168-146 BCE]: *The Histories.* Vol. 3. Cambridge, Mass.: Harvard University Press.

POSNER, R. A., 2003: *Law, Pragmatism, and Democracy*. Cambridge, Mass.: Harvard University Press.

RAHE, P., 1992: *Republics Ancient and Modern: Classical Republicanism and the American Revolution*. Chapel Hill: University of North Carolina Press.

RATNER, C., 2013: *Cooperation, Community, and Co-Ops in a Global Era*. New York: Springer.

RAWLS, J., 1987: "The Idea of an Overlapping Consensus", *Oxford Journal of Legal Studies*, 7 (1): 1–25.

RAWLS, J., 1993: *Political Liberalism*. New York: Columbia University Press.

RAWLS, J., 1999: *A Theory of Justice – Revised Edition*. Cambridge, Mass.: Harvard University Press.

RAZ, J., 1986: *The Morality of Freedom*. Clarendon Press; Oxford University Press.

REIFF, M., 2020: *In the Name of Liberty: The Argument for Universal Unionization*. Cambridge: Cambridge University Press.

RICARDO, D., 1817: *On the Principles of Political Economy and Taxation*. London: John Murray.

RODRÍGUEZ ADRADOS, F., 1993: *La Democracia ateniense*. Madrid: Alianza Editorial.

ROUSSEAU, J. J., 2002 [1762]: *The Social Contract and The First and Second Discourses*. S. Dunn (ed.). New Haven/London: Yale University Press.

ROXIN, C., 1976: "Sentido y límites de la pena estatal", in *Problemas básicos del derecho penal* (trans. D. Luzón Peña). Madrid: Reus: 11–36.

RYLE, G., 1946: "Knowing How and Knowing That", *Proceedings of the Aristotelian Society*, 46: 1–16.

SAEZ, E., ZUCMAN, G., 2020: "Taxing the Superrich: For the Sake of Justice and Democracy, We Need a Progressive Wealth Tax", *Boston Review*, available at https://bostonreview.net/forum/gabriel-zucman-taxing-superrich/ (last accessed: September 3, 2025).

SAHLBERG, P., 2013: *El cambio educativo en Finlandia: ¿Qué puede aprender el mundo?* (trans. Rodolfo Biekofsky). Buenos Aires: Paidos.

SAMUELSON, P., 1954: "The Pure Theory of Public Expenditure", *The Review of Economics and Statistics*, 36 (4): 387–389.

SARTORI, G., 2014: *¿Qué es la democracia?* 2nd edition. Madrid: Taurus.

SCHMIDTZ, D., BRIGHOUSE, H., 2020: *Debating Education: Is There a Role for Markets?* New York: Oxford University Press.

SCHMIDTZ, D., 2023: *Living Together: Inventing Moral Science.* New York: Oxford University Press.

SCHOTTER, A., 1981: *The Economic Theory of Social Institutions.* Cambridge: Cambridge University Press.

SCHUMPETER, J. A., 1950: *Capitalism, Socialism, and Democracy.* 3rd edition. New York: Harper Perennial.

SEN, A., 1979: "Equality of What?", in *Tanner Lectures on Human Values*, Stanford, Stanford University Press, 197–220.

SEN, A., 1985: *Commodities and Capabilities.* Amsterdam: North-Holland.

SEN, A., 1999: *Development as Freedom.* Oxford: Oxford University Press.

SEN, A., 2004: "Capabilities, Lists, and Public Reason: Continuing the Conversation", *Feminist Economics*, 10 (3): 77–80.

SEN, A., 2005: "Human Rights and Capabilities", *Journal of Human Development*, 6 (2): 151–166.

SEN, A., 2006: *Inequality Reexamined.* New York: Oxford University Press.

SHUGART, M. S., CAREY, J. M., 1992: *Presidents and Assemblies: Constitutional Design and Electoral Dynamics.* Cambridge: Cambridge University Press.

SIMHONY, A., 2021: "Positive Freedom and Freedom of Contract", in J. Christman (ed.): *Positive Freedom: Past, Present, and Future.* Cambridge: Cambridge University Press: 65–82.

SIMMONS, A. J., 1979: *Moral Principles and Political Obligations.* Princeton, NJ: Princeton University Press.

SKILES, A., 2015: "Against Grounding Necessitarianism", *Erkenntnis*, 80 (4): 717–751.

SKINNER, Q., 1991: "The Paradoxes of Political Liberty", in D. Miller (ed.): *Liberty.* Oxford: Oxford University Press: 183–205.

SKINNER, Q., 1998: *Liberty Before Liberalism.* Cambridge: Cambridge University Press.

SKINNER, Q., 2002: "A Third Concept of Liberty", *Proceedings of the British Academy*, 117: 237–268.

SKINNER, Q., 2008: "Freedom as the Absence of Arbitrary Power", in C. Laborde and J. Maynor (eds.): *Republicanism and Political Theory.* Oxford: Blackwell: 83–101.

SMITH, A., 1981 [1776]: *An Inquiry into the Nature and Causes of the Wealth of Nations. Volume I.* Indianapolis: Liberty Fund.

SMITH, N., DERANTY, J. P. (eds.), 2011: *New Philosophies of Labour: Work and the Social Bond*. Leiden: Brill.

SOWELL, T., 2015: *Basic Economics: A Common Sense Guide to the Economy*. 5th edition. New York: Basic Books.

SPECTOR, E., 2018: "Aspectos filosóficos del matrimonio", in D. M. Papayannis and E. Pereira Fredes (eds.): *Filosofía del Derecho Privado*. Madrid: Marcial Pons: 233–252.

SPECTOR, H., 1992: *Autonomy and Rights: The Moral Foundations of Liberalism*. Oxford: Clarendon Press.

SPECTOR, H., 2006: "Philosophical Foundations of Labor Law", *Florida State University Law Review*, 33 (4): 1119–1148.

SPENCER, H., 1960: *The Man Versus the State*. Caldwell: The Caxton Printers.

SPITZ, J. F., 1993: "The Concept of Liberty in "A Theory of Justice" and Its Republican Version", *Ratio Juris*, 7 (3): 331–347.

SPITZ, J. F., 1995: *La liberté politique: Essai de généalogie conceptuelle*. Paris: Presses universitaires de France.

STEINER, H., 1994: *An Essay on Rights*. Oxford: Blackwell.

STIGLER, G., 1971: "The Theory of Economic Regulation", *Bell Journal of Economics and Management Science*, 2 (1): 3–21.

SUGDEN, R., 1984: "Reciprocity: The Supply of Public Goods Through Voluntary Contributions", *The Economic Journal*, 94 (376): 772–787.

TALISSE, R., 2011a: "A Farewell to Deweyan Democracy", *Political Studies*, 59 (3): 509–526.

TALISSE, R., 2011b: "Toward a New Pragmatist Politics", *Metaphilosophy*, 42 (5): 552–571.

TAYLOR, C., 1979: "What's Wrong with Negative Liberty?", in A. Ryan (ed.): *The Idea of Freedom: Essays in Honour of Isaiah Berlin*. Oxford: Oxford University Press: 175–193.

TAYLOR, C., 1989: *Sources of the Self: The Making of the Modern Identity*. Cambridge, Mass.: Harvard University Press.

TAYLOR, C., 1991: *The Ethics of Authenticity*. Cambridge, Mass.: Harvard University Press.

TAYLOR, M., 1976: *Anarchy and Cooperation*. New York, NY: Wiley.

TAYLOR, R., 2017: *Exit Left: Markets and Mobility in Republican Thought*. Oxford: Oxford University Press.

THALER, R., SHEFRIN, H. M., 1981: "An Economic Theory of Self-control", *Journal of Political Economy*, 89 (2): 392–406.

TIEBOUT, C., 1956: "A Pure Theory of Local Expenditures", *Journal of Political Economy*, 64 (5): 516–524.

TIMBERLAKE, R., Jr., 1984: "The Central Banking Role of Clearinghouse Associations", *Journal of Money, Credit and Banking*, 16 (1): 1–15.

TOBAR, F., 2010: *¿Qué aprendimos de las reformas de salud?* Buenos Aires. Fundación Sanatorio Güemes.

TOMASELLO, M., 2014: *A Natural History of Human Thinking*. Cambridge, Mass.: Harvard University Press.

TOOLEY, J., DIXON, P., 2006: "La educación privada es beneficiosa para los pobres: Un estudio sobre las escuelas privadas para los pobres", *Cato Institute*, available at https://www.elcato.org/la-educacion-privada-es-beneficiosa-para-los-pobres-un-estudio-sobre-las-escuelas-privadas-para-los (last accessed: September 3, 2025).

TROGDON, K., WITMER, D. G., 2021: "Full and Partial Grounding", *Journal of the American Philosophical Association*, 7 (2): 252–271.

TUCKER, I., 2009: *Survey of Economics*. 6th edition. Mason, OH: South-Western Cengage Learning.

VAN PARIJS, P., 1992: "Why Surfers Should be Fed: The Liberal Case for an Unconditional Basic Income", *Philosophy & Public Affairs*, 20 (2): 101–131.

VIROLI, M., 2002: *Republicanism* (trans. A. Shugaar). New York: Hill and Wang.

VON HUMBOLDT, W., 1993 [1852]: *The Limits of State Action*. Indianapolis: Liberty Fund.

WALL, S., 1998: *Liberalism, Perfectionism, and Restraint*. Cambridge: Cambridge University Press.

WANNISKI, J., 1978: "Taxes, Revenues, and the "Laffer Curve"", *The Public Interest*, available at https://nationalaffairs.com/public_interest/detail/taxes-revenues-and-the-laffer-curve (last accessed: September 3, 2025).

WEST, E.G., 1994: *Education and the State: A Study in Political Economy*. 3rd edition. Indianapolis: Liberty Fund.

WILLIAMS, B., 2001: "From Freedom to Liberty: The Construction of a Political Value", *Philosophy and Public Affairs*, 30 (1): 3–26.

WISS, M., MAUREA FARIA, T., 2007: "Public Private Partnerships in Latin America: Governmental Salvation or Deception", *Business Law International*, 8 (2): 186–206.

WÖSSMANN, L., WEST, M., 2006: "Class-Size Effects in School Systems Around the World: Evidence from Between-Grade Variation in TIMSS", *European Economic Review*, 50 (3): 695–736.

YOUNG, P., 1998: "Social Norms and Economic Welfare", *European Economic Review*, 42 (3–5): 821–830.

Index

E. Spector, *Freedom as Social Cooperation*,
https://doi.org/10.1007/978-3-032-12217-9

FSC
www.fsc.org
MIX
Papier | Fördert
gute Waldnutzung
FSC® C083411

Kolibri 360 GmbH
Ferdinand-Jühlke-Straße 7
99095 Erfurt, Deutschland
produktsicherheit@kolibri360.de